W0259785

BABY NAME ENVY

BABY NAME ENVY

The New Way to Choose a Baby Name You'll Love

SJ Strum

Vermilion
LONDON

VERMILION

UK | USA | Canada | Ireland | Australia
India | New Zealand | South Africa

Vermilion is part of the Penguin Random House group of companies whose addresses can be found at global.penguinrandomhouse.com

Penguin Random House UK
One Embassy Gardens, 8 Viaduct Gardens, London SW11 7BW

penguin.co.uk
global.penguinrandomhouse.com

First published by Vermilion in 2025
1

Typeset by Six Red Marbles UK, Thetford, Norfolk
Text design by seagulls.net

Printed and bound in Great Britain by Clays Ltd, Elcograf S.p.A.

The authorised representative in the EEA is Penguin Random House Ireland, Morrison Chambers, 32 Nassau Street, Dublin D02 YH68

A CIP catalogue record for this book is available from the British Library

ISBN 9781785045585

Penguin Random House is committed to a sustainable future for our business, our readers and our planet. This book is made from Forest Stewardship Council® certified paper.

CONTENTS

For my sister Naomi, always

WHAT'S IN A NAME?

Picking a baby name is a huge decision – it's the name you'll whisper in lullabies and sing loudly and joyously with loved ones on your baby's birthday. One day, far in the future, it's the name you'll see light up on your phone screen and know your baby is calling home. It's your first love letter to them and will always be a token of when they were a dream that was about to become true. They will carry this choice for a lifetime, and you want to love it now *and* forever.

You may have arrived here liking a whole bunch of names, you could have a top contender or two, or you may be at a total blank - don't worry, they're *all* great places to start. Welcome to this unique book that I've poured my years of baby name consulting experience into. As a consultant and a parent, I know there are also a lot of common battles or road bumps that can occur when making this huge decision, and so you'll also find my tools and tips for navigating dilemmas. Here you'll discover traditional and timeless names as well as modern and unusual choices. The huge difference from a regular baby name A-Z is that the names in this book are listed by themes and interests, so you can find *your unique style*. A name can tell your love story of how your baby came to be; all your passions, experiences, your style, your interests, your home and family and their special place within it. This is where their story starts. This is where their heart will lie, and where yours will find new meaning. Within these pages I've included features that will help to guide you in finding those names that have true personal meaning.

I get how huge and daunting picking a name can feel. I've always been a proud name nerd - my childhood teddies' names were themed around towns in Surrey. I like to think Chertsey and Woking were the most hipster bears on the cul-de-sac. As a seven-year-old I felt I'd nailed it calling my pets Cuddles and Kisses (my dad was less than impressed when calling for the cat). I often insisted on going by Sally-Ann, Dorothy, Maria von Trapp, Kylie or Tiffany, depending on who I was most infatuated with at the time.

My lifelong obsession has now turned into a job as a Baby Name Consultant. I love nothing more than finding gorgeous names by researching history, aesthetics, trends and meanings to curate inspiring lists. Over the years, I've worked with thousands of parents-to-be to become the UK's leading name consultant, opening their eyes to a whole new way of choosing a baby name that is both personal and meaningful. It's a skill to come up with that perfect name, one that entirely captures the essence of the little person you already love so much. I've carefully collated this book so that you will enjoy the experience of choosing your baby's name, giving you the answer to that inevitable question, 'how did you pick your baby's name?'

It's almost a little wild and daunting that we get to choose such an important part of someone's life. There are endless possibilities and so many gorgeous name choices, it's hard to know where to start. Imagine arriving at your dream restaurant, but you can go there only once. You've been on the waiting list for ages and have been so excited for this day, everything on the menu looks so good on paper and suddenly . . . you just cannot decide on a dish. How do you pick? Go for a tried-and-tested favourite, take a risk on something a bit different or choose the most popular dish of the day? A–Z baby name books always feel a bit like that unwieldy menu - a lot of options, but nothing that stands out as perfect. What do you do? Frantically flip through the list, phone a friend for a recommendation, throw ideas at one another until someone yells 'bank' before the time's up? Then, once you've chosen, sprinkle on top pregnancy hormones, a pinch of other people's opinions and a handful of friends stealing all your favourites before you can get to them, and welcome to the minefield of picking a baby name.

This book is designed to make the experience so much easier and give you tips to navigate the common issues that may pop up along the way. Just like selecting from that dream food menu, we'll focus on all the ingredients that are important to you that make that one name stand out and shine.

It was in imagining that difficult menu at my 'Baby Name Restaurant' that I created *Baby Name Envy*. Just as I get food envy, I've heard many names over the years that I wish I'd discovered and they all give me baby name envy. So many names that I loved, but not enough babies of my own to use them on, and they all made me think, 'If I'd seen it, I'd have chosen that.' Those are the names I used to start making my YouTube videos during my third pregnancy, which spun into a series called *Baby Name Monday*; weekly videos that have gained millions of views and sparked the baby name consultancy trend on social media.

I adore creating the bespoke name lists you'll find in this book. It's endlessly fascinating and I have laughed and smiled so much along the way, especially when I receive birth announcements. I've been honoured to be a part of naming thousands of babies over the years.

Parenthood, however you arrive at it, is a once in a lifetime experience. Whether it's your first or your seventh baby, your baby after previous baby loss, through IVF, adoption or as a solo parent bringing your much-loved child into the world, I hope you to truly enjoy this name book. Spend time here. Start to believe this is really going to happen and how good it's going to be. Allow for the butterflies, calm the anxieties and bring your baby into your mind's eye as you navigate the thought starters, BIG conversations, prompts and name lists. Your baby is on their way, and they are waiting for you to find their name in this book.

How to Use This Book to Find Your Perfect Name

You don't need to read *Baby Name Envy* in any particular order. I recommend delving into the themes that immediately grab you and I've added pointers to where names cross over into other themes you might wish to explore. For example, if you like the vintage name Marigold, you might want to know that it also features in the Colours section of the book where you could find other names to inspire you. You can create your own path through the book. If you've underlined a Water Name that has a minimalist vibe, like Coast, I'll let you know where to find similar names on other lists. It's the ultimate 'pick-your-own ending', or really a 'pick-your-own child's beginning'.

I've included an even number of girl and boy names, though some themes may skew towards one more than the other. Floral names for instance are more traditionally feminine, but you'll also find nature-themed lists like Wilderness Names where there are stunning choices for boys. If you want to explore names that are not assigned to a particular gender there's plenty of gorgeous ideas in the Neutral Names lists. Many parents love gender-neutral names mainly because we don't want our children to be raised to a gender stereotype, plus the explosion of name inspiration means there's plenty of stunning picks that don't fall into any historic gender bias.

While the chapters in *Baby Name Envy* appear by theme, to make it easy to navigate, each list is ordered alphabetically, but this isn't an alphabetical guide where I pick a name for each letter. I've added detail next to each name because having more than just a one-word meaning helps *so* much to find that personal connection. Whether that's the name's heritage, its style and sound or what the meaning symbolizes. I've researched the meanings across multiple sources; online ancestry records often have meanings and history sites record names of the decade. Where a name is made up of Latin, Greek or words from a specific language, you will get to know its true meaning. Also, where notable, I'll let you know if a name is rising or falling in the name popularity charts, which are created by the Office for National Statistics in the UK. They keep a record and total of each name registered and I love to keep track, as it indicates how rare or common the name will be for your little one.

Your copy of *Baby Name Envy* is also a keepsake of how your baby got their name, one they will treasure as they grow up, seeing their own name-story unfold before they even arrived. I imagine them pulling this book down from the shelf in many years to come, smiling as they read your notes and hearts and underlines. The aim of this book is for you to create your own Baby Name List while you read, picking your favourites and creating a list packed with names you love and can consider for your baby. Ultimately one will then rise to the top and I've got tips along the way to help you decide. *Baby Name Envy* is yours to scribble in, so grab a pen and underline the names you love as you read through. Add hearts and ticks to remind you to revisit them. Use a notepad for name ideas so you can write down all the ones you like and begin to curate names that are perfect for you. By writing them on paper you can add your surname, mix and match middle and first names and begin to get closer to naming your baby.

In *Baby Name Envy* I've included names from indigenous communities with rich and diverse cultures. They aim to inspire those of you who may have a particular heritage or feel deeply connected to specific names, with full respect and understanding of where the name originated. For some of these names, however, it could be potentially offensive for a person not of that heritage to use them, especially unknowingly and without acknowledgment. I urge you to be sensitive to others and make informed choices, but like me, I know you'll really welcome the inclusion of so many beautiful and special names that broaden our appreciation, inclusion and acknowledgment of indigenous people and the names and land they own.

Quiz, Discussion Guides and Tips

Baby Name Envy offers loads of invaluable tips and hacks gleaned from my experience as a Baby Name Consultant, so you get all my favourite games and conversation starters that I love to include in a consultancy.

The opening Style Quiz is there to help you refine what kind of namer you are. It's a brilliant base to start from, whether you already favour certain names or have never even considered names before - you will quickly get a sense of where your tastes lie.

There are also tips on how to match sibling names or how to honour loved ones, living or passed on, even when you may not like their name as much as you adored the person (sorry grandad). I suggest when to announce your baby name and how to pick the perfect middle name. Plus, at the end of the book, I help you navigate the big dilemmas and conflicts that can occur along the way, for example if your family don't like the name you've chosen or it's stolen by a friend - yes, that happens and I'm here to guide you.

Becoming a parent is not always an easy path and there are names dedicated to those extra special babies bought to your life through IVF, surrogacy, adoption and after baby loss. Visit the Rainbow Baby, Virtue and Names That Tell a Story chapters for heart-hitting names that recognize the events along the way that bought them to you.

I've included some hacks on how to agree on a name if you're in a couple, but lots of my friends are solo parents and of course, I'm here to be your naming buddy with plenty of tips.

On the last page I invite you to add a dedication to your baby. I'm here to support you, encouraging you to capture those names you love, further explore why you are drawn to them and help you settle on 'The One' that most readily fits with your style. Grab your pen and notepad, let's find your baby's name.

For My Sister, Naomi

This book would never have happened had it not been for the *Baby Name Envy* podcast I co-hosted with my sister Naomi.

The podcast launched at number one in the Apple parenting podcast charts and remained in the top ten as we navigated the real world of baby name dilemmas, as sisters. Naomi was the second half of *Baby Name Envy*, a happy recruit as my naming buddy for the podcast. Although she was a successful estate agent and had no experience doing anything on social media, I knew her brutal honesty and hilarious sense of humour would resonate with everyone trying to pick a name. And ultimately it was just us getting to hang out together.

A few months after launching the podcast Naomi was diagnosed with terminal bowel cancer and the podcast recordings, name dilemma polls and reading your messages became our most favourite, happiest thing to do together as a distraction. We often whizzed into the studio before hospital appointments or sat in her bed as she recovered from chemo thinking up games and ideas, holding hands and genuinely laughing out loud and loving our sister time. She adored this community, I cherished getting to share her sense of humour with you and most of all she loved her family - Lee, Summer Dorothea Rose and Lottie Loveday - very much.

She was my sister, my best friend, my naming buddy, the one who I had the privilege of joining in the delivery room when her first child Summer arrived and sharing her whole labour experience when her second daughter Lottie appeared. Eight years later I lived with her at the hospice for her last few weeks. To each and every one of you holding this book, thank you for making my sister so proud of me. This book represents our sisterhood joy poured out onto paper and I can't wait to see what name you pick from its pages.

HOW TO DISCOVER YOUR 'BABY NAME STYLE'

Considering your name style is often overlooked in the process of picking a name but your style is that secret essence that can take a name from 'like' to 'love. It's also why when people announce a baby name we like, we often comment that it's a name that really suits them. However, knowing what suits us is often hard to articulate or even recognize in ourselves, so I've created a quiz to help jump-start your name picking process. Knowing your style will help you make decisions throughout the book because a name choice is always more than just how they sound; it's how they *feel* to you.

If you're naming as a couple it's important you both take this quiz. It really illuminates why one of you may love a name that the other doesn't - often it's simply outside their style. And if so, I've got tips coming up on how to pick a name you both agree on.

QUIZ – FIND MY NAME STYLE

Grab a pen and jot down how many A, B or C answers you get, then reveal your name style at the end of the quiz.

1. What's in your wardrobe?

a. I have my own unique style and my wardrobe is full of one-off pieces. I love to mix and match and be creative, my accessories are a key part of my look and I enjoy spending time putting an outfit together and expressing myself.

b. I adore fashion and update my wardrobe with a couple of key trends for each season. I like looking at what other people are wearing for ideas and adding a bit of flair to my everyday outfits makes me feel happy.

c. I know what suits me and have clothes in my wardrobe I've worn for years. My wardrobe is full of staples and classics so I can grab whatever's clean and comfy and get on with my day.

2. My home

a. I have an aesthetic for my home and display curated artwork and decor that reflect the vision I have for my space. I love finding pieces no one else has and designing to a colour palette as my home is an expression of my personality.

b. I like to be stylish and enjoy a browse around the shops to update corners of my house and add a little pop of something special – like wall art, a blanket or a decorative piece I've seen online to bring my home up to date.

c. I like keeping my home practical and welcoming, it's got everything I need and I only update things if I have to. I choose classic items of furniture with a simple, tasteful décor that doesn't date.

3. Personality

a. I'm a creator. I'm inspired by a blank piece of paper so I can let my ideas flow. People have always described me as creative and imaginative and I feel most lit up when I'm bringing my ideas to life, whether that's writing, performing or putting together looks.

b. I'm an experience hunter. I love finding new ideas so am always up for joining in, whether that's a book club, going to a mini festival or dissecting a TV show in the group chat. I've always got something planned, as I come alive when I'm excited about a new passion.

c. I'm happy-go-lucky. I love my daily routines and keep my life as drama-free and comfortable as possible. I thrive in places I know well and enjoy the simple pleasures in life, like cooking my favourite meal, rewatching a classic movie or phoning an old friend.

Circle your favourite names below according to how likely you'd be to pick them if no one else had an opinion.

a. Rosenwyn
b. Rosalie
c. Rose

a. Obsidian
b. Orson
c. Oliver

a. Enya
b. Elodie
c. Emily

a. Hamlin
b. Hudson
c. Harry

Count if you are mostly A, B or C to find out what type of namer you are.

Mostly As – STAND OUT & SHINE

You love names that are unique and ideally that no one else has thought of using. It might take a bit more sifting through the rails, but it's worth the hunt to discover something that feels like a one-off, but isn't whacky or frivolous. It's harder to know what you do like than what you don't, but when you see it, you just know. Keep an eye out for the rarer and more unique names throughout *Baby*

Name Envy. Those you haven't heard before will stand out, and if it appeals, jot it down on your name list.

Mostly Bs – TRENDY WITH A TWIST

You know what's in style but always like to make it your own. You can put names together in a way other people might never have thought of, but totally match your unique personality. You like being playful, are always up for switching things around and trying new combinations, and when it feels right, you won't be able to stop smiling. In *Baby Name Envy* I've included lots of names I know you'll love; keep a look out for upcycled vintage gems, plus there's hundreds of modern names that are newly in fashion. Write down all those you love on your own name list to mix and match later.

Mostly Cs – TIMELESSLY TASTEFUL

You have an effortless style and are drawn to names that aren't overly complex and don't need to try hard to have star power. You know what you like and can spot what suits you; however, you need to know you'll love it forever before making a commitment and there's no bigger investment piece than your baby's name. *Baby Name Envy* is packed with names that have that classic appeal; look out for vintage names that have stood the test of time, plus new names that are simple to say and easy to spell. Pop down all your favourites on a Baby Name List.

How to Use Your Style to Pick Names

Throughout *Baby Name Envy* you'll find names that appeal to each Name Style. I'll point you in the right direction as you read. Use your style as a barometer, particularly if you're struggling to get started. Write down those names you read that immediately feel like a good fit, as it can help to get your list flowing. You can always shorten it later.

If you're naming as a couple and came out with different styles at the end of the quiz, use your styles as a discussion point when writing or comparing name lists. It's frequently the case that clashes happen later on because you didn't realize you were essentially shopping for one item in two different shops! One of you is at the tailors looking for an elegant classic and one of you is sifting the antique shop for a daring one-off. Knowing this early on can really help prevent those disagreements and lead you to find a compromise. Can your partner make their Timelessly Tasteful name choice more Trendy with a Twist to suit you? Are you able to elevate your trendy name to make it Stand Out & Shine more to match their style?

And my top tip if you're clashing is to read the full themed list where your favoured name appears and discuss whether there's another name within the same theme that you both agree on. The theme can often be enough of a 'style tick' to unite you and elevate all the names within it.

For example, I'm a Stand Out & Shine but my husband is Timelessly Tasteful. I loved literary names like Atticus and Gatsby - being an English Literature graduate they captured my creative spark. However, Henrik couldn't get onboard with the daring names. Eventually we agreed that we both liked Finn, which had the literary twist of Huckleberry Finn for me and was just classic enough for him.

If your partner favours Timelessly Tasteful Hugo but you're not sold, you can revisit the chapter on Vintage Names and perhaps upgrade to a less common Trendy with a Twist Frank.

NATURE

Nature is a huge inspiration for a beautiful baby name. We've been naming babies after flowers for generations but are now starting to see trends that explore the great outdoors.

The natural world is an amazing place to pluck ideas from and a gorgeous way to bring the wild and free essence of nature into your child's name. When we think of childhood, we think of freedom, play and family time and names drawn from nature are so evocative of ocean swims, sandy toes, mountain views and blossoming flowers.

Throughout history our ancestors attributed meaning to the natural world around us - the Victorians created emotional meanings for flowers, so a Rose came to express love and a Lily expressed empathy when gifted. Further back in time, the name Asher taken from the Ash tree was revered as warding off evil by the Gaels in historic Ireland. I've included those meanings below so you can pick a name on sentiment which might hit your heart in a special way. The natural world is an amazing place to pluck ideas from and a gorgeous way to bring the wild and free essence of nature into your child's name.

My own middle name is a word inspired by nature. I love being out in the woods with my family and we always pick holidays where we can stay surrounded by trees - for me it's about slowing down, playing and getting messy, feeling protected from the stresses of life. So, when my parents surprised me with the super-fun gift of a deed poll voucher a couple of years ago to pick my own middle name, I chose Forest. I absolutely cherish having such a meaningful middle name.

FLOWER NAMES

Flowers have always inspired baby names. The Victorians created a secret code for every flower so they could communicate their feelings discretely by sending blooms to each other - flowers were the 'swipe right' of our ancestors' love lives. Each month also has a birth flower attached to it depending on what's in season. I was always certain I'd have children with flower names, I've loved them since I was almost called Daisy and coveted the name all my childhood. Flower names are a walk in a country garden, a bouquet bought in celebration, a single bloom that brightens up your table. I cannot lie, I'd have chosen any one of these names for my own children, and I think they're as hard to pick from as a wildflower garden. I hope you find a few you adore. Flower names have mostly been given to girls historically, however there are a number of gorgeous picks for boys here as well.

GIRLS

Azalea - 'Azalea', pronounced Azay-Lee-A, is such a cool sounding floral name with the modern 'z'. Native to Japan and China and the national flower of Nepal, this bloom is so bright and cheerful, full of petals in crimson, pink and white. Azalea flowers are just as stunning and vibrant as their name is.

Blossom - 'To bloom'. I chose this as a middle name for my daughter and it would have been her first name if it hadn't been vetoed. I'd always loved the name Blossom since the nineties kids' TV show of the same name. Each spring, my daughter Evelina Blossom and I enjoy going to see the pink and white blossom trees in London parks, and the name just grows on me more and more. That's why I've also included it in my Spring Names list (see page 40)

Bluebell - Not commonly used as a name, it could tick the box for a Stand Out & Shine namer. There are many folklore tales about bluebells, one being that if you picked a bluebell you'd be led astray by fairies, giving it a bit of rebellious cool. I love a unique name that is easy to say and spell and Bluebell does both.

Calla - 'Beautiful'. The Calla Lily is a stunning flower shaped like a chalice. Its unique shape led to its ancient Greek meaning of 'beautiful'. They really are gorgeous flowers and so distinct. Calla makes for a fashion-forward name, as it hasn't been used as often as some vintage flower names - perfect for Trendy with a Twist namers.

Cataleya - 'Orchid'. Pronounced Cata-Lay-A. This vibrant purple flower is a genus of orchid from Costa Rica. Cataleya makes for a really bold name with a distinct Spanish character.

Dahlia - 'Valley'. Named after Swedish botanist Anders Dahl, the flower is so popular it's making the name bloom as well. Pronunciation is either Day-Lee-A, which is more common here in England, or traditionally Dahl-e-ah in Swedish origin.

Daisy - 'Day's Eye'. The name Daisy was hugely favoured in Victorian times, symbolizing purity and innocence. Enduringly popular, I love it - it remains not too serious while still being vintage and it stands out in a modern setting too. See my Vintage chapter for more like Daisy (page 201).

Edelweiss - The flower symbolizes strength and adventure but will always be linked to classic movie *The Sound of Music*. For any Stand Out & Shine namers who, like me, were raised on this film, it makes a daring name or a brave middle name choice based on a passion. See my chapter on Middle Names for more ideas.

Fleur - 'Flower' in French. This one-syllable name has a timeless beauty that would work so well as a soft first name or trendy middle name. Understated but enduringly beautiful, I'd recommend Fleur for all lovers of floral names.

Flora - 'Flower' and the Roman goddess of springtime and flowers. Flora is such an upbeat and joyful name, it takes me straight to bright and cheerful gardens and that feeling when spring arrives and the natural world bursts into colour again. A very traditional name that sparks joy.

Heather - 'Evergreen plant'. This evergreen flowering plant with pink, purple or white flowers thrives in Scotland and has been a popular girl's name. It peaked in the nineties and feels due a revival.

Hyacinth - 'Purple'. Hyacinths are such stunning flowers and make me think of vibrant purple. The name got lost somewhere in time and is now totally unranked, but can *Bridgerton* help me bring this special name back into fashion? If you love a rare name, pick Hyacinth quickly so you can feel proud to have thought of it before anyone else. It's giving me massive Baby Name Envy.

Iris - 'Rainbow'. Iris was the Greek goddess of the rainbow. She's depicted with wings on her back and was said to be a messenger for the gods. The flower is a gorgeous purple colour and has three main petals said to symbolize valour, wisdom and faith. It is one of February's birth flowers. Iris has a vintage charm; it was most used in the 1900s then dropped out of the charts completely before having a recent revival.

Jasmine - 'Fragrant flower'. The flower Jasmine got its name from the Persian word *yasmin*, which was in reference to the perfume of the flower. Symbolizing love and grace, Jasmine is known for its strong scent, earning it the name 'Queen of the Night' in India where it is smelt in the air after sunset.

Jessamine - 'Jasmine Flower'. A bright yellow bloom, Jessamine is a variant of the Jasmine flower which is found in southern USA. This unique flower name sounds vintage. It really hits the spot if you love longer girl names.

Jonquil - 'Reed'. A member of the Daffodil family. I love Jonquil as a name. It's very original sounding with the pretty 'quil' ending that could make a cool nickname.

Lavender - This purple flower is so popular for its scent and colour. Lavenders are used in lots of oils and beauty products as they are famous for being calming. The character 'Lavender' in the *Harry Potter* and *Matilda* books could help it hop onto your name list.

Lily - 'Pure'. Lily is one of our favourite flower names for its gentle 'L' sound. Perfect for Timelessly Tasteful namers, Lily has been enduringly popular, having been in the top 20 girl names registered as far back as 1904. I adore Lily - it's delicate but punchy and feels lively even though it has soft sounds.

Lilja - The Finnish version of Lily pronounced Lil-Ya adds a trendy twist on traditional Lily.

Linnea - 'Twin flower'. Known as the twinflower due to it having two flowers at the top of each stem, Linnea always makes me do a double take, as I love the sound. It was named after the Swedish botanist Carl Linnaeus and is pronounced Lin-Ay-Uh. The name has been wildly popular in Sweden but is rare elsewhere, making it ideal if you want a unique name that has classic roots or, of course, if you're naming twins!

Magnolia - 'Excellence'. If you're looking for a rare floral name, Magnolia is a perfect pick. There are many species of magnolia and they bloom in white, yellow, pink, purple and green, making it such a vibrant name with a modern feel even though it hasn't been popular since the 1900s.

Marigold - 'Golden flower'. Marigold was totally unranked in the UK baby name charts until 2010 where it began to get modest use after *Downton Abbey* burst onto our screens with Marigold as a main character. Goldie makes a trendy nickname, adding a cool edge to this forgotten vintage gem.

Peony - 'Praise giving'. Symbolizing happiness, this flower has a celebratory feel with its big round petals looking so special in a bouquet. Pronounced Pee-on-ee, Peony is a statement name that is as soft and pretty on the page as the flower itself. It creates just as much impact too, being unique and underused as a name.

Petunia - Petunia as a name hasn't hit the classic heights that a lot of the floral names have, making it perfect if you're after a rare name. There are hundreds of varieties of Petunia in all colours and as a name it has a certain old-school glamour.

Posy - 'A small bouquet'. A bunch of blooms is called a posy, we carry them on wedding days and a posy is also the name for a ring with an inscription. Two special reasons to choose this playful name as an alternative to the more common Rosie.

Poppy - This vibrant red flower is another popular girl's name that is wonderfully upbeat and cheerful. We've worn poppies to remember those lost in war since 1921, inspired by John McCrae's famous poem 'In Flanders Field'. They symbolize both remembrance and hope.

Primrose - 'First rose'. One of the birth flowers for February, it is among one of the first flowers to bloom after winter. I absolutely love this name - it is a classic that hasn't become as iconic as some of the other flower names, giving it a bit of that Trendy with a Twist style.

Rose - A moment for our heroine of the chapter, the enduringly popular flower name Rose. The symbol of love of course makes this a top girl name that has so many variations. The simplicity of Rose has my heart, but what about the more spirited Rosie, which has a less formal feel? Other variations of this beautiful name are: Rosalie, Rosa, Primrose, Rosamund, Rosanne, Rosario, Roisin, Rosabella, Rosemary, Rosenwyn, Penrose and Rosebay. Shakespeare wrote, 'A rose by any other name would smell as sweet' and it seems we rolled with his advice.

Tansy - 'Protection'. The Tansy flower is a vibrant round yellow flower. It's also useful to know that popping a Tansy flower in your shoe will guarantee a safe journey, phew! I love the protection meaning and Tansy feels fashionable and modern.

Tigerlily - Tiger Lilies are bright orange flowers that grow in Asia. Tiger has been a sweet name pick for boys and girls and the addition of the popular 'Lily' balances it for a more traditional namer. Tigerlily has a hippy and bohemian vibe that so many of us love for our little girls.

Tulip - 'Turban'. The meaning of Tulip comes from this pretty flower's unique shape. Ever since one of my children was in 'Tulip' class at school, I became obsessed with how perfect this flower would be for a baby name, especially as they symbolize a perfect and deep love. Choose Tulip for a loveable, stand-out girl name.

Violet - 'Purple'. A pretty flower that has a striking colour. The strong 'V' makes Violet stand out. A truly stunning name!

Zinnia - 'Flower'. The zinnia symbolizes friendship and it's so bright and colourful, it is no surprise that it's bursting onto the name popularity charts with its cool 'Z' initial.

BOYS

Bud/Buddy - A cheeky name with a nod to a new flower about to bloom into your world. A buddy is of course also a term for friend, so it's got a sunny feeling that makes it a great choice for a happy name.

Callyx/Callix - Inspired by flower anatomy, the Callyx are small leaf-like sepals that protect the flower while it's blooming. It's a strong boy name that is a cool twist on the more traditional Alex.

Florian - 'Blossoming'. A pretty boy name that has a fashionable, bohemian feel. Florian is also the name of the prince in *Snow White*, so it's got romantic hero engrained into its charm.

Oleander - 'Evergreen tree'. Pronounced Olly-Ander. I love this as an alternative to popular Oliver. It's rare but easy to say and spell which makes it a great choice. With nicknames Olly or Anders, I think it ticks a lot of boxes.

Rosen - 'Rose or burning bush'. It sounds a bit cowboy cool.

Ren - 'Lotus flower'. This Japanese name has a minimalist sound and is packed with meaning. A lotus blossom holds a lot of significance as a symbol of purity and enlightenment.

Zephyr - The Zephyr lily means 'flower of the west wind'. Pronounced Zef-Ear it's a trendy choice for a little boy. The flower is sometimes called the rain lily as it emerges after a rainfall - I love the name, and the story of the flower feels like hope after a rainy day. I've included Zephyr in my Air Names list, so check it out for more similar options (see page 84).

NEUTRAL

Aster - 'A star'. The bright purple, star-shaped Aster flowers are September's birth flower. This stylish name has that blend of nature and celestial meaning. The flower also has a magical origin story from Greek Mythology where the goddess Astraea was placed by Zeus amongst the constellation of Virgo and cried because there weren't enough stars in the sky. Her teardrops were said to have turned into Aster flowers when they hit earth. I love to imagine telling these tales to little Aster, a true Stand Out & Shine name.

Bloom - 'Flower'. A middle name favourite and brave first name that is so special as your baby blooms and blossoms into the world. Strong and packed full of sentiment, it's a name that gives me serious Baby Name Envy.

Linden - 'Flax hill'. From the gorgeous Linden tree, Linden flowers are one of the UK's edible plants and are often made into tea. Known to have a calming effect, I love the idea of bringing that same essence of peace and restoration into your baby's name.

TREE NAMES

The woods and forests of the world have inspired both traditional names throughout the ages as well as some more recent modern gems. The idea of magical and mystical forests has given rise to many a fairy tale adventure, reinforcing that whimsical, playful feel - some trees were considered sacred or were thought to be pathways between two worlds. Regardless of whether you believe in the mystic symbolism of trees, you are guaranteed to be coming home with many a stick and twig once your little baby is a toddler, so let's begin our exploration of the woods.

GIRLS

Acacia - 'Thorny'. The Acacia tree grows fragrant yellow flowers which are used for making honey and believed to reduce stress. From the Greek *akis*, meaning thorn, I love to think of it as a name that celebrates protection, something we all relate to feeling as parents. Acacia, pronounced A-Kay-Sha, makes a feminine but not overly frilly name with that special meaning of being delicate yet tough.

Elowen - 'Elm tree'. I fall in love with all names ending in the 'wen' sound and Elowen is a stunner. If you love names like Olivia and Amelia but feel they are too popular, then choose rare Elowen instead and prepare for the compliments.

Holly - 'Holly tree'. Holly is so pretty with the double 'LL' adding softness to the name of this spiky tree with red berries. Druids believed that fairies lived in Holly trees to keep protected by their spiky branches, so they bought the trees indoors during long winters to offer protection. As a first name it's been in use since Victorian times and stayed high in our charts, making it a beloved classic. See more on Victorian Naming Traditions in my History section.

Juniper - 'Evergreen tree'. Juniper gives me huge Baby Name Envy. I love the hippy vibe of fun 'Juni' and the youthful mood of this evergreen tree name - full of life with a huge dose of outdoorsy spirit.

Laurel - Laurel is so whimsical with its double 'L' sounds. This evergreen tree feels celebratory and joyful as a name choice, it being the plant used for victory wreaths and garland crowns people still love to wear today for festivals.

Sequoia - 'Sparrow'. Pronounced Se-Coy-Yah. This epic tree is the third oldest tree in the world, named by an Austrian botanist who may have named the tree after Sequoyah, a nineteenth-century Cherokee who invented the Cherokee writing system. The tree symbolizes wellness and safety, which is gorgeous for your little baby girl who will always feel safe in your arms.

Sylvie - 'Forest'. From the word Sylvanus, a vintage name that is still rare, giving it extra sparkle and this gorgeous link to the forest.

Willow - 'Willow tree'. One of our most popular names, the Willow tree is the tree of enchantment with its flexible branches. Willows are beautiful to look at and also symbolize resurrection, as they regrow branches quickly. As a name, it began as a bit of a celebrity pick in the late nineties but has lived up to its symbolism of fast resurgence by climbing quickly to one of our favourite girl names. To me it is stylish with a sprinkling of magic, a winning choice.

BOYS

Cedar - The cedar is a tree *and* a flower. The trees are huge evergreen conifers found in our royal parks. I love the idea of Cedar as a quirky name that evokes the British countryside and playing outdoors. I've included it in my Autumn Names list, so you may find similar inspiration there (page 46).

Darragh - 'Oak tree'. A popular Irish name, Darragh is from old Irish 'daire', meaning 'Dark Oak'. A figure in Irish mythology, the name connotes a rugged cool.

Delamere - 'Forest of the lake'. A French place name introduced to England as a surname, 'la mere' means' by the water'. It's a grand name that fits the 'surname as first name' trend that's become popular. It sounds romantic and elegant with the picture book forest setting meaning.

Elon - 'Oak tree'. A rare Hebrew name, Elon could make a great alternative to Noah with a similar vibe.

Ewan - 'Born of the Yew tree'. The yew tree symbolizes everlasting life. A delicate and soft name, Ewan pronounced You-En is of Celtic origin.

Jarrah - 'Eucalyptus tree'. A tree native to the south west of Western Australia, the Noongar people used the Jarrah tree to make tools, shelters and bedding.

Koa - 'Warrior'. The Koa tree is the largest tree in Hawaii and the name evokes that island style. The Koa tree would be used to create canoes, ukeleles, spears and warrior weapons and is extremely beautiful, growing to huge heights. I love the idea of pouring all those qualities into your little baby's name.

Oakley - 'Oak tree clearing'. This takes me straight into the woods. Names with the 'ley' ending always blend so well into most surnames and this modern little boy name should hit your list if you're after that outdoorsy, fun vibe.

Oran - 'Pine tree'. This Irish boy name has a subtle earthy meaning. You can opt for Orran to help with pronunciation and the emphasis is on the 'r' sound, like a boat oar. A unique name with plenty of spirit and sparkle.

Silas - 'From the woods'. This name is strong and outdoorsy from the long form Silvanus. Silvanus was the Roman god of the forests and a disciple in the New Testament. It's calming and soft with the gentle 'S' sounds, and is easy to spell and write. A stunning pick that makes me want to go for a walk holding his little hand and play with sticks under the trees.

Woodrow - 'Row of houses by the woods'. I love how Woodrow takes us to a little village or urban treelined avenue.

Woody - 'From the woods'. The playful name Woody burst onto the scene as we all started to embrace these rarer nature names. This cute boy name makes a brilliant free-spirited choice.

Yves - 'Evergreen tree'. From the yew tree. Pronounced without the 's' like feminine Eve, it's a super-trendy name if you're after something minimal and sweet.

NEUTRAL

Ash - 'Tree of life'. One of the most spiritual trees, Ash makes a cool name for a boy or girl. Longer form Asher also links to the tree and has the extra bonus of meaning 'happiness', which your little one will bring so much of. I also love Ashby which is more modern and means Ash Tree Farm.

Aspen - 'Shield'. The Aspen is a beautiful tree, known also as the quaking aspen, as it moves so beautifully. The name means 'shield' and its lightweight wood was used for making shields. People also believed the tree had a protective magic that would keep them from harm.

Forest - 'Woodland'. I chose this as a middle name for myself a few years ago, as I didn't have one. Forests are magical, vast places where deer, wolves and bears make their homes. I'm never happier than playing amongst trees with my children, and it makes for an outdoorsy namesake you'll love together, forever.

Kiri - 'Bark'. This Māori name means the skin or bark of a tree. Kiri is a short and sweet name that would complement a longer surname.

Perry - 'Pear tree'. Perry is a gender-neutral name with an English countryside vibe. Also used as a nickname for Peregrine, meaning 'traveller', it's a charismatic name for a lively child.

Rowan - 'Red berries'. The name's meaning comes from the red berries on the Rowan tree. The Rowan tree symbolizes protection, some say because of when the Vikings came across and carved their Rune protection symbols into the tree's bark, which gave it the 'Rune Tree' name. That warm feeling of protection elevates the name to a place that can truly touch your heart.

Xylon - 'From the forest'. This Greek name appears in ancient literature often as a woodland deity. Pronounced Zy-Lon, the word originally included anything created from wood, including the trees, or a wooden horse. 'X' names always have added edge and Xylon would suit a Stand Out & Shine namer looking for that nod to nature.

BOTANICAL NAMES

Botanical Names are inspired by the lush plants and open natural spaces all around us. Lots of these would have once been surnames, given to those people actually dwelling by meadows, fields or even by peaty bogs - don't worry, the names get five stars even if the venue doesn't. Historically topographical names helped link people to where they came from, and now they give us some creative first name ideas. I know that in every home renovation show you've ever watched someone will suggest ways of 'bringing the outside in' - and I'm about to do just that with names. Plant-inspired names celebrate the great outdoors and all the fun you'll have in nature's playground with your baby.

GIRLS

Abilene - 'Stream or meadow'. A Hebrew name, also the name of a city in Texas which gives it a Southern vibe. Abilene is grand and spirited just like its nature meaning.

Ardith - 'Flowering meadow'. The sound of Ardith is just so special and fills a space on your personal name list with something unique and super vintage. I get serious Baby Name Envy with Ardith.

Briar - 'Brambles'. Briar-Rose was the name of Sleeping Beauty during the years she spent living in the forest. Briar has a very cool, botanical vibe and is mostly used as a hyphenated name like the fairy tale character, Briar-Rose.

Briony/Bryony - 'Sprouting plant'. Inspired by the Bryonia plant, Briony was first recorded as a name in the 1700s and peaked in the nineties in England. The name is now as rare as the plant, so it's perfect if you're looking for a gentle option that she won't be sharing with many of her peers.

Delavigne - 'Dweller in the vineyard'. An old French surname pronounced 'Dela-Veen', meaning 'from the vine', this topographical name would have been given to people who lived and worked in the gorgeous French vineyards. It's a complex but worth-it stylish idea for a first name.

Demetria - 'Earth mother'. From Demeter, I find the name softer with the longer ending. Demeter was goddess of plants, crops and harvest and the story of her daughter Persephone was used in mythology to explain the cycle of seasons. During autumn and winter Persephone was taken by Hades to live in the underworld and spring and summer came when she returned to live with her mother.

Evanthe - 'Good flower'. Pronounced E-Van-Thee, this Greek name has a bohemian feel, being strong and creative in sound with such a whimsical meaning. See my Bohemian Aesthetic Name list if you love names in this style.

Georgia - 'Earth worker'. The feminine form of George is a timeless classic. A stylish moniker, Georgia can also have some fun nicknames like GiGi or Gia.

Ivy - 'Vine'. This botanical name is pretty without being too frilly. The creeping ivy has symbolized fidelity for centuries and is popular to adorn wedding venues. Ivy oozes style in its simplicity and elegance. See Minimalist Names for similar ideas.

Meadow - 'Field of grass'. I have always loved the name Meadow, it's not a word we use very often so it feels natural as a name. If you love the image of meadows full of wildflowers then you're brave enough for this stunning name.

Myrtle - 'Evergreen shrub'. This Victorian favourite hasn't bloomed in a few years in the name charts, but with Margot and Mabel hitting top spots, Myrtle could be on your list.

Nettie - 'Plant'. Taken from the ending of Jeanette and Annette, Nettie is a really playful name with such a sweet meaning.

BOYS

Bailey - 'Berry clearing'. An old French name, Bailey has a wild nature meaning, reminiscent of being out berry picking. I've always loved the name, it's down to earth but fashionable.

Brody - 'Ditch'. A handsome name with an interesting history. The Brodies were a Medieval Scottish Clan, dwelling at Brodie Castle, so it's got that grand and iconic feel as a name too. Brody has continued in popularity, being both earthy and distinctive.

Byron - 'Place of the cow sheds'. I love the juxtaposition of this poetic sounding name and its countryside meaning. Byron is a dashing name - a little bit stately home and a little bit farmer's help - it's a period drama of a name all by itself.

Florens - 'Blossoming'. This Italian boy name is very cool. Pronounced floor-enz, the emphasis is at the end of the name. It sounds right out of an Italian garden.

George - 'Farmer'. A British classic, this royal name never goes out of style for good reason. It has a fascinating history. The Greek god Zeus gave the name its 'earth worker' meaning; originally known as Zeus Georgos, he was god of the harvest. In Greek *Ge* means 'soil' and *ergon* means 'to work'. In 303 a Roman soldier called Georgos was martyred, and the name took religious significance for Christians; we now know him as Saint George, the Patron Saint of England. The name George was reserved solely for religious leaders as a baptismal name until King George made it a top spot for British baby boys, where it's stayed ever since.

Hemlock - 'Poisonous plant'. Hemlock is easy to say and spell and has a gothic vibe due to it being a poisonous plant. It would suit you if you love the sound and find the meaning a little magical.

Logan - 'Little hollow'. Scottish Logan is a warm and inviting name and its meaning takes me outside to a mystical wood or animal burrow.

Reed - 'Grass plants'. Although not as obvious a nature word, it's got that marshland, rugged vibe with a traditional slant. I love that Reed can also mean red-haired.

Whittaker - 'White field'. It brings to mind a lovely image of a snowy field. Whit is a cool shortened version of the name.

NEUTRAL

Dallas - 'Meadow dwelling'. This place name has become more synonymous with Texas in the US, but its origin is a Scottish habitual name from *dol* 'meadow' and *gwas* 'dwelling'. It also means 'valley house' when translated from Norse. Dallas was the 1980s hit TV show, so this place name is one of the most iconic and a great pick if you want a stand-out name.

Hollis - 'Dweller at the holly trees'. I love names ending in 'S' and with Ellis and Holly being so popular, Hollis is putting its roots down in the charts as a trendy gender-neutral alternative. I think it's on the right side of edgy - not trying too hard while still feeling naturally fresh. Perfect for Trendy with a Twist namers.

Moss - 'A peatbog or Son of Moses'. A super-trendy choice with a vibrant green colour at its heart. I imagine you would always associate moss with countryside walks with family. It also has stylish links to supermodel Kate Moss, which creates a minimalist nature name that has both glamour and earthiness.

WILDERNESS NAMES

Wilderness Names celebrate the huge resurgence and trend of rewilding urban areas and getting back to basics. There's so many of us who choose to spend our free time and holidays going off-grid, detoxing from technology and living a simpler life. It's like our souls really want to live that way. With this Wilderness Names list, I chose names that are outdoorsy and spirited but not too frilly or fussy. Just like a cabin in the woods, you are your baby's sanctuary, where they feel they can be truly themselves and your heart is their home, always.

GIRLS

Artemis - 'Goddess of the wilderness'. I have such a name crush on Artemis, goddess of the wilderness; it's such a spirited and adventurous name. Pronounced Arta-Miss, it's not overly complex which gives it such wearability in today's world and it has a strong and independent spirit that makes a really cool namesake.

Avani - 'Good earth'. Ticks all the boxes for fans of more popular Ava, so stylish with a grounded feel from its meaning. Avani has a classy vibe and will turn heads with its beauty. It could jump to the top of your name list for its gorgeous eco meaning.

Clover - 'Meadow flower'. Growing wild across meadows, gorgeous clover is associated with good luck, as they are one of the rare trefoil plants that typically have three leaves or occasionally four. Clover ticks my box for being a unique name that's easy to say and spell and has the word 'love' in the middle, which really feels special for your lucky and beloved baby girl.

Fauna - 'Young deer'. Fauna was the Roman goddess of the woodlands and gave her name to the baby deer fawns. Pronounced Faw-Na, it's a soft and delicate name that is perfect for a Trendy with a Twist namer looking for something special but classical.

Fiadh - 'Wild and free'. A stunning Irish name, full of fun and energy. Pronounced Fia, it's ideal for your free-spirited baby girl.

Kayla - 'A beauty only a poet can capture'. Pronounced Ky-la, this feels very bohemian with the meaning being drawn from the indescribable beauty of nature. An Irish name, the traditional spelling is Cadhla, which was anglicized to Kayla and both are beautiful. Kayla is barefoot and fanciful all at once.

Nesrine - 'Wild rose'. This Persian name perfectly captures the wilderness vibes of a wild rose. A gorgeous name that brings that wildflower soul right into her story.

BOYS

Brent - 'High land'. Of Celtic origin, Brent is a beauty of a name. Simple but stylish.

Digby - 'Ditch by the farm'. A unique boy name that despite its down-to-earth meaning feels classy and scholarly. If you're after a classic British name with a twinkle in its eye, Digby is perfect.

Harlan - 'Hare's land'. Harlan was a place name for those living a little 'off-grid' in ancient times - Harlan dwelt on the boundaries in less cultivated areas. Just like the olden days' hipsters, it's off the beaten track.

Heath - 'Uncultivated land'. So outdoorsy with the literary allure of Heathcliff, I love the romance and unspoilt style of the name Heath.

Lathan - 'From the barn'. An old Norse name, Lathan has a striking sound.

Leland - 'Meadow land'. We don't often get the 'Le' sound at the beginning of boys names and I love this old English name and its connoations.

Mostyn - 'Moss town'. If Moss alone is a little daring, Welsh name Mostyn gives you a longer form that is more traditional.

Parker - 'Park keeper'. An occupational surname, now an established first name, it shows a love and care for nature wrapped up in a trendy name.

Yulin - 'Jade forest'. A Chinese name, Yulin has magical wood vibes meaning 'Jade' or 'Feathered Forest'.

NEUTRAL

Arden - 'Great forest'. There were two great forests named Arden, one named the Ardennes which stretches across France, Germany, Luxembourg and Belgium and one in Warwickshire, which inspired the Forest of Arden in Shakespeare's *As You Like It*. Arden was Shakespeare's mother's maiden name. It feels poetic and mysterious.

Glen - 'Valley'. Glen is the Scottish term for a valley. The name was a hit in the eighties and nineties and with such a lovely nature meaning it is a short, sweet choice for a girl or boy.

Hartley - 'Deer forest'. A Hart is a male deer or stag, so this name evokes strength and power and the vast nature of a forest.

Hunter - 'To hunt'. Booming into the charts in the seventies, Hunter has been at an all-time peak in our top 100 names in the UK recently. The hunter/gatherer nature vibe has made it a playful but vintage choice for parents who value what the great outdoors means to childhood.

Lavern - 'Land of trees'. Lavern has a retro style that feels edgy and unique. I love the image of a land of trees that reaches as far as you can see. With an 'e' at the end, Laverne means 'born in the spring'. See my Spring Names list for more ideas if you're having a spring baby.

Marley - 'Marshy meadow'. Marley is an English surname that's made its leap onto our first name lists. It's a very cool name that makes me think of Bob Marley or Jacob Marley from *A Christmas Carol*. Marley is perfect if you love gender-neutral names with a trendy twist.

Montana - 'Mountain'. A gorgeous name synonymous with showing strength. Meaningful for so many reasons, it could make an ideal name, capturing the strength a lot of us need in our journey to parenthood.

Quigley - 'Unkempt'. An Irish surname that has the best meaning of being unruly, which I take as an invitation to get messy and have fun. Quinn has been popular for a few years, so the more quirky Quigley may be just the name you've been looking for.

Valley - 'Between the mountains'. A unique place name that conjures up adventure and depth. Valli is another spelling with the slightly different meaning of 'healthy'.

Wilde/Wilder - 'Uninhabited land'. A newly popular baby name that stands out for evoking a back-to-basics, off-grid childhood for your baby. Hitting the 'surname as first name' trend, this stylish option is wearable, playful and spirited for your little wild child. Get ready for an adventure.

BABY NAME LAWS

The UK is quite relaxed when it comes to how to legally name your baby, but there are some laws and customs it's good to be aware of. You will have a few weeks in which to register your baby's name after birth. The registrar will then create their legal birth certificate. It is possible to make changes afterwards, but this does involve some extra paperwork and small fee. There are different laws about baby names all over the world, and some are amazingly strict.

Denmark has a list of 7,000 preapproved names parents must choose from. It's still law in some countries like Switzerland and Germany that the gender be obvious in the name so as not to cause confusion; though this book shows there are plenty of names that are gender neutral, this law is there to stop parents naming a boy Sarah-Jayne, for example, and causing the child embarrassment if they identify as male.

As a legal rule all over the world, every child needs a first name and a surname, and the name shouldn't be offensive. Cancel culture is rife in the world of names and can happen either through historic events or popular culture; poor Karen has had it hard lately.

Word names should be wearable. There are reported cases of parents trying to register Santa Claus in America, Nutella in France and Ikea in Sweden; each of which were rejected by the country's authorities. Misleading titles such as President, Messiah or Sir would not make it past UK registration guidelines. In France, parents who tried to name their baby Prince William were swiftly rejected. Justice and Judge are banned in New Zealand and Lord, Lady and Baron could be contested in lots of countries, as they are titles that give authority. Most countries also ban symbols which I'm fully onboard with; so, scrap #blessing and @las from your list right now. In the UK the guidance is not to use names that are excessively long, meaning names with more than one hyphen risk not being approved. So, if you love three names, it's best to move some to the middle, though a limit on the number of names is often enforced too.

A strange new phenomenon is occurring where a few parents have been told their baby name is trademarked. Rumour has it Jay-Z and Beyoncé have trademarked Rumi Carter, Sir Carter and Blue Ivy, which doesn't mean you can't use the name/s, but it might mean your child has trouble creating a social profile or business named after themselves. A mum from my hometown Swindon had to fight for her daughter's passport when it was rejected, as her daughter's name Khaleesi was deemed to have been trademarked by Warner Brothers. It was later overthrown, but shows that it's a brave new world out there.

CAN I CHANGE MY BABY'S SURNAME?

In the UK you can register any surname for your baby. It's a custom not a law that you pass your surname onto your child. However, most people use their own surname from birth or a shared name through marriage. We also see 'double-barrel' surnames or even blended names made up of two surnames.

Using a double-barrelled surname has come full circle into popularity again. The double-barrel used to be reserved for the upper classes to ensure the bride's name carried the wealth and estate of her heritage on through the generations. It then went out of style in the decades of the nuclear family; but now we often don't share surnames as a family, whether that's due to being a blended family with multiple surnames, unmarried parents or a married couple choosing to keep their own surnames. What's interesting is that the double-barrel has come back into style recently for our children and I hear a lot more of my friends and school families who have given both surnames to their children.

It's a great idea to have the chat with loved ones. One recent trend that needs consideration and some further thought is that when two double-barrelled people 'couple up', what then becomes of their four surnames if they choose to have kids?

Same-sex couples, blended families and modern marrieds are also looking into the option of choosing a whole new 'family' name.

My married surname and maiden name Ljungstrom-Whitcher could become Whitstrom or my friends Sealey-Vaughan could become Hanley. I love this freedom we have when creating our families and it's special to see Naming Ceremonies for not just the baby's name but the new joint surname. It's an easy deed-poll form to change the adult's surnames alongside the baby's. So have those chats early on and decide what surname you're going with.

SEASONAL

Your baby's due date is one of the things you'll get asked a lot, with the next question being, 'Do you know what you're having?' and then an unsolicited piece of advice about labour or parenthood. 'Sleep now, while you can.' Ha ha ha! Your due date is one of the best places to start when looking for a baby name. It's beautiful to be named after the season you arrived into the world, and there are so many other ways to be inspired – birth stones, seasonal holidays, the cosy feelings of autumn or the warmth and light of summer. The season will also have standout events, moments and changes in nature which are packed with inspiration.

SPRING NAMES

Spring names celebrate all the new life coming into the world. It's when our days grow longer and plants and flowers begin to bloom after winter. I've chosen names that really celebrate the sun breaking through and all the fresh new beginnings of the season.

GIRLS

Anastasia - 'Resurrection'. This was the name of so many of my dolls growing up. I love the name Anastasia - it's long and elegant, traditional but not as popular as some others, so it might be your perfect name, and the meaning is spot-on for a spring baby.

April - 'To open'. From Latin *Aprilis,* the name for the fourth month of the year has its roots in the word *aperire* meaning 'to open'. It's a meaning that makes me think of being open-hearted and alert to adventure. The name would work for a Timelessly Tasteful namer who wanted something a little less common.

Aurora - 'Dawn'. The goddess of the dawn brings renewal and new life, perfect themes for spring, and it's such a pretty name (a princess name too, see Disney names for more).

Aviva - 'Springtime'. From *Aviv,* the Hebrew word for spring, Aviva really complements the season, sounding fresh and vibrant.

Avril - 'April'. The French name for April, Avril has a more whimsical sound to punchy and vibrant April.

Blossom - 'To bloom'. Perfect for the season where flowers bloom, the name Blossom makes a pretty alternative to Lily, Rose or Poppy. My daughter is called Evelina Blossom and she loves her middle name. I have, of course, also included Blossom in my Flower Names list (see page 17).

Florence - 'Flourishing'. From *fior* meaning 'flowering' in Italian. I love the significance of the word 'flourish' for spring. A place name which has long been used for girls, Florence is joyful and positive wrapped up in a vintage bow.

Iola - 'Violet dawn'. This makes me think of lovely spring mornings. Pronounced Eye-Oh-La, it could be another pretty option if you've listed Isla or Olivia, as it's got a sprinkle of both as well as a beautiful meaning.

Oriana - 'Sunrise'. Oriana couldn't be more stunning in sound or meaning, with the open 'a' ending pronounced Orry-Ah-Na. It gives me a lot of Baby Name Envy. From the Latin word for sunrise, it's full of magic.

Persephone - 'Goddess of fertility'. In Greek mythology, Persephone brought the spring with her when she returned from the underworld every six months. Alongside a lot of long, interesting names, Persephone has been slowly growing a following with brave namers.

Rachel - 'Ewe or female sheep'. Classic Rachel will always sound elegant but down to earth. I love the sheep symbol for a springtime baby.

Sakura - 'Cherry blossom'. Sakura is a stunning Japanese name. Cherry blossoms, with their distinctive pink flowers that bloom in spring, are always celebrated in Japan with family walks and picnics. Sakura brings that spring flower to life in a pretty name.

Verda - 'Green'. A Spanish girl's name, Verda oozes cool. I particularly like the symbol of green, associated with renewal, life and beginnings.

BOYS

Albert - 'Bright'. The brighter and longer days of spring perfectly suit Albert. A classic that has been steadily rising up the charts, it's a great pick for Timelessly Tasteful namers.

Denver - 'Green valley'. An English place name, now maybe more well known as an American one. Denver has a wonderful outdoorsy meaning, and place names always exude a sense of exploration.

Inizio - 'New beginnings'. A super-interesting and exciting Italian name, new beginnings is the perfect meaning for your newborn.

Jarek - 'Spring born'. Jarek is a Slavic name after the God of spring and harvest. A classic name with a lovely sound - the 'j' pronounced as a 'y' for British speakers. I also like the alternative Jarilo.

Mika - 'New moon'. I always think of new beginnings in spring and Mika is a gorgeous name heralding a new season with a new moon.

Omar - 'Flourishing'. This stylish Arabic name is perfect for the flourishing countryside in spring.

Stanley - 'Stony meadow'. Stanley can be traced back to 1264 as a typographic name for someone dwelling near the stony meadow. Since then it's been in and out of style, but it's definitely back, bridging the vintage and nature trend, making it perfect for spring. I think it's super-sweet as little Stan and will grow with your baby.

Vernon - 'Alder tree'. A vintage name that hasn't come back into fashion, it's not dissimilar to Oliver and Noah in tone. The Alder Tree symbolizes safety and protection, which adds so much care and love into the name.

NEUTRAL

Genesis - 'Origins'. A brave choice, but we're moving towards words like 'saint' and 'psalm' being used as names, and Genesis fits the trend. For springtime it's perfect for that sense of a new beginning and creation.

Laverne - 'Born in spring'. Laverne appears in both Celtic and Roman mythology. The name sounds so glamorous and quirky. See Lavern without an 'e' as other spelling option in Wilderness Names.

Pascale - 'Easter born'. For the male version it's Pascal without the 'e'. This takes me to a spring day in Paris, a French name that is high-fashion and will turn heads.

Usha - 'Dawn'. From Ushas, the Hindu deity of the dawn and the child of heaven. Usha celebrates new beginnings and new life.

SUMMER NAMES

Summer is a season of friends and family, time off work and lots of togetherness, plus it's evocative of the long endless holidays of our childhoods. My lovely niece Summer perfectly suits her name, being the most full of life, resilient and warm little girl. This Summer Names list is inspired by sunshine and happy times; may your little baby have plenty of both.

GIRLS

Aavya - 'First ray of sun'. An Indian girl name, Aavya is dazzling, with such joy in its meaning.

Avalon - 'Island of apples'. With thousands of people flocking to Glastonbury in the summer, the name Avalon should take centre stage this season. Glastonbury is also called 'The Isle of Avalon' where King Arthur went after his last battle and the Avalon stage and Avalon fields at the festival celebrate this link.

Holiday - 'Holy day'. Holiday originally meant Holy Day from the Christian calendar but then went on to mean any celebration. It could fit in other seasons' lists but it feels most fitting in Summer. As a name it feels retro and a little kitsch, upbeat and fun, ideal for a Stand Out & Shine namer.

Kupala - 'Bathing'. Whether you're bathing in the sun, forest or lake, Kupala is such a wonderful but rare name. Kupala Night is a festival around Europe dedicated to the deity Kupala. Celebrations are held on riverbanks where people bathe in the water and it's also folklore that this is a day the sun plays. Your little

Kupala - pronounced like Koala, just adding the 'p', which yes, makes me love it even more - would be an outdoorsy spirit who loves to swim in the sun with you.

Pearl - 'Precious'. A vintage gem of a name, it's also the birthstone for the month of June. See the Quiet Luxury Names list for more on the name Pearl.

Posy - 'A small bouquet'. Flower names are stunning for a summer baby, as picking wildflowers is a tradition on midsummer. Find more floral names in my Flower Names list.

Solana - 'Sunny place'. A warm and inviting name, a sunny place evokes feelings of warmth and also somebody with a sunny nature.

Soleil - 'Sun'. The name Soleil also links in meaning to solitude and takes me to solo days on the beach, my dream. Soleil is pronounced So-Lay, so it's an intriguing name, very soft and beachy.

Summer - 'Summertime'. With Summer Solstice happening in June, Summer makes a bright and vibrant name and is divine for your little girl.

Tess - 'Summer'. Tess comes from the name Teresa which means both 'summer' and 'to harvest'. It also has a satisfying one-syllable appeal.

BOYS

Bay - 'Body of water'. I love the beachy vibe of the name Bay and adding it to my Summer list is giving Australian Soap associations. Anyone who loves a summer's day on a quiet beach will get a lot from the sweet name Bay.

Dashiell - 'Sky, Heaven'. Originally a French surname, Dashiell sounds romantic and elegant. The meaning is evocative of a sunny blue sky.

Dayton - 'From the bright and sunny town'. Dayton is a place name appearing around the world, with a summer's-day-out, laid-back essence.

Elio - 'Sun'. From Helios, the God of Sun, who drove a chariot from east to west each day bringing the Sun, Elio has emerged as the modern boy's name. Pronounced Ee-Leo it's got that something extra that makes an impact.

Frasier - 'Strawberry'. The perfect summer baby name, whether it's strawberries and cream at Wimbledon or the June full moon, known as the Strawberry Moon. It's a lovely happy name.

Jared - 'Rose'. One lovely meaning of the name Jared is Rose. Roses are the birth flower for the month of June, so a subtle nod to the special month you first meet your baby boy.

Lucien - 'Light'. With June holding the longest day of the year, it's really lovely to share the light and joy of the season with your baby's name.

Ravi - 'Sun'. This stunning Hindi name literally means 'sun'. Ravi is warm and inviting just like it's meaning; a timeless gem that will never go out of style.

Samson - 'Bright as the Sun'. Samson has legendary strength. The name can also mean Sun Child, perfect for your summer born babe. It makes a great Trendy with A Twist name, as it's really classic but hasn't got the popularity of other biblical names and you get cool Sammy or Sonny as nicknames.

Somerled - 'Summer Sailors'. An old Irish name that was also picked up as a Viking name. Traditionally it's pronounced with a silent 'd', however it would feel most natural to me to pronounce it, so go for it if you like the sound. If you're looking for a nautical, vintage gem, Somerled could be for you.

Tommy - 'Twin'. The 'nickname as first name' trend is really thriving for our boys. Tommy is a delightful June name, as this is the month of Gemini, the symbol of twins. So, double the love with a name celebrating their zodiac sign.

NEUTRAL

Bertie - 'Bright'. The nickname for Robert and Albert, Bertie is a great vintage nickname. I'm hearing it more and more for girls too and it works so well. For brighter days and sunny times, Bertie is a good bet.

Devon - 'Divine'. Devon is best known in the UK as a place name, but it has various meanings, including Divine, from the French word *devin*. Devon has both a seaside holiday style and a glamorous movie edge to it. For more place names, see my Travel-inspired names lists.

Juno - 'Youthful'. This modern-sounding name is the namesake of the month of June. Juno is the ancient Roman deity of love, which makes it a perfect name for your little loveable baby.

AUTUMN NAMES

Autumn is the most picturesque season. It's when everything turns copper and everyone gets excited to swap sandals for slippers and puts pumpkin spice in everything. My autumn baby Finn was born during the craziest September heatwave, and I was mostly found at our local lido pool at 41 weeks pregnant with a toddler in tow, which was probably a terrifying sight for those hoping to escape delivering an impromptu water birth. But the weather cooled once he was finally here, so we enjoyed long buggy walks around the park, and I bought all the cosy onesies for him. Autumn names bring all the comfort and warmth of the season into a name. It's the golden hour of the year and the perfect inspiration for a special name.

GIRLS

Aurelia - 'Golden'. Beginning with the same letters as the season and with the sound 'ray' right at its centre, Aurelia really brings the golden hues of autumn leaves to life. So vibrant, romantic and enthralling, Aurelia always gives me a pop of envy when I hear it, as it would have been a really strong contender for my daughter's name.

Ceres - 'Goddess of the grain'. Pronounced 'series'. The harvest season predominantly falls in Autumn, and this goddess name has taken off in the trend for ancient names that feel thoroughly new again.

Ginger - 'Spice'. Ginger was one of the original spices to come over to England. It's a warming name, evoking the rich colours of autumn with its deep orange hue. You'll be sipping on your gingerbread latte next autumn feeling very content with baby Ginger tucked in beside you. You may even get 'girl power' or 1930s movie icon associations - a brave pick but I think one you may love.

Jorah - 'Autumn rain'. Jorah's charm for me is that it's close to Norah. The meaning is very romantic, and you'll relish getting out your wellies and splashing in puddles with your little Jorah.

Maple - 'Maple tree'. For both the stunning tree leaves which are vibrant red and the golden-hued syrup, the name Maple was *made* for autumn.

Orla - 'Golden princess'. This Irish princess name is a rare alternative to Olivia (our top spot) and reminiscent of Isla. The traditional spelling is Orlaith and is perfect for the golden leaves of autumn.

BOYS

Cedar - 'Cedar tree'. A cone-bearing tree, the cedar leaves turn sunset-coloured during autumn, so it's a name at the heart of the season and makes a cool choice. See my Tree Names list for more tree-inspired ideas (page 24).

Flint - 'Stream'. I think nature names work perfectly for the season and Flint is a bang-on-trend boy name. Flint stones are used to spark fire and it feels like getting cosy for autumn.

Keifer - 'Pine tree'. Pine trees were the symbol of a long life and Keifer is a charismatic name of German origin. Its other meaning is 'barrel maker'.

Radley - 'Red meadow'. Radley sounds classy and inviting with the vibrant colour evoked by a red meadow. It's a surname that can be traced back to Berkshire in England, but then travelled far and wide.

Van - 'Cloud'. A Vietnamese name that brings an autumnal cloudy day to mind. Spelt Vân traditionally, it's used mainly for boys but can be gender neutral. An alternative spelling, Văn, means literature. Both stunning, cosy-day vibes.

NEUTRAL

Indra - 'Possessing drops of rain'. Indra was the warrior of rain and the sky and it's a great weather-inspired name for this season. I've always loved the name India, but it felt too brave (although my granny was half Indian). Indra is a striking alternative with nickname Indie, too.

Lennox - 'Elm tree grove'. Tree names feel ideal for autumn and Lennox is one of my favourite hidden nature names, the 'x' makes it so cool.

Wyndham - 'From the windy village'. If country village walks are your vibe, then Wyndham, to rhyme with Kingdom, will be so up your lane.

WINTER NAMES

Having a winter baby is special, as you get to really enjoy that cosy season and of course hibernate during the fourth trimester as much as you can. It's also a season full of holidays and family time. My daughter, who was born on Winter Solstice, loves seeing all the fairy lights go up as it nears her birthday. I must admit the night feeds in her first few days were a lot more fun with left-over Christmas snacks and TV specials to keep me going. I still remember her first bath by the fire under the Christmas tree in one of those bucket baths; it's a magical season. These winter wonderland names are inspired by the weather, the traditions and the new year we enter each winter. Next year perhaps your little winter-named baby will be nestled beside you.

GIRLS

Apricity - 'The warmth of the sun in winter'. I was thrilled when I heard there's a word meaning 'the warmth of the sun in winter'. It makes for a beautiful name. It's the best feeling when you pop on a beanie hat and sunglasses for a walk - you know you're at peak whimsical weather. Apricity is pronounced A-Pree-City.

Dagny - 'New day'. I love the name Dagny for a winter baby as we move into the new year. It's Scandinavian and has a fashionable, contemporary feel despite dating back to Norse mythology. A strong, empowering girl name full of the hope and wonder of a new beginning.

Eira - 'Snow'. A pretty Welsh name that could be an alternative to Isla with deep winter vibes.

Enya - 'Fire'. We always think 'cold' when we think of winter, but I enjoy the cosy fireside vibe of the season. Enya is a warm hug of a girl name.

Iclynn - 'Dream or vision'. Aisling is a stunning Irish name meaning Dream or Vision, and Iclynn, the Scandinavian version, brings frost and icy lakes to the name.

Joy - 'Great happiness'. Merriment and Joy are celebrated all winter. This vintage name has been used so many times as a middle name, I'd elevate it to first place.

Lumi - 'Snow'. I adore this Finnish girl name, pronounced Lou-Me. With Luna (meaning 'moon') being a rising star in baby names, Lumi adds that extra winter sparkle.

Noelle - 'Christmas'. Synonymous with Christmas carols, Noelle comes from a Latin word for birth, relating to the Birth of Christ.

Reeva - 'One who guides'. Star names sparkle strongly in winter, but Reeva means 'a guiding star'. It's a stunning name for a baby girl who will always be guided by you, but who is also the star you follow when you need to make decisions. Reeva will always shine brightly.

Tanzy - 'Tanzanite'. The birthstone for December, Tanzy is a lovely 'nickname as first name' idea for a winter baby.

Winica - 'Christmas orchid'. Winica gives me major Baby Name Envy. A type of Orchid found in New Zealand, Winica also means vineyard. Two botanical meanings for a Christmas baby with vintage Winnie just waiting to be snapped up as a nickname.

Zima - 'Winter'. This beautiful Eastern European word for winter sounds so fashionable.

BOYS

Aiden - 'Little fire'. This Irish name is so romantic and brings to life cosy fireside evenings during those colder months.

Aquilo - 'North wind'. Aquilo was the god who blew winter across the earth. With the 'o' at the end it's a brave pick with the most evocative meaning.

Caldwell - 'Cold stream'. A 'surname as first name', it transports me to wild swimming and ice baths. I love water-themed names for their calm and power. See the Water Names list for more on this theme if you are drawn to them too.

Cole - 'Victorious people'. I really like the name Cole, it feels handsome and grounding. I also think of coal used in the past to make fires during winter and a convenient quick-grab for Santa who, legend tells, would leave a lump of coal for naughty kids.

Douglas - 'Black stream'. The most popular type of tree for adorning at Christmas time is the Douglas Fir and I think it makes a cute nod to the season. Douggie is the sweetest nickname for a Christmas baby.

Everest - 'Dweller on the Eure River'. The mountain summit covered in snow feels like a cool pick for a winter-born baby, with a winter wonderland vibe. The mountain was named after a British Surveyor - read more about Everest in the Names Inspired By The Earth list.

Fraser - 'Fraser tree'. A Fraser is a scented and lush Christmas tree variant. The name is sophisticated and cool and you'd always have so much fun picking your Fraser tree.

Hart - 'Brave stag'. A hart is a male deer. Reindeers are such a huge part of winter, I adore the idea of the name Hart for your little love. Or maybe a brave middle name choice paired with a more traditional first name.

Shepherd - 'Sheep herder'. Shepherds are a huge part of the Christmas story, with a Shepherd symbolizing divine guidance. I think it makes a trendy name and with Shep as a nickname, you're guaranteed a role in the nativity.

NEUTRAL

Aspen - 'Shaking tree'. The Aspen tree, also known as the shaking tree, gets a winter double tick, as it's also the name of the famous ski resort. So many reasons to use trendy Aspen for your little winter baby. For a girl, Penny could make for a quirky vintage nickname.

Aubrey - 'Elf ruler'. It's got to be Elf season, surely? Aubrey is a beautiful vintage name I see on so many name lists. Although traditionally male, it works on both lists and makes a playful nod to the season they are born in. My daughter would be over the moon with this name's meaning - who doesn't want to work in Santa's workshop with the elves? Find Aubrey in my Fantastical Beasts & Mythical Creatures Names list as well (page 107).

Flóki - 'Flake of snow'. Icelandic name Flóki was one of the first Vikings to discover Iceland's name and it captures that Icelandic style so perfectly. This name would have been a definite contender for me had I discovered it when I had my babies, for its special sound and evocative meaning.

Nevada - 'Snow-capped'. A Spanish adjective which became an iconic place name, Nevada makes an inspiring and memorable name that takes you right up high to snow-capped mountains.

Robin - 'Bright'. The Robin is a pretty little red-breasted bird. One historical reason they became associated with winter is during Victorian times when sending Christmas cards began as a tradition. The cards were delivered by postmen who were nicknamed 'Robins', as their uniforms had red breasts. Robyn with a 'y' for girls is a personal favourite of mine. See my full list of Bird Names for other bird options, as they are always so symbolic.

HOW TO FIND NAMES BASED ON SPECIAL MOMENTS

I love thinking back over special moments, places, people and experiences that stand out to find a truly meaningful baby name. It could be a hidden meaning or a word but it ultimately tops the name list if it reminds you of the happiest and most emotive times of your life so far. In a journal, jot down your top three stand-out moments as a couple that brought you joy and bring you happiness when you think about them. Don't start with a name - just where you were, and why you loved it.

A date in the calendar is also a fun place to start - what season, event, festival or tradition can you pinpoint that feels like a part of your DNA?

A pivotal memory provides so much food for thought and will spark a list of ideas you hadn't thought to investigate yet, like the flower in your bridal bouquet, a special street name or a treasured walk on the beach that will stay with you forever. Your child doesn't share your identity, but your life experience is their story too. I've picked names from the champagne at people's weddings, a favourite cake has been used in a middle spot more than once and one couple used a street name from Soho because they had their first date in the London district. It's a super playful and personality-fuelled way to bring that sparkle of 'you' into their name.

SPACE & STARS

'I love you to the moon and back' must ring out at kids' bedtimes around the world. The moon is still an icon of mystery and guidance and the story of a shining star, bright, happy and totally unique, is everything we want for our children.

The popularity of this theme is growing and I've explored far and wide in space for name ideas as diligently as Galileo (I imagine this service to humankind will be just as pivotal to history!) You'll hear a lot about Greek and Roman mythology in the following lists: the ancient Greeks named many of the stars and we've kept those names, or their Roman equivalents. Our star constellations were named after the gods' favourite heroes or beasts and early astronomers in Roman times then named the planets based on the qualities of Roman gods. Mars was red, named after the god of war. Venus was bright, named after the goddess of beauty who shone the brightest. Not only is the space race inspiring name lists everywhere, but these ancient god- and goddess-inspired names are gaining so much popularity as we get braver in going further back in time with our name picks.

SPACE-INSPIRED NAMES

Space names look up to the planets and universe for name inspiration. If exploring space was high on your wish list or you want a name that captures the mystery and wonder of the greater galaxy we live in, this list is full of ideas.

GIRLS

Celeste - 'Heavenly'. The meaning says it all. Celeste is a gorgeous name with vintage vibes that takes you right out to space with it's celestial meaning.

Evren - 'Universe'. How stunning is this name? It's a Turkish name with that beautiful 'Ev' sound that's so popular for girls. Universe is a magical meaning for a baby who will be at the centre of yours.

Olivine - Olivine is the mineral found in the dust of young stars as they form in the sky and in the tails of comets. Pronounced Oli-Vine, it makes a stunning name alternative to Olivia or Olive if those have been pinched by friends or feel too popular. A bright, shining magical name for the shooting star you get to always call yours.

Solstice - 'When the sun stands still'. The time twice a year when the Sun is either closest or furthest from the Earth makes a whimsical girl name that is perfect for planet lovers.

Soraya - 'Cluster of stars'. Soraya is a stunning name and it represents a cluster of stars known as The Pleiades, which are also nicknamed the Seven Sisters. This gorgeous Arabic name for the Pleiades makes a rare choice with that mysterious feel of looking up at the starry sky.

BOYS

Apollo - Apollo is the iconic Greek and Roman God of sun and light. America chose Apollo for their space modules which NASA famously said they named 'as carefully as a baby' - Apollo 11 being the most iconic for the first moon landing. The name Apollo seems daring but is popular as an inspiring boy name full of wonder.

Atlas - We know an Atlas as a collection of maps, but the word was originally inspired by the name of a Titan god. Atlas was given the burden of holding the heavens on his shoulders for eternity. The celestial sphere he's holding was one used by sailors to navigate the earth and eventually became the collective name for a group of maps we know today. I love its sense of adventure and travel for your little one.

Galileo - 'Of Galilee'. The namesake of the famous father of observational astronomy would be a brave pick that isn't more 'out there' than Atlas. Galileo could be shortened to Leo. making it a great mix of an unusual long name with a traditional nickname.

Jovian - 'Of Jupiter'. Jovian planets are the outer planets of our solar system: Jupiter, Saturn, Uranus and Neptune. I love Jovian as an unexpected space name. Joe is a vintage name, and this feels like the modern twist we've been waiting for.

Rocket - 'Jet propelled'. Rocket is a brilliant name for anyone with a passion for space exploration. It's got an adventurous style, but I love a rare name that's a common word, as it's so easy to say and spell, making it really wearable. Rocket is a perfect Stand Out & Shine name.

NEUTRAL

Astro - 'Outer space'. Astro is a really bold space name. Ideal for space lovers who also want a name to Stand Out & Shine.

Cielo - 'Sky, Heaven'. Cielo - pronounced See-Low - is a gorgeous Spanish name alluding to the skies and Heaven. I love the trendy 'o' ending, making it fresh, bold and truly special.

Cosmo - 'Order, beauty and the universe'. Literally meaning 'the whole universe', Cosmo makes a wonderful name for the baby who will soon become the centre of yours.

MOON NAMES

From the Moon cycles to lunar landings, we're obsessed with the Moon. Powerful and spiritual, these names have that same sense of mystery.

GIRLS

Amaris - 'Child of the Moon'. A beautiful alternative to the more traditional Amelia, any name meaning 'child' is always special to a parent. Adorable Amaris with its allusions to the Moon is a true Stand Out & Shine name.

Ayla - 'A halo of light around the Moon'. A halo is angelic and this name matches up to it as a divine discovery. Magical and wearable, it could be 'The One'.

Callisto - 'Most beautiful'. One of the moons of Jupiter, Callisto was a nymph coveted by Zeus whose wife promptly turned her into a bear. To keep her beauty visible, Zeus transferred her to the sky as a constellation, now known as The Bear. It feels playful and unusual, one of a kind, just like your baby.

Elara - One of the moons that orbit Jupiter, this name is so pretty. Reminiscent of the name Ellen, it's a gorgeous pick.

Esmeray - 'Dark moon'. I adore this mysterious and unusual name, pronounced Ez-mur-ay. It sounds exotic and perfectly suits a baby born at night. Esmeray elevates the more frequently heard Esme while still being easy to say and spell.

Kamari - 'Moonlight'. A Swahili name with an evocative meaning for your magical baby girl.

Luna - 'Moon'. In Roman mythology, Luna was the personification of the Moon. The name has become a modern classic. Luna Lovegood from *Harry Potter* bought it to the masses and the name Luna took off. I know many Lunas and it never fails to turn heads for its simple beauty.

Mahina - 'Moonlight'. A Hawaiian name that conjures up the glow from the moon, Mahina is very elegant and magical.

Neoma - 'New moon'. A beautiful new beginning and a new life. Parenthood changes life for the better and Neoma encapsulates that in an ethereal name for your darling daughter.

Phoebe - 'Bright and radiant'. Phoebe is often associated with being the light the moon gives off. Effortlessly beautiful and well-loved, the earliest document of the name Phoebe being used in England was 1566. However, it really took off in 1995 - yes, one year after the launch of iconic TV Show *Friends* where Phoebe Buffay starred as the most eccentric and quirky of all the characters.

Quilla - 'Mother Moon'. In Inca mythology, Quilla is a goddess who was worshipped, especially by women for her beauty and role as a protector.

Rhiannon - 'Great queen'. This Welsh name refers to the Welsh Goddess of the Moon. Still popular today, it's a stylish and timeless girl's name that would work well for a Timelessly Tasteful namer.

Selena - 'The Moon'. The Greek counterpart to Luna in Roman mythology, Selene is the Goddess of the Moon. Selena comes from the Greek noun *selas* meaning 'brightness' or 'to gleam', which make it perfect for your baby girl who will shine so brightly in your world.

BOYS

Badr - 'Full moon'. Representing the bright light and strength of the moon, Badr is an Arabic name pronounced Bar-Dra.

Francisco - 'Free man'. One of Uranus' moons and also synonymous with the city of San Francisco, it's a name of Spanish origin that has real strength to it. See Place Names for more city-inspired ideas for your baby.

Jericho - 'City of the Moon'. If you know me, you know this is a *huge* name crush of mine and my sister's. Naomi once lived near Jericho, Oxford, and it just works so well as a strong boy name that feels both urban and otherworldly.

Mani - 'Moon'. The Norse God of the Moon is called Mani and it's this myth that is thought to have inspired the phrase 'The man in the Moon'.

Munir - 'Illuminating'. With the word moon embedded in it, the Arabic name Munir, pronounced moon-ir, has a delicate sound that will appeal to Stand Out & Shine namers.

Oberon - The second largest of the Uranian moons, popularized as a name by Shakespeare in *A Midsummer Night's Dream*. 'O' names are high hitters in the name charts for boys and girls. Oberon feels daring but is really easy to say and to spell - look to the moon at night and if it draws you in, list it.

NEUTRAL

Anwar - 'Collection of lights'. I love the Arabic name Anwar for the light of your life.

Chandra - 'Moon, in Sanskrit'. Chandra means 'bright or shining'. Many rituals are held around the moon cycles and Chandra is a great name for anyone who loves a more spiritual vibe.

Moona - 'Radiates light'. Moona is a really trendy name and the meaning makes it so loveable. Someone who radiates light makes for a name that will always Stand Out & Shine.

Shashi - 'Moon'. A really striking Indian name, Shashi can also mean 'having a hare'. which relates to the dark patches on the moon looking like a hare. Many cultures, including East Asian, Chinese and Native American, have told the story of the mythical Moon Hare.

STAR NAMES

Stars are the most magical place to look for a baby name. We name stars for loved ones, knowing how enduring they are. The names of stars are so full of history, it makes me feel connected to everyone who came before us. I'll always remember my lucky window bed on the maternity ward after having my first baby. The ward was full of new baby cries and machines beeping. I looked outside, saw the stars and realized, wow! I'm a mum now. I needed to romanticize that moment; I essentially felt I'd invented motherhood that day and that we were the only two beings to ever have experienced it. And I love that about us all - at every school concert, piano recital and play, every one of us will only have eyes for our baby. We all live under the same sky, and we all see our own children as our own little stars.

GIRLS

Andromeda - 'Leader of humankind'. Andromeda is a constellation named after a princess in Greek mythology. A grand and strong name choice, I love the warrior princess edginess of the name; perfect for a Stand Out & Shine namer.

Astrea - 'Star maiden'. Pronounced A-stray-uh, this beautiful name is whimsical and magical. Astrea feels like a softer take on well-known Astrid for Trendy with a Twist namers.

Bellatrix - 'Female warrior'. Bellatrix is the name of a star in the Orion constellation and it's the first star to rise in the East. Harry Potter fans will also know it from the infamous Bellatrix Lestrange (née Black). An unusual twist on popular Beatrice and a great long name for Bella, list it or lose it. Find more Harry Potter Names in the Passions chapter (page 153).

Cassiopeia - The largest constellation in the Northern Sky makes an exciting name choice. Cassia, Cassie and Pia as shortened nicknames make it special. It's important to note that in the Greek myth, Cassiopeia is a vain and arrogant queen who gets punished for stating she was the most beautiful woman alive - but she did have a great name, so who's judging!

Danica - 'Morning star'. A very stylish name from Slavic mythology. Danica was a star that was worshipped in the morning and said to be the Sun's sister. A wonderful name for a baby born early, it feels classy and strong.

Estelle/Estella - 'Star'. Two variations of Stella, adding the beautiful 'E' at the beginning. Estella Havisham is also the lady protagonist in *Great Expectations,* which gives it a literary bonus.

Esther - 'Star'. This Old Testament name has a beautiful starry sky meaning. Hugely popular in the 1930s, the name shines brightly today as a vintage moniker that I think is underused. It's old-fashioned in the best way - a vintage rose painting with its head in the stars. My niece is called Ester spelt the Swedish way and she shines so brightly in our family. See Vintage Names for more classics that are due a revival.

Nova - An astronomic term for bright stars that appear in the sky and give off huge energy. What could be more perfect for your baby to really let her shine?

Ostara - 'Bringer of dawn'. This lovely name gives you the hugely cool nickname Star.

Seren - 'Star' in Welsh. If you're honouring a Sarah this also works so well. It's top on many Welsh baby name lists and shines out as delightful choice for a girl.

Sidra - 'Of the stars'. In Latin Sidra means 'goddess of the stars'. It is also an Islamic name that refers to the tree in heaven.

Starla - 'A star'. If Star is too much of a word name for your style, Starla adds the extra syllable to make it feel more robust while still connected to its starry meaning.

Stella - 'Star'. A special girl's name known worldwide, it ticks the vintage box and movie buffs will know it from *A Streetcar Named Desire*. Enduringly popular and memorable for your baby girl.

Tara - 'Light of the soul'. Tara has a deep spiritual meaning as the name of an important female deity in Buddhism. She is said to guide souls across the ocean of existence to enlightenment. It's a name that brings this message to your baby in a beautiful, understated way.

Twila - 'Twilight'. Twilight is such a romantic time of day, and it gives the name Twila a really cosy, whimsical vibe.

BOYS

Aster - 'Star'. Also the name of a flower, Aster is a variation of vintage Esther. It sounds so spacy with its astronomy connotations. A little Aster will become your whole universe.

Columba - 'Dove'. A constellation named after the dove who warned Noah the flood was coming.

Izar - 'Star'. A super-trendy Basque name, pronounced Ee-zar.

Lucero - 'Light or star'. This Spanish boy name is so lyrical in sound, pronounced Lu-sey-ro. I love that it means both light and star. Illuminating the sky is just what your new baby will do.

Orion - Orion the Hunter is one of our most famous constellations in the sky, named after the god Orion. The biggest and brightest constellation visible all around the world makes Orion a popular baby name. Not unlike popular Ryan in sound, it's wearable and brave all at once.

Sirius - 'Burning star'. Harry Potter fans unite for this powerful baby boy's name.

NEUTRAL

Antares - 'Brightest red star'. Antares is also known as a 'red supergiant', being one of the largest stars visible to the naked eye. The name feels right out of a novel, so vibrant, grand and unique in sound.

Lynx - 'The Lynx constellation'. This constellation symbolizes sight or vision as it's so dim astrologers say it can only be seen with someone with the vision of a Lynx. It makes a cute one-syllable name that feels modern and fresh.

Vega - 'Stooping eagle or meadow'. Vega is one of the brightest stars in the sky and it's twice as large as the Sun. As a name it is as memorable and as impressive as the star, perfect for a child who will shine brightly in your life. If Vegas is a special place to you, it's also a nod to Las Vegas. Book your Vegas naming ceremony now!

Vesper - 'Evening star'. A super-trendy name, it just makes me smile every time I see it. Looking up to the stars together with your gentle and magical Vesper would always be a special moment as new parents.

ZODIAC-INSPIRED BABY NAMES

The zodiac is a belt-shaped region of the sky made up of the Moon and brightest planets. The zodiac was divided into 12 equal parts and the zodiac calendar refers to when the Sun passes through each part. This is how time was measured, and each equal part was given a name by early astronomers. They chose Roman gods as the titles, and people born within each moment of that calendar were given what we know as a 'star sign'. As the gods all have character traits and personalities, those were said to transfer onto babies born at that specific time in the astrological calendar. In this section I've looked at each sign and curated names that match the character traits assigned to them.

Aries (21 March–19 April)

Aries is the sign of the ram. Aries rule the roost and can butt heads, but that makes them amazingly loyal friends. Mars is the ruling planet of Aries, so battle and warfare make them good at conflict, and an Aries will stand up for causes and people they believe in.

Aries (n) - 'Ram'. Aries is one of the zodiac signs that really works as a name. It sounds both edgy and whimsical all at once.

Athena (f) - The Goddess of Wisdom and War and Craftwork, Athena shares the values of these strong Aries attributes. I love how fierce this girl name is. If you love Athena, I've included it in my Main Character Energy list, so pop to that next for similar names.

Dillon (n) - 'Loyal'. Irish Dillon reflects the loyalty of the Aries zodiac sign. It's a gorgeous choice for any gender.

Elda (f) - 'Warrior'. An Italian name, Elda brings the fighting spirit and courage of Aries to this powerful name.

Finnian (m) - 'Handsome warrior'. Finnian is a charming name with a bit of swagger in its step due to its warrior meaning. I love the bounce in Finnian, it sounds playful and edgy.

Fremont (m) - 'One who will protect liberty'. Fremont is a place name in France and the US, and makes a very cool first name with the spirit of fighting for others.

Taurus (20 April–20 May)

Taurus is an Earth sign on the zodiac and has the symbol of the bull. Earth signs are thought to be grounded and a Taurus child loves their home comforts and feels a lot of contentment in everyday pleasures. They love beautiful things and are drawn to music, great food and pretty places.

Drew (n) - 'Strong-willed'. Gender-neutral Drew is so stylish, and its meaning perfectly fits the stubborn side of the Taurus personality.

Farley (m) - 'From the bull's pasture'. A rugged Irish surname, Farley is super-grounded and playful. It definitely stands out as a cute and quirky nature name.

Jay (m) - A Jay is a songbird famed for its rejoiceful song. Taurus are known for talking about their feelings and being good communicators, so I love the songbird connection to this zodiac sign.

Tirzah (f) - 'Delight'. Biblical Tirzah was used as a verb to describe something that pleases you, a perfect pick for the Taurus personality and a rare, gorgeous name.

Venus (f) - Venus is the moon of Taurus. It is a Stand Out & Shine name, full of character with that strong goddess vibe.

Gemini (21 May–20 June)

The twin sign, some people say this can be negative, as two-faced has become a phrase for people who cannot be trusted, but Geminis are great at creating bonds, as they look for their twin companions in life and friendships. Geminis love to learn and are always curious.

Evangeline (f) - 'Bringer of good news'. Mercury is the moon of Gemini named after the Roman messenger god. Mercury could be a daring name, but Evangeline is more classic with its meaning of bringing good news, which feels like it has a special connection to bringing a new baby into the world.

Gabriel (m) - 'Messenger'. One of the familiar Archangels, I've always loved Gabe as a shortform. The name means 'messenger' and Gabriel is the Patron Saint of Communicators - if this feels like you, the name could be perfect for your little one.

Kenji (m) - A stunning Japanese name meaning 'healthy second'. It seems like a spot-on personality name for the twin symbol.

Oakley (n) - The Oak tree is the tree of the Gemini zodiac sign, a stable balance for the inquisitive mind. Oakley is a modern name that feels fresh.

Tamsin (f) - 'Twin'. A female version of Thomas, Tamsin feels so fresh although it's a classic British name. The pretty 's' in the middle makes it a brilliant pick for Timelessly Tasteful namers looking for something a bit special.

Cancer (21 June–22 July)

The crab symbol, someone born under this zodiac is thought to be deeply intuitive and sentimental. A Cancer type can be very open to other people's feelings and once attached they stay close, but they can be challenging to get to know.

Chester (m) - 'Fortress'. This is a vintage surname that has been registered in the UK as far back as the twelfth century. It's a place name meaning 'fortress', which echoes the slightly guarded nature of a Cancer personality type. I love Chester, it's so traditional but hasn't ever exploded in popularity, meaning it's great for Trendy with a Twist namers.

Lina (f) - 'Delicate'. Lina's tender or delicate meaning and the soft sound of the name is great for those who are open to others' feelings.

Manan (n) - 'Thought'. Manan is an Indian name meaning to be in thought, or meditating. I love the sentiment of this choice for a deep and spiritual soul.

Maven (f) - 'Expert'. Maven makes Raven seem old-fashioned and I think it's the coolest name. Cancers are intuitive, deep thinkers who can often become an expert in their passions. As a baby name I'm giving Maven a huge tick for being trendy without trying too hard. A great choice for Trendy with a Twist namers.

Wade (m) - 'Crossing the sea'. Cancer is a water symbol and Wade, with its quite literal meaning of crossing water, complements the zodiac sign splendidly with its one-syllable charm.

Leo (23 July–22 August)

Leos are known for being feisty, generous and creative people. Leo has the symbol of the lion and the Sun, making them fiery and larger than life. They are people magnets and have a lot of confidence. They go for their goals and don't like failure.

Leander (m) - 'Man of lions'. I adore this historic name. In the Greek legend *Hero and Leander,* Leander, in love with Hero, swims a treacherous sea to her each night until a storm takes his life. A rugged romance encapsulated in a name.

Lenni (n) - 'Brave as a lion'. Lenni is the perfect Leo name, brave as a lion but also meaning 'light like the Sun' if taken from Helena. It's become a real name crush of mine. There is nothing better in my mind than a vintage 'nickname as first name' and Lenni makes a charming choice for any gender.

Lucia (f) - 'Light'. Pronounced Loo-Chee-Uh. This Scandinavian name is so lovely and, as Leos are said to shine really brightly with their larger-than-life personality, Lucia matches brilliantly.

Millicent (f) - 'Gentle strength'. Millicent is a vintage name that is familiar but not common, although we do hear the shortform Millie more frequently. With its meaning 'to labour', it strikes me as an ideal name for hard-working Leos, but its 'gentle strength' echoes that inner confidence. Millicent is a great choice for Trendy with a Twist namers.

Napoleon (m) - 'Naples lion'. Napoleon matches someone with confidence and suave who has the magnetitic power of the lion.

Virgo (23 August–22 September)

A Virgo likes order, business and leading and can be quite bossy. They like to be of service to others and being part of a community rather than being introspective. Virgos are perfectionists, so are prone to self-criticism. They need support, as they put pressure on themselves. Connected to Demeter, responsible for the cycle of change and plants growing, Virgo is an Earth Sign.

Annona (f) - 'Harvest goddess'. The personification of the Harvest Grain in mythology, Annona worked hard for Demeter as they changed the seasons. Annona is a distinctive name that's very lively and punchy, like the Virgo personality.

Cody (m) - 'Helpful'. This Irish boy name means someone who protects and shields others. It's such a wonderful characteristic to be encapsulated in a name, not to mention how much of a smiley and cheerful option it is.

Fritz (m) - 'Peaceful ruler'. Fritz remains a popular alternative to Fredrik around Europe. It was my husband's grandfather's name and has a quirkiness and confidence that is full of life.

Miller (n) - 'Grinder of the grain'. Miller is a surname that makes a stand-out first name for earth-worker Virgos. I love the double 'll' sound in Miller, it's stylish yet simple.

Zola (f) - 'Earth'. In Italian, Zola translates as 'a mound of earth and soil', which fits this earthy sign. I love how strong it is as a name, fitting the leadership quality of Virgos. Zola is a super-fashionable name for Trendy with a Twist namers.

Libra (23 September–22 October)

This is the sign of judgement and scales. Libras are very fair and moral and have a strong sense of what's right and equal. They seek peace and want to bring harmony to people around them, valuing partnership and balance with others.

Adilah (f) - 'Just'. Adilah brings the balance of a Libra to life in a name. Simple and elegant.

Blake (n) - 'Black and white'. A very confusing meaning - some scholars say it comes from Blac meaning 'fair' and some from the darker black. I love the blend of both meanings for those seeking harmony and seeing things clearly.

Joaquin (m) - 'God will judge'. Joaquin is a Spanish variation of a Hebrew name that speaks to god being judge or establishing what's right. A stylish name that reflects having good balance.

Kanisha (f) - 'Beautiful one'. An Arabic name whose translation is synonymous with its pretty sound. Kanisha has the dual meaning of 'having all-seeing eyes', which is so interesting and perfect for the fair judge sign, Libra.

Zedekiah (m) - 'Justice'. An Old Testament name, Zedekiah is a striking choice that could be a great alternative to the more common Zachary.

Scorpio (23 October–21 November)

Scorpios are determined and decisive, although they can sometimes be closed off and mysterious. They are great secret keepers. Their mystery makes them quite magnetic to others - they often work as therapists or mentors, but you might not get to know them and their thoughts as much as they know yours.

Aldous (m) - 'Wise'. Aldous is an Old English boy name meaning wise, like a sage. It also has an 'old soul' feeling and is an unforgettably cool name with literary allusions.

Delyth (f) 'Beautiful'. Irish Delyth gives me huge waves of Baby Name Envy, it's just so stunning and unexpected. The name was originally given in Irish folklore to fairies before it became a more common first name. Packed with the mystery and magnetism of the Scorpio sign, see Goth Glam list for more options in a similar style.

Ernest (m) - 'Working with intent'. A vintage name, to be earnest is to be honest and to work with intent. Its adorable nickname of Ernie stands out amongst some of the more common classics.

Sloane (f) - 'Warrior'. An edgy name that really matches the Scorpio vibe. Sloane is Irish in heritage and sounds very fashionable with urban city edge. Meaning 'warrior' or 'raider', it's great for a determined and decisive little girl.

Zillah (n) - 'Shadow'. Such an enigmatic meaning - connotations of shadow or shade make Zillah a mysterious and intoxicating name.

Sagittarius (22 November–21 December)

The bow and arrow symbol is the sign of Sagittarius. Said to be ethical but very impulsive, Sagittarians are known for their generosity, compassion and great pride in themselves.

Archer (m) - The occupational name for a bowman, Archer is still in use as a surname and it's making its way into our top boy names with short form Archie. It's hugely playful and upbeat.

Ascella (f) - 'Armpit'. One of the most hilarious name meanings, Ascella is a beautiful flowing name with a slightly less appealing definition. It comes from the Sagittarian Archer, who nestled his bow and arrow in his armpit. It could make a fun naming story for your little Ascella.

Bo (n) - Meaning 'home' or 'abode' in Scandinavian and pronounced Boo rather than Bow. This is one of my son Finn's middle names after his Swedish Farfar (father's father).

Valentina (f) - 'Strong and healthy'. Valentina is a chic and graceful name with Spanish origins. Valens was a Roman word used to wish someone well - a great word we should bring back. And Valentina brings that compassion and strength of character in a stunning name.

Capricorn (22 December–19 January)

Capricorns are very strong characters who can be extraverted. They are often considered 'old souls', displaying determination and grit for reaching their goals. Their symbol is the goat, which feels really appropriate for this outgoing and high-achieving sign.

Luella (f) - 'Female warrior'. Luella is an upbeat, charismatic name that has the strength and determination of a warrior wrapped up in its meaning.

Montgomery (m) - 'Mountain'. Monty sounds so sweet while Montgomery, its long form, has the grandness of a mountain. We often describe challenges as like climbing a mountain, and this name has that strong sound.

Quinn (n) - 'Wise chief'. An Irish heritage name that has boomed and is perfect for a high-achieving Capricorn. Quinn sounds preppy and happy while carrying a bit of edge with the 'Q' initial.

Zion (m) - 'Highest point'. For high-flying Capricorns, Zion is a bold name that feels aspirational and meaningful.

Aquarius (20 January–18 February)

Aquarians are deep thinkers, known for being highly intellectual, and this is complemented by a strong need for time alone. An Aquarius type is known to follow their own path; they will go against the norm if needed and will stand up for causes they believe in. Progressive thinkers and loyal humanitarians, Aquarians are the rebels and change makers.

Franklin (m) - 'Free man'. Someone who speaks freely and brings change to the world around them.

Gwen (f) - 'Holy'. This sense of giving and humanitarian spirit suits an Aquarian. A stylish Welsh girl's name.

January (f) - From 'Janus' the Roman God of new beginnings, this is a great name for a new year baby.

Rebel (n) - 'Defiant'. I love the parents who choose this name, as I know you'll be raising your child to be a loyal, big thinker who is full of ideas.

Riordan (m) - 'Royal poet'. This Irish name brings to life the sensitive side of the Aquarian and their role as advisors and leaders.

Pisces (19 February–20 March)

Water signs are very friendly and like to be in company. They are selfless, sensitive and highly emotional. Always faithful and caring, a Pisces makes a great friend, as they are never judgemental.

Auden (m) - 'Old friend'. Nordic name Auden has a poetic feel and I really like the soft sound of Auden. The meaning brings that open and friendly company-loving personality to the forefront.

Buddy (m) - 'Friend'. Buddy is a colloquialism for a friend that has a 1950s feel. It's really open and warm in sound and echoes that 'faithful friend' vibe of the Pisces personality.

Cordelia (f) - 'Daughter of the sea'. Cordelia is a literary name from Shakespeare's *King Lear*. A loyal and emotional character, Cordelia has a gorgeous flow to it, perfect for this deep-thinking water sign.

Jocelyn (f) - 'To pour'. Someone who pours out love, Jocelyn embodies the giving personality of a Pisces. Jocelyn is a vintage name that hasn't made a comeback, but I adore Joss or Cici as nicknames for this unexpected gem with a gorgeous meaning.

Lake (n) - 'Water'. A lake is one of nature's most whimsical places, representing both depth and calm. It's a perfect name for a Pisces-born child with an old-school glamour that will Stand Out and Shine.

CRYSTALS, ROCKS & MINERALS

Precious stones and crystals are rare to find and beautiful to look at, and they also have gorgeous names. Many people love learning about the spiritual properties of crystals and that's also a fun place to find special meaning that aligns with your life and experiences. I've done all the digging for you and curated this list of popular and more unusual ideas inspired by this glistening world of crystals, rocks and minerals.

GIRLS

Beryl - 'Sea-green jewel'. Beryl was used as a feminine name since the late nineteenth century, then fell out of style. However the jewel is among one of the most expensive gems. I'm all for a throwback vintage name and think Beryl epitomises that quirky vintage name which would surprise then delight your family and take the top spot as a cool name.

Coral - Corals are actually animals, small polyps that gather together and create habitats in reefs under the sea. The Egyptians would place coral in their tombs to keep souls safe on their travel to the afterlife. In the late 1800s, children were given coral necklaces to prevent illness - you'll notice a lot of red coral beaded necklaces in Regency paintings - and Coral then started to gain use as a first name. It's as rare a name as it is a sea creature and is just as special.

Gemma - 'Precious jewel'. We call them gems, and in Italian these precious jewels are called Gemma. The name became really popular, peaking in the eighties, but since then it's dived down the charts. This classic is well overdue a revival and would now make a unique choice.

Jewel - The name Jewel has such a bohemian vibe. Crystal names were extremely popular in the 1970s during the hippy movement and Jewel feels totally of that era. It's a one-syllable name that will stand out and shine bright.

Lazuli - Lapis Lazuli is a sky-blue stone that was ground by painters as the only way of creating a vibrant blue. With links to the Persian word meaning 'Heaven Stone', Lazuli makes a rare and interesting name.

Opal - 'Jewel'. This stunning name hits a lot of my criteria for a girl name. The name Opal peaked in the early 1900s, so it's a rare vintage name that hasn't become overly popular yet. It's simple, classic and the jewel gives it an elegance.

Ruby - A beautiful crystal name, Ruby is a gorgeous red which links it to love and it's often used in commitment rings and wedding rings. The birthstone of July, rubies were historically reserved to adorn royalty, as they were expensive and believed to bring the wearer protection. Ruby has a festival girl vibe - if she's like her gemstone, she's passionate, easy to love and fiercely protective of those around her. All reasons to list this sparkler of a name.

Sapphire - Meaning 'blue', ancient Greeks believed the sky was blue as a reflection of a giant Sapphire the world was placed on. Sapphires are a symbol of wisdom, with wearers said to have enhanced creativity and ideas. A gem of a name to pop on your list.

BOYS

Flint - Flint is a type of rock used since the stone ages as a tool to spark fire. It's such a great name that has inspired characters in *Spiderman* and *Marvel,* plus the pirate in *Treasure Island*. It's a name that evokes a sense of adventure and is memorable amongst the more popular Finn and Finley.

Gabbro - This dark green or black rock makes a super-edgy boy name. Gabbro is the most abundant rock in the deep oceanic crust, giving it a mystery aligned to the unexplored sea. You'll recognize the mottled appearance of Gabbro, as it's used for countertops and floor tiles. Hardy and strong, it sounds stunning as a unique baby name.

Jasper - The Jasper gemstone is thought to be a powerful healing stone. Jasper was also one of the three kings said to have visited baby Jesus - he carried the gold, hence the name meaning 'Treasurer'.

Jett - Jet is a dark black gemstone that has inspired the name Jett. It's a fun and playful name, with its quirky double 'tt' spelling.

Kito - 'A rare jewel'. The name Kito has travelled the world with different meanings, but in Swahili it means 'rare jewel'.

Slate - A balancing stone used by some to bring harmony to the chakras. Slate makes for an urban-sounding boy name with spiritual significance.

NEUTRAL

Jade - Typically green, but Jade can come in a variety of colours. It's been used since the neolithic days to carve tools, and spiritually it's linked to compassion and self-love. A great gender-neutral name.

Ochre - This clay pigment is a gorgeous yellow or deep red and it's getting picked up as a unique baby name. Pronounced Oak-Er, it refers to a pigment that has been used by humans to decorate themselves and communicate on cave walls since the beginning of time. See my Earth Tone Names list if you like the sound of Ochre and want similar names (page 121).

Onyx - A dark gemstone in black or red. Onyx works so well as a name as it's both short and strong. It is similar to familiar names like Opal or Alex. The meaning of Onyx is 'claw' or 'fingernail' - according to legend, the fingernails of the Goddess Venus turned to onyx when they were cut, as every part of her was immortalized. This bizarre history is almost as fun and memorable as the name.

Topaz - A well-known gem, Topaz is the symbol of love and affection, making it a meaningful choice as a daring first or middle name. Topaz is the birthstone for November and it's an eye-catching name.

PICKING A NICKNAME OR AVOIDING ONE

At some point during picking a baby name, the topic of nicknames will come up. Some people love a name that can be shortened and some of us want to ensure that it never ever does. When our baby is little we can have a bit of control over that; a steely glare anytime a family member calls Eleanor, 'Ellie' or shortens Barnaby to 'Barney' can nip it in the bud quite quickly. But there may come a time when their friends play around with the name and it's out of your control. With my children, Freddie goes by 'Fred' to his mates. Finn has oddly been lengthened to 'Finley' by his friends. And Evelina . . . she's still Evelina, thank goodness - no steely glares necessary!

A nickname is also sometimes described as a pet name or an endearment name and that's a lovely way to show our familiarity and love for each other. Sometimes people just shorten a long name out of laziness though - I inherited the nickname 'SJ' as soon as texting became prevalent and friends couldn't be bothered to spell out my full name.

When choosing a name for your baby, it's important to try out all the nickname variations and ensure there's nothing there you really dislike. It's also a chance to get creative with a name. Here's some of my tried-and-tested tips and tricks for finding a perfect nickname if you're keen to control the narrative and want to get in there early and find an option that you all love.

Top Nickname Tips

- My top tip when choosing a nickname is that it doesn't have to be simply a shortened version of the name. For example, Lottie can be Lulu, Lo, Ottie or Lola. Harrison could be Sonny, Rizzo or Harris. Taking just the prominent sounds, you can create some fun and unique nicknames for any name.

- For traditional names you can get creative and give a more unisex nickname. Liberty can be Bertie, Aurora makes a great Rory. Or consider fun word nicknames that give edge to a name - Lucas can be 'Lucky' or Felix lends itself well to 'Fox'.
- Nicknames are all about personality, so have fun with them. It's also an idea once they've arrived into the world and you've got to know them to give them a nickname that celebrates a part of their personality. My cousin David is called 'Huggy' by our group of friends. He's a tall, bearded country-living guy who loves a big embrace when he says 'hello'.
- You could use their middle name as a nickname. I often call my daughter Blossom. There are more great tips on how to get the perfect middle name in my Mastering the Middle Name feature coming up (see page 198).

ELEMENTAL NAMES

The four elements of nature are those that life depends on to exist – earth, wind, fire and water. These elements naturally align themselves with personality types and are often used to describe character traits. Whether you're drawn to the deep and powerful force of water or feel close to the earth, your heart is bound to be more connected to one of these elemental names. Some people are airy and love to go with the flow, some are fire types showing lots of passion. One character trait doesn't exclude the others, so you may find parts that appeal to you in each chapter. Have a read of each list and make a record in your notepad of the names that stand out.

EARTH NAMES

These earth-inspired names are taken from the natural world around us. As a new mum, the highlight of my week was the days I managed to get outside, pushing my pram along the street and stopping to look at every leaf or let my baby feel the grass with their toes. It's the simplest activity but suddenly you're introducing the world to this totally precious new set of eyes and it feels awe-inspiring again. Our planet Earth is a great place to search for a meaningful name.

GIRLS

Alanis - 'Little rock'. Taken from the name Alan came the melodic feminine form Alanis, which has flown more under the radar - it's a stunning name for your little girl.

Avni - 'Earth'. One of the names of Hindu goddess Bhumi (*see* below), Avni makes a stunning name with classic roots.

Bhumi - 'Earth'. The Hindu goddess personifies the earth and Bhumi is a gorgeous name. She is often portrayed with four arms representing the four elements.

Demeter - 'Goddess of the Grain'. Demeter was the goddess of agriculture. It's short form Demi is delightful if you love strong, modern girl names. Another variation that feels fresh and unusual is the very pretty Demetria.

Gaia - 'The Earth'. Pronounced Gy-Ah, she is literally Mother Earth in Greek mythology. Known for being caring and nurturing and 'down to earth', the name Gaia is still popular around Europe.

Gigi - 'Earth worker'. Taken from the male form George, Gigi has the same meaning of 'Earth Worker'. A real modern classic with its roots firmly in the top charts, Gigi works for both Timelessly Tasteful and Stand Out & Shine namers.

BOYS

Arlo - 'Fortified hill'. The name Arlo is a modern favourite. From unranked in the year 2000 to a Top 20 boy's name in 2020, it's climbing up the name chart with no signs of slowing down. Catch it while you can.

Brent - 'High place'. Brent feels like a modern name but dates to the Anglo-Saxon period when it meant 'from the high place' or 'steep hill'. If you love to hike and climb, Brent makes an ideal name.

Everest - We call the famous mountain Mount Everest after explorer Sir George Everest. Its local name is Sagarmatha, meaning 'forehead of the sky'. A well-known name that has plucky courage for adventurous parents.

Hamilton - 'Flat-topped hill'. For musical lovers, 'surname as first name' fans and people who love a view from the top . . . this makes a confident, trendy name that's unexpected.

Mason - 'One who works with Stone'. A trendy occupational name, Mason has that modern edge coupled with its old-school traditional surname charm.

Peter - 'Rock'. Peter is one of the classic English boy names that has been popular since Simon Peter, an apostle of Jesus. The root of the name means 'Rock', which I love as a term of endearment - when someone is our rock, they give us stability and care. Peter appears across the world, so it travels well if you're after a truly international name.

Stanford - 'Stony ford'. A scholarly name, Stanford makes a modern alternative to traditional Stanley without too much edge. A great pick for those Trendy with a Twist namers.

Vermont - 'Green mountain'. What a vibrant place name Vermont is. It gives you vintage Monty as a nickname while sounding much more modern in its long form. Its lush meaning foretells the exploring you'll do together once little Vermont has arrived.

AIR NAMES

Airy names are sometimes strong and powerful and sometimes gentle and soft, just like the element they are inspired by. This is a really evocative name list with so many options that are giving me baby name envy. Pop the ones you love on your own name list.

GIRLS

Audra - 'Storm'. Stylish and punchy, just like it's meaning. A unique alternative to vintage Audrey, Audra has a modern edge to it.

Auretta - 'Light wind'. From the Latin *aurum*, meaning gold, or Italian meaning 'light wind', Auretta feels like Audrey and Etta - two gems joined up to create an incredible name perfect for vintage name lovers.

Brontë - 'Thunder'. Pronounced Bron-Tay. With its literary sensibility from the esteemed Brontë sisters and its Greek meaning, this is a loud and proud name with a lot of beauty.

Fei - 'To dance in the air'. Pronounced Fay, how beautiful is this Chinese name? There's four intonations in Chinese so the word has multiple meanings, including 'fragrant', 'to fly' and 'to dance in the air'.

Kasumi - 'Mist'. A Japanese name with a whimsical meaning encapsulating the ethereal beauty of mist over mountains and rivers.

Nolani/Noelani - 'Mist of Heaven'. Hawaiian names have gorgeous meanings and names are a very precious part of the culture. It's a language that is rich with words and deeply connected to expressing ways of seeing the natural world. Noelani is a beautiful example of a Hawaiian name.

Thora - 'Thunder'. From Thor who controlled lightening, thunder and storms, I have a lot of love for vintage Thora. It's coming back out of its hiatus in the charts and there's such a modern, cool-girl element to this strong name.

BOYS

Abel - 'Breath'. Gaining popularity, this name is understated and classic. It would suit Trendy with a Twist and Timelessly Tasteful namers seeking a fresh take on a biblical name. 'Breath' brings life into its airy element for a stunning option.

Akash - 'Open air'. Our expectation for our baby is that the sky's the limit when it comes to love and their potential. Akash is a Sanskrit name from ancient Indian texts, where it represents the vast expanse of the sky and the realm of the gods.

Guthrie - 'Windy spot'. What a cool name. With its Gaelic origin, it sounds unique but sits firmly aside popular picks like Albie and Auggie.

Keanu - 'Cool breeze over the mountain'. An unforgettable Hawaiian name with a beautiful and soothing meaning.

Zephyr - 'West wind'. A trendy boy name inspired by the seasonal breeze controlled by the ancient god Zephyrus.

NEUTRAL

Corentin - 'Tempest'. Corentin comes from the Breton word for hurricane, *coruentenn*. It's an ancient saint's name too and I think has a gorgeous sound to it that's rarely heard.

Skye - 'Sky'. A hippy vibe of a name, the sky is ever-changing and ever-inspiring, which makes a wonderful metaphor for a new baby coming into the world.

Wyndham - 'Windy village'. Wyndham has a very classic sound, a topographical name that makes me think of a gorgeous seaside village and taking a blustery walk beside the shore. Both whimsical and charming, Wyndham is a solid choice for a Trendy with a Twist namer.

FIRE NAMES

Energetic and sparkling, a fire name is great if you want a name with big personality. We often associate fire with the emotions of being passionate, expressive and bold, which are amazing character traits and values to pass on to your little one in a name. Whether you're basking in the blazing hot sun or curled up by a cosy log fire, these fire names give all of the warm and inviting vibes you'll need.

GIRLS

Ember - 'Spark'. What a name, what a meaning! I adore Ember and it makes a great alternative to an Emma or Amber. Embers are the small sparks in a fire, and the meaning makes the name feel glowy, warm and lively - ideal for a Trendy with a Twist namer.

Enya - 'Little fire'. Many of these fire names have Irish heritage - the name Enya comes from the traditional spelling Eithne, an Irish saint known as 'of the golden hair'. Enya sounds soft and ethereal and its meaning is perfect for raising a determined and bold little girl.

Hestia - 'Goddess of the Hearth'. Hestia sometimes appears as meaning 'fireside'. It's such an ancient name that would make an intriguing and alternative version to the more well-known Hester.

Idalia - 'Behold the sun'. It's such a lyrical name, pronounced Id-ah-lee-uh. Idalia was an epithet for the Goddess Aphrodite, the goddess of love and beauty. Aphrodite's main place of worship was the ancient city of Idalium in Cyprus, which gave rise to the gorgeous name. The flow of sounds in Idalia with the long 'a' at its core make it a real Stand Out & Shine beauty.

Vesta - A pretty variation of Hestia (see above), Vesta feels like curling up by the fire together with your baby girl.

Zora - 'Dawn'. This feels like the bright orange sky at sunrise, a delightful meaning for your little fireball. Iconic writer Zora Neale Hurston is a wonderful literary namesake.

BOYS

Aiden - 'Little fire'. An adorable traditional but not overused boy name. Aiden is a form of Aodh, the Celtic god of sun and fire, a perfect Timelessly Tasteful name choice.

Brantley - 'Forest fire'. From the Swiss-German surname Brändli. Names ending in 'ley' are always popular and Brantley is a cool alternative to lots of more common names with the same sound.

Fintan - 'White fire'. A more unusual idea for a longer form of Finn, Fintan is cheery and interesting. Fintan is the name of a Celtic mythological figure who was the personification of old age and knowledge. I like the 'old soul' mystery of the myth with the up-to-date sound.

Ignacio - 'Fiery one'. I see this on so many modern parents' name lists. It's Spanish and the name of several saints and leading thinkers. Ignacio is great if you love longer boy names with special meanings.

Inigo - 'Fiery'. Ignatius of Loyola was the patron saint of spiritual retreats, a role I'd like to job share on. Spanish Inigo is a very hip name.

Keegan - 'Fire'. An Irish boy name, Keegan is an Anglicization of the clan name Mac Aodhagáin. It's strong and unique and harks back to its Irish roots.

NEUTRAL

Bobbie - 'Bright fame'. From Robert and Roberta, Bobbie is such a striking name that has a lot of lively character.

Cyrus - 'Sunshine'. Cyrus could be a summer name, but it also radiates the warmth and crisp feel of an autumn day when the sun's out. It's of Persian origin with loads of positive, joyful vibes.

Sorin - 'Sun'. Sorin is a Romanian name. Although traditionally a male name, it works just as well for any gender and is a very stylish alternative to Sonny or Summer.

WATER NAMES

Water-inspired names often evoke calm, and the meanings can be so stunning. The depth of the ocean, the romance of a lake, the liveliness of a brook, a cold-water swim or baby's first bath - there are endless fantastic names that have the flow and feel of water.

GIRLS

Calypso - 'Hidden'. Calypso controlled the sea with Poseidon in Greek mythology and her moods were as rocky as the waves. The name has a fun, festival girl vibe for someone with a big personality.

Delta - 'River's mouth'. Delta was genuinely a name that stood out to me as I helped my son with his geography homework. It's a gorgeous name - a little Delilah and a touch Etta. A river delta is where the mouth of the river flows into the sea and settles.

Genevieve - 'White wave'. A beautiful and elegant name with French origin, it translates from the older name Genovefa. It also means 'kin' or 'woman of the family' in some translations. Genevieve always sounds stylish and works well for Timelessly Tasteful namers.

Jorah - 'First rain' or 'autumn rain'. A seriously stunning name with a pretty, evocative meaning, pronounced Jaw-Rah.

Maren - 'Sea'. Pronounced Mare-En, this is the Danish variation of the name Marina. It's a vintage name in Denmark and Germany that sounds like the seaside - outdoorsy and fresh.

Marisol - 'Sea and sun'. I'm already packing my suitcase. If you're a travel lover, then this Spanish name will brighten up your daughter's world.

Marissa - 'Of the sea'. From the Latin *maris,* meaning sea, Marissa feels lively and happy, like a day at the beach.

Meredith - 'Protector of the sea'. I've always felt the name Meredith is so underused - it's very understated, traditional yet beautiful. With its Welsh roots, I'd suggest popping it on your list if you love vintage names that aren't top of the charts. I've included it in my Quiet Luxury Aesthetic Names list, so see page 278 for similar ideas.

Moana - 'Ocean'. Made popular globally by the success of the Disney movie, Moana has a strength and power to it reinforced by its namesake character and its meaning. Immediately list it as a classic or see the Disney name section for more ideas.

Moselle - 'Drawn from the water'. If you're having a water birth this would be such a pretty name. I had two water births and had to get out to deliver, but I'd still lay claim to this lovely name and go with the sweet nickname Moss.

Nahla - 'First drink of water'. I love the meaning of Nahla, thought to be the name for water in a desert and that feeling of your first sip. The name also translates as 'honeybee', so the gorgeous meanings are endless and the name has that vibe of Noa with the pretty addition of a soft 'L' sound.

Nerida - 'Sea nymph'. In ancient Greek the Nereids were mermaids. The name has a nautical feel and any little girl will relish being named after the mermaids. Luring sailors to their doom or falling in love with the human world in the Disney classic, it was the eighties movie *Splash* that made me want to live under the sea and would encourage me to list this name in honour of the iconic imaginary creature.

Polly - 'Star of the sea'. Once a pet name for Mary, Polly has become a well-loved first name. It has so much charm and feels like a spirited name that is always memorable.

Talise - 'Lovely water'. How special is the name Talise? If you're having a water birth or your baby is born in her amniotic sac (which I was amazed to hear happens just one in 80,00 births), then Talise could make a stunning name choice for your little water baby. Plus, with this unique name you avoid my experience of baby swimming classes where my daughter Evelina was joined by similar-sounding Evie, Ava and Evelyn - I doggy paddled out of there as quickly as you could get their names confused.

Tallulah - 'Leaping water'. A *wow* of a name meaning, and with the lovely double 'll' sounds, it's almost like the name itself is leaping across the page. Tallulah also has Bugsy Malone gangster's moll vibes. It's a confident name with a special meaning.

BOYS

Aalto - 'Wave'. Aalto is a Finnish name taken directly from the word wave. The double 'Aa' is reminiscent of Aaron, but Aalto has more of a Nordic-cool edginess.

Bayou - 'Small stream'. Like Beau and Bodhi, it's such a cool name with a beautiful meaning thought to originate from the Native American Choctaw tribe word *bayuk*. Bay is strong as a nickname - imagine sitting at the dock together looking over the water.

Caspian - The Caspian Sea between Asia and Europe has been widely used as a name and it's so cool. If Casper is on your list, but you crave something more associated with the water, then this could be ideal.

Devereux - 'Banks of the river'. Such a sophisticated name, it makes me want to meet them. With its French heritage, it oozes the style and suave of the Parisian river Seine.

Dewi - 'Beloved or favourite'. This Irish name is pronounced Deh-Wee to rhyme with Berry. It's probably better to stick with the first meaning if you're going to have more than one child. Although not strictly a water name, it does have the word Dew in it, which adds a twinkly charm.

Dylan - 'Born from the ocean'. Dylan is a Welsh boy's name that's enduringly popular. I love the meaning, as it comes from the root word 'to flow'. A laid back, effortlessly stylish name.

Fen - 'Marshland'. A fen is a type of wetland that is home to many plants and small mammals. It makes a cute, short name for lovers of the English countryside.

Ford - 'A shallow body of water to cross'. This 'surname as first name' sounds trendy and the meaning is very beautiful, as it gives a sense of your baby crossing the waters and appearing in your arms. However, it's also a vehicle brand name, which could be something to consider.

Kai - 'The sea'. In Hawaiian culture, it's a name that means 'the Sea' and is a modern and deservingly popular option pronounced to rhyme with 'sky'.

Lachlan - 'Land of the lakes'. Pronounced Lock-Lan, it's no surprise this is originally a Scottish name. The name has travelled far and wide and is popular around the world. Lockie as a nickname is very cool and 'L' names always get my vote.

Murphy - 'Sea warrior'. One of the most common Irish surnames, Murphy is a great boy's first name option that takes on the spirit of the sea warrior Murchadh, its namesake in Irish history.

Murray - 'Sailor or seashore'. A Scottish and Irish surname that's made its leap into a much-deserved first name spot.

Musa - 'Drawn from water'. Musa is Arabic. Linked to Moses, it means to draw someone out of the water, giving it a sense of protection and bringing to safety.

Neptune - 'Roman God of the Sea'. Neptune is a brave name pick but a perfect choice for a family connected to the sea.

Rafferty - 'Flood tide'. This Irish name has a little twinkle in its eye. It feels lively and confident, with its flood tide meaning linked not only to water but to prosperity and good fortune. Let's welcome all the abundance in this quirky name.

Reef - 'Jagged rocks below the surface of the sea'. A coral reef protects so much in the sea - the other creatures and the shoreline and it also provides food and medicine. Protection credentials aside, the name is so 'surfer dude', I can see why it's popular.

Usher - 'River mouth'. From the old Latin word meaning 'river mouth', we also use the name 'usher' for a doorkeeper, just like the opening path of a river. Usher is a gentle-sounding, unusual name and I love the guiding path meaning for a new baby.

NEUTRAL

Arizona - 'Small spring'. From the Native American people of the O'odham tribe who primarily lived in Arizona, the place got its name from their word *ali sonak,* meaning small stream.

Beck - 'Brook or stream'. A nod to a Rebecca in your life, Beck would make a trendy water-themed name for a family looking for a short, sweet baby name.

Brook/Brooke - 'Small stream'. This water name has been in use for decades as a first name with bags of style.

Cove - 'Coastal inlet'. There's nowhere happier than a cute cove, they are all over Instagram and a hidden cove is every traveller's beach dream. This word name associated with the sea has been so popular with modern parents. I adore that it also looks like the word 'love' and suggests protection and cosiness.

Harbor/Harbour - 'Shelter'. The meaning has led thousands of parents to use this stunning name linked to the water. We also harbour feelings of love that are so strong for our baby, making this instantly listable if you're looking for a water-themed name.

Indra - 'Possessing drops of rain'. This must be the most poetic way to say it's raining. Indie is enduringly popular as a gender-neutral name, but Indra makes a stunning alternative. Indra is the Hindu god of rain and storms, a powerful name that works perfectly for a modern style.

Lake - 'Body of water'. The name Lake has been documented since Anglo-Saxon times as a surname and makes a glamorous first name. Lakes are truly romantic places and it's a whimsical water name, solitary and social all at once.

Marlow/Marlowe - 'Hill by a lake'. If you know me from YouTube, you'll know this was my close second contender for my daughter Evelina. I absolutely love its beautiful sound and it makes a soft alternative to Margot. I always encourage people to find personal links to names, and for us it was because my husband's family live in a stunning Swedish house on a hill by a lake and we met in Canterbury, home of Christopher Marlowe. It was enough to get my traditional husband to list it, but his heart lay with the more traditional Evelina. So, I'll gift it to you, but I'm envious.

Ocean - 'The sea'. There's no place I feel more relaxed than by the sea. Its power, depth and beauty mean something to every one of us. Giving the name Ocean to your baby will remind them every time they stand at the shore of how wide, deep and strong your love is for them.

Raine/Rain - 'Abundance from above'. Another quite positive meaning for rain, but we know how much we love to romanticize our lives. Learning to dance in the rain is something we love to share about the human condition and no British rom com is complete without a rain-soaked declaration of love. Raine with the 'e' means 'Queen', as in 'reign', but feels more wearable as a name.

Rio - 'River'. This Spanish name is perfect if you love a short name that packs a lot of style into its two syllables. It has a sense of adventure borrowed from Rio de Janeiro in Brazil, is super-lively and always memorable.

River/Rivers - 'River'. I love adding an 's' to the end of the name River to give it a little more edge and individuality.

Sailor - 'Sea-farer'. The occupational name for someone working on the sea makes a quirky but popular name for a baby. It's not too 'out there', as it's been quite high profile as a name, but it is daring.

Skipper - 'Ship's captain'. Also Barbie's little sister. It's daring, but cute.

Thames - The River Thames is an iconic landmark, and Thames makes a smart and quirky choice that would be a great name.

VETO TAX **HACK**

HOW TO SAY NO TO A NAME CONSTRUCTIVELY

A struggle I hear so often when chatting to couples is when one person constantly says 'no' to the other's ideas. In my own baby naming journey, I was constantly coming up with baby names – but Winnie was walled, Oakley got the chop and even my absolute favourite Lily was refused by my husband Henrik . . . but he wasn't offering anything as an alternative, so I created the VETO TAX. Here's how to apply it.

- If someone doesn't like a name, the answer can't be 'I just don't like it.' They need to explain why they are vetoing the name. Is it the length, the sound of the letters, an association? Is it too popular or too 'out there'? Getting more specific feedback will help you adapt the name or find a new one that doesn't fall into the same veto trap.
- If you veto a name your partner loves, the rule is to bring two more options to the table. Using the theme or style of the name, delve into this book to find two or more names you *would* consider and bring them to the table.
- Visualize. It's super hard to connect instantly to a name and could mean you're passing up on a great choice. If one of you really loves a name that the other doesn't like, try this visualization idea. Write the name, surname and any middle names on a sticky note or piece of paper and pin it up around your home. Practise saying the name out loud in your environment (don't feel silly) and if it hasn't landed after a few weeks, pop it on your long list as a backup until you both

agree on something else. This is how I ended up with 'Freddie' for my baby after I initially vetoed it. I began to love seeing the name stuck up next to the shower and walking into the nursery, I'd say 'hello Freddie' along with other names and it started to really grow on me. My brother-in-law did a similar hack of saying the name Otto over and over after his partner Stina had vetoed it. In the end she couldn't think of the baby as anything other than Otto - ha-ha. A bit more of a hardcore approach than I'm recommending.

ANIMAL KINGDOM

There are so many reasons to pick a name from the animal kingdom. Bear, Fox and Tiger have already become modern classics, and playful baby animal names like Kitty, Joey and Bunny were favourites in the fifties. Our kids, cubs and little monkeys bring out the protective Mama Bear in all of us, and they have just as much energy. When our boys were toddlers racing around the house, we always used to joke we needed to walk the puppies. From the Big Five to Delicate Butterflies, let's see what names you find – underline or star your favourites and add to your own name list.

BIRD NAMES

Bird names have such a deep connection to us, especially when raising our little ones. We use the term 'nesting', and phrases like 'spreading their wings' and 'helping them to fly' are synonymous with the parenting we see in the bird world. Nurseries everywhere have owls, doves and garden birds flying across their walls. I love bird names for that whimsical reason, and there are so many wonderful choices. Pretty Wren or cute Dovie are an absolute dream, and the classic Robin will always be enduringly popular.

GIRLS

Alouette - 'Lark'. This French name means Lark and is just stunning. It's not being used often, so add it to your list and feel very smug about it. It's a true Stand Out & Shine name.

Ava - 'Birdlike' or 'to breathe, to live'. I adore this vintage name which stays atop the charts year upon year. One root to the name is Avis meaning 'birdlike'. A classy, glamorous choice that will never go out of style for someone looking for a Timelessly Tasteful name.

Aviana - 'Birds'. This name is so like my daughter's name Evelina, I can't help but love it. Ava makes a gorgeous nickname.

Birdie - 'Bird'. Retro kitsch is such a vibe and if you love it too, then Birdie is the poster-girl name for the trend. If you prefer it as a nickname, it would be a pretty short form for Bridget, Beatrice and even Delilah at a stretch.

Doli - 'Bluebird'. Doli is a name from the Navajo Tribe, a Native American people who live in the southwestern United States. This name jumped straight onto my name-crush list - pronounced Doh-Lee. If you have roots with the Navajo people, it could make an amazing name choice.

Dovie/Dove - 'Peace'. Dovie was a popular name in the 1940s winging its way back into the charts. I adore how vintage it sounds - a beautiful dove that symbolizes peace. I can't pick a favourite between Dovie or Dove and paired with another vintage name, you will be in name envy territory very fast. If peace stands out to you as a meaning, visit Virtue Names next.

Kittiwake - A seabird named after its distinctive call. I'll admit I've been sneaking this onto a lot of name lists for clients who want something unique. In its short form, Kit or Kitti are delightful and it would be a fun middle name for a sea-loving family.

Lark - 'Songbird'. Lark or Larkin work brilliantly as a name and I also think Skylark would make for a more daring choice. There are lots of sayings about this gorgeous bird - 'as happy as a lark' for its cheerful song or 'up with the larks', which might cause a slight eyeroll if your baby is an early riser. I like to think their cry will at least make you smile if they have this name.

Luscinia - 'Nightingale'. Luscinia is a type of Nightingale, famous for their unique song. Although reminiscent of Lucy, it remains an unusual name and has cool Lulu as a nickname. See Maximalist Names for more of these longer names.

Mavis - 'Songbird'. I predict this quirky name is due its revival. It's been out of style since its peak in the 1920s but shrug off any associations and revisit this old-fashioned winner. Vintage Gold or Vintage Old? You know where I stand.

Paloma - 'Dove'. Paloma is a Spanish girl name. Doves are symbols of peace. In biblical times, a dove was depicted carrying an olive branch back to Noah in his ark as a sign that dry land was near. Doves also represent love with their pure white colour. Paloma is perfect if you love unique names that are easy to say and spell but still stand out from the crowd.

Raven - The Raven is one of our most poetic birds, symbols of prophecy and insight due to being a 'talking bird' with their trademark croak. The negative association of ravens being a symbol of ill-fate or the ghost of people passed over hasn't stopped the name becoming a popular one.

Rhea - 'Flowing'. This flightless bird (like an Ostrich) is native to South America with impressive feathers. Rhea was the daughter of the earth goddess Gaia and the sky god Uranus and it ticks a lot of trends with its gentle, elegant sound.

Usoa - 'Dove'. This Spanish name is pronounced You-So-Uh, a pretty three-syllable girl name that isn't often heard outside of Spain.

Zenaida - A Zenaida is a species of dove. Doves are monogamous and mate for life and at weddings you'll often see doves released, as they have a great sense of navigation and always return home. As someone who plans to be a 'ready nester' not an 'empty nester', this name appeals to me in so many ways.

Zipporah - 'Bird'. Wow, what a name - the wife of Moses in the bible, this rare name is achingly cool. Birds are loved for the sense of freedom they inspire and this name does just that.

BOYS

Altair - 'Flying eagle'. This name should soar onto your name list if you want a unique option that stands tall and proud.

Arvis - 'Forest of eagles'. This Old Norse name evokes the Scandinavian forests, which gives the name a rugged feel. Arvis is also popular in Latvia as a name, and sounds hipster and vintage all at once. I love the 's' ending - maybe a great alternative to more popular Arlo.

Azio - 'Owl'. I recently learnt, since taking my children to a birds of prey display, that owls are in fact not at all wise, despite being depicted throughout literature as scholarly due to their large, all-knowing eyes. Azio is an interesting name with a cool 'o' ending derived from the Latin word for owl.

Branwen - 'Blessed raven'. Bran is the Celtic god of the underworld, whose symbol is a Raven. It's a strong name that oozes style and Bran makes a trendy short form.

Callum - 'Dove'. The Scottish variation of the name Columba, meaning Dove. Callum is a classic which never goes out of style, perfect for Timelessly Tasteful namers.

Finch - 'To swindle'. There's lots of different types of finches and I think the name sounds like an urban, edgy, cool moniker. Finch could be an alternative to popular Finn if that was on your list but someone has stolen it or it feels too mainstream for you. A group of goldfinches are called a 'charm', and all finches are super-sociable, so it evokes the idea of a popular character with lots of friends.

Hamza - 'Lion'. An Arabic name, Hamza is edgy with its 'lion' meaning representing qualities of being steadfast and strong.

Hawk - 'Bird of prey'. Hawks are huge birds, a symbol of independence and strength. It's a bold and brave name pick that could be perfect if you feel connected to what it stands for.

Jay - 'Rejoice'. A sweet one-syllable name that's handsome, the jaybird is a characterful bird who is famous for mimicking other birds and even cats when under threat.

Kestrel - 'Rattle'. This bird of prey has a gorgeous name meaning 'rattle' due to the sound of its call. Britain's most common bird of prey, a master of riding the wind, it's the ideal name for your baby who will soar through life.

Lonan - 'Blackbird'. An Irish boy's name, Lonan is unusual but engaging. The name was used by several early saints, as the blackbird was a symbol of wisdom and knowledge.

Peregrine - 'Traveller or wanderer'. The Peregrine Falcon is known to fly far and wide and Peregrine has long been used as a boy name. It's just the right side of quirky to be called traditional. If you love strong, vintage boy names, the journeying meaning might make this name wander right into your heart.

Shikoba - 'Feather'. A Native American name from the Choctaw tribe, Shikoba means to be like a feather. I've been asked a few times to find a name with 'feather' in the meaning, as many people associate it with the fluttering feelings of pregnancy or in remembrance. While being mindful of cultural appropriation, if the name fits a piece of your story, I think it would make a deeply meaningful choice.

NEUTRAL

Quill - 'Scribe'. I often get asked for feather-inspired names, as feather is a popular bump nickname, along with 'pip' (go, Pippin!). Quill is a rare one that sounds wearable.

Robin - One of our most popular gender-neutral names is Robin. A robin redbreast is the symbol of remembrance: When a Robin visits you, it's said to be a visit from someone who has passed on, making it a loving nod to anyone missing a loved one. I also like the spelling Robyn with a 'y', which is the feminine form.

Sparrow - 'Small, chirpy'. This sweet name is a garden bird that symbolizes joy and love of community.

Wren - The symbol of luck and happiness, the name Wren has flown up the charts in recent years. Wrens were associated with poets and songwriters due to their distinctive song. A really on-trend, short and sweet name for Trendy with a Twist namers.

ANIMAL NAMES

Choosing an animal name for your baby is not only a good idea for animal lovers - animal names bring the characteristics of that creature and can really help pack meaning and value into a name. Whether that's a peaceful Fawn, busy Bee or fierce Tiger, animals

have been inspiring baby names more and more, and I've put together a list of my favourites. I've also included names that have hidden animal meanings. I'm a huge sucker for a themed nursery and collecting items with their special animal on; so have a read and pop the ones you love on your own personal name list.

GIRLS

Agnes - 'Lamb'. I love the vintage girl's name Agnes and it can mean 'lamb' and 'pure'.

Bindi - 'Butterfly'. In Noongar, the official language of the Aboriginal people in the south-west of Western Australia, this name can mean 'little girl' or 'butterfly'. A bindi is also a significant mark worn by Hindis, representing the third eye and worn as an adornment for marriage.

Birdie - A retro nickname, Birdie was used as a short form for Bridget traditionally, but a modern trend is for using the nickname itself as the full name. Birdie makes for an upbeat name and one for golf fans everywhere.

Deborah - 'Bee'. The name Deborah was most popular in the seventies, so it's a few years away from its retro revival, but I love biblical Deborah with the sweet image of a bee.

Ebba - 'Brave boar'. A Scandinavian name that's very popular in Sweden, Ebba makes a lovely twist on traditional Emma for Trendy with a Twist namers.

Everly - 'Wild boar meadow'. Everly is a topographical name, from an old English word *eorfor*, meaning 'boar', and *ley*, meaning 'clearing' or 'meadow'. The name would have come from the settlers who lived near these tusked wild pigs. With a variant spelling of Everleigh, it has such a pretty sound.

Fauna - 'Young deer'. The Roman goddess of woodlands brings this stunner of a name.

Fawn - 'Baby deer'. The image of a baby deer is super-popular for babywear and nursery décor and it's a name that is just as delicate and charming.

Kitty - 'Baby cat'. I adore Kitty and would have given anything to have been called it when I was little. Its vintage charm is happy and retro - how sweet for your little girl.

Nyala - 'Mountain antelope'. A Nyala is a twisted-horn antelope native to southern Africa. The name is as striking as the animal.

Pippa - 'Lover of horses'. Iconic for any horse riders, the short form of Phillipa is strong and playful as a name.

Rachel - 'Ewe'. Rachel is a biblical name, meaning ewe or female sheep, possibly as a follower of Christ and part of his flock. It's a name that has stood the test of time, with an example of it being registered as far back as the 1600s.

Tabitha - 'Gazelle'. Named after the small antelope, Tabitha was a name bestowed on those who showed qualities of the grace of the animal.

Ursula - 'Little bear'. Although this Spanish name means 'little bear', it is also associated with the sea and is a lovely pick for Timelessly Tasteful namers.

BOYS

Ari - 'Lion or eagle'. A double pick when it comes to hidden animal names is Ari, pronounced Arr-Ee. In Hebrew it means 'lion' and in Scandinavian it means 'eagle'. Both amazing creatures, I love the minimalism of Ari if you want a softer-sounding boy name that packs a punch.

Bear - Bear brings out both the cuddly and sweet teddy bear icon of childhood into a name, plus the strong and powerful spirit of the mammal. It makes a great first name or perfect one-syllable middle name paired with a traditional moniker. Scandinavian name Bjorn also means Bear, as does English Arthur, so if you love the idea of Bear but it's a bit too on the nose - they are both great alternatives.

Bjorn - 'Bear'. Scandinavian Bjorn is well-known but unexpected, which could be the perfect combo for Stand Out & Shine and Timelessly Tasteful namers who can't agree.

Caleb - 'Dog'. Man's best friend, the name Caleb also means 'whole-hearted' or 'faithful', the characteristics of lovely dogs. Although traditional, Caleb still remains in the sweet spot of not being too high in the charts.

Conall - 'Strong wolf'. Shared by both a Scottish and Irish king, Conall has great heritage. I love the double 'll' ending, giving it a warmth as well as strength.

Conor - 'Lover of dogs'. We all know a dog lover and this name would be so wonderful for your child if that's you.

Giles - 'Young goat'. Giles is quite grown-up, but I think it's a very handsome, traditional name. Ideal for Timelessly Tasteful namers.

Harley - 'Hare's meadow'. The brown hare is Britain's fastest land mammal. If you enjoy zipping through the countryside, Harley has perfect name potential.

Jonah - 'Dove'. Jonah was on my name list, as I liked how established the name is while still having an unusual sound. It ticked my criteria of being stylish, yet was traditional enough for my husband and the symbol of a dove is so special.

Kobe - 'Turtle'. The Swahili meaning of fashionable Kobe is turtle or tortoise.

Leo - 'Lion'. Associated with courage, the name Leo has been a mainstay in the charts for years. Both a constellation, a zodiac sign and the brave symbol of a lion means that it ticks a lot of boxes for a traditional boy name that always sounds special.

Leon - 'Lion'. Leon is a French boy name, associated with the constellation of Leo and representing strength and bravery.

Ralph - 'Wolf counsel'. Ralph has been adapted from the medieval name Rædwulf, which is said to have been given to people who displayed leadership qualities, like the head of a pack of wolves.

Rudy - 'Famous wolf'. Rudy is a vintage nickname short for Rudolph and it's having its revival. It's such a fresh sound for a name that was out in the cold for a while due to the Rudolph the Red-nosed Reindeer associations; but Rudy would make a perfect pick for Trendy with a Twist namers.

NEUTRAL

Fox - Mainly used for baby boys, the name Fox has the benefit of being a well-known surname and it's springing to the front spot. A fox is always depicted as cunning and intelligent - and your unique little fox will certainly have a spring in their tail.

Kit - A baby fox is called a 'kit'. Also known as a short form of Christopher or Christine, it has become a modern classic.

Lynx - 'Wild cat'. Just as Tiger and Fox have become popular names, I love the idea of Lynx as a daring one-syllable name.

Tiger - This powerful cat makes for one of the most gorgeous names. Any child named Tiger would grow up loving their name and forever remain playful and fearless.

Wolf/Wolfie - Both of these names have been used historically as short forms of German name Wolfgang, which has such a cool, vintage vibe. Wolves are linked to spirituality and moonlight and are known for being loyal to their pack, making it an adorable name for your little wolf cub.

FANTASTICAL BEASTS & MYTHICAL CREATURES NAMES

If you want to sprinkle some magic over your baby, a fantastical creature name does just that. The names Phoenix and Griffin may sound rare but have actually been in the baby name charts for years, and there's plenty more inspiration within the world of mythical creatures. You don't need to be a sci-fi and fantasy fan to love the vibe - the world of dragons, fairies and elves is jam-packed with dreamy names.

GIRLS

Amalthea -'Tender goddess'. The foster mother of Zeus in mythology and the pretty name of *The Last Unicorn*. The name Amalthea is dreamy and special, just like your baby girl.

Celestia - 'Heavenly'. A celestial name inspired by Princess Celestia in *My Little Pony*.

Cleodora - 'Gift'. The mythical nymph Cleodora could tell fortunes by throwing pebbles. The name is just as magical, and its nickname Cleo sounds so whimsical and vintage.

Ella - 'Fairy maiden'. Ella translates as many things and is often used in its short form for Gabriella or Isabella. But in its simplicity, Ella is a sophisticated and effortless girl name.

Lorelei - 'Alluring'. Lorelei was a famous siren. The German myth comes from the Lorelei rock in the Rhine River, a site of maritime disasters and shipwrecks. The myth goes that a beautiful maiden named Lorelei lured sailors to their doom with her beautiful song. Pronounced Laurel-eye it's a brilliant way to honour a Laura.

Nessie - 'Pure'. From the name Agnes, Nessie is best known as the Loch Ness Scottish mythical creature. A cool vintage nickname as first name, check out the list of Vintage Names for similar ideas.

Nixie - 'Water sprite'. In German mythology, a Nixie was like a mermaid, being half fish, half woman. A magical choice for your little water sprite.

Pixie - 'Little fairy'. In Celtic mythology, pixies lived in the moorlands and were known for being mischievous. It's a playful name that would suit a sparkly, free-spirited little girl.

Selkie - 'Seal folk'. In Scottish folklore, a selkie was a shapeshifting creature who could turn from a seal into a human. A powerful tale of reclaiming feminine power for your daughter.

Titania - 'Giant'. Most well-known as the queen of the fairies in Shakespeare's *Midsummer Night's Dream*, Titania feels so fairylike and delicate, yet with a power and strength. The name originated from the daughters of Titans who were called Titania and Shakespeare borrowed it.

BOYS

Aslan - 'Lion'. This ancient name was once the title of Turkish Emperors and was famously used by C.S. Lewis in *The Lion, The Witch and The Wardrobe*. It has been on a slow but steady rise in recent years and a modern baby Aslan would be adorable.

Castiel - 'Angel'. Castiel is a variation of the name Cassiel, both of which I love, but the 't' adds a bit more to the name. Cassiel was one of the archangels who preceded over Seventh Heaven, the most holy.

Drake - 'Dragon'. Meaning both 'dragon' and 'serpent', Drake is a modern boy name that has a fantasy twist in its hidden meaning.

Fenrir - 'Giant wolf'. The famous wolf from Norse mythology, Fenrir sounds adventurous and full of magic.

Griffin - 'Lord'. A mix of a lion and an eagle, the Griffin was created as the king of animals and birds and was said to protect treasures. I have a Finn and wish I'd thought of using Griffin as a longer form version, as it really elevates the name to something more distinctive.

Loki - 'Lock'. The infamous Norse god of mischief, Loki was a shape shifter. This cheeky name has been getting increasingly popular and could be a super-playful pick for your baby boy.

Nuno - 'Grandfather'. Nuno in the Philippines are nature spirits. The meaning 'grandfather' comes from the ancestral spiritual belief in these bright and wise mythological creatures.

NEUTRAL

Aubrey - 'Elf ruler'. From Alberich, an elf in Old Norse mythology, came Aubrey. With a powerful meaning and long history, Aubrey has that touch of magic and you can also find it in my Winter Names list (see page 49).

Haizum - 'Pegasus'. In Islam, Haizum is the name of the Pegasus ridden by archangel Gabriel. This winged white horse flying across the cosmos makes a super-trendy name.

Phoenix - 'Crimson'. The name means 'red' and the mythological bird is known for dying in red flames and being reborn in the ashes. Phoenix has rockstar edge and symbolizes rebirth, a very cool name.

MY TIPS ON **SPELLING**

TRADITIONAL OR YU'NIQUE

I love a unique name but prefer a traditional spelling. The hardest thing for a person to navigate as they introduce themselves isn't being called Winter or being a girl called Finley. It's having to be Wynter or Finleigh that trips people up. Being Sarah-Jayne with a 'y' myself, it's not too complex a spelling, but I still always need to spell it out.

The biggest reason I recommend a traditional or phonetic spelling is that we're increasingly starting to hear how having your name constantly misspelt or misheard can make the wearer feel insecure. I recently read a study on people whose name is a 'typo' and the constant necessity to correct others left them feeling frustrated. There is a bit of backlash online about yu'nique spellings, as many feel it is about incorrect spelling or trying to be too stylish.

On the flip side, our name is our calling card and it's refreshing that we now have the freedom to broaden our horizons when it comes to naming and draw upon more unusual inspiration when we think of a name for our baby.

Three quick checks to make before going with a different spelling:

- Does the spelling make the name easier to say and spell? For example, in the UK we have Esme registered, but then also Esmay, Esmee, Ezmae, Ezmee and Ezme. Esme is the traditional spelling, but if you preferred the stronger Esmee as the pronunciation then it would work to add the second 'e'. Ezmae would always need to spell her name, so consider if it's worth it. If it is, then go for it.

- Is the original spelling less common but more meaningful to you? My son Fredrik is spelt the Swedish way while Frederick, Fredrick, Frederick and Frederic are all more commonly used in the UK. However, it was my Swedish husband's favourite name and it didn't feel right for us to not go with his spelling.
- Does the alternative spelling you're considering really make the name more special or just more complex? Often our rationale for wanting to change up the spelling is to make the name extra special. Although it may look 'prettier on paper' with the extra letters, if it adds too much complexity, I advise that you take it back to basics.

COLOURS

It's childhood law to pick your favourite colour, though my daughter Evelina has totally cheated and always picks 'rainbow' as hers. Colour names range from vintage classics like Scarlett to modern favourites Indigo and Violet. In this list I've split them into groups of aesthetics. Vibrant colours have always been popular, but what's your own colour palette? Are you a mix-and-match bright patterns kind of person? Is your wardrobe and home made up of neutral earth tones? Muted colours are soft and modern and then there's gilded silvers and metallics which add a sequins-and-sparkles vibe.

VIBRANT & COLOURFUL NAMES

From gorgeous greens to beautiful blues, these vibrant colour names will add a glow to your personal name list. Jot down your favourites.

GIRLS

Aya - 'Design, colourful'. It couldn't get more stylish. Aya can also mean 'beautiful' in Japanese.

Cherry - 'Red'. The name Cherry has retro, fifties kitsch vibes.

Ebony - 'Dark black'. The name Ebony is very classy and the black keys of pianos were traditionally made of polished ebony wood, so it has musical links that could make it just perfect for your baby girl.

Fairuza - 'Turquoise'. With its Turkish meaning, Fairuza is such a special name, a gemstone of bright turquoise. I love the unique 'z' ending reflecting its uplifting, vibrant colour paired with its fairy tale charm.

Lavender - 'Purple flower'. Evocative of the colour and scent and used as a name in *Harry Potter* and *Matilda*, it's got literary credibility and timeless appeal.

Mulberry - 'Deep purple'. The fruit is spelt 'Mulberrie' whereas the colour ends with a 'y'. Also the name of a fashion brand, this would be a fun pick for your little girl.

Myrtle - 'Green'. The myrtle plant is a lovely green colour with pink flowers. Mabel, Margot and Maeve are back, so why not Myrtle? I think it has such a pretty sound and it's always fashion forward to go back in time.

Olivine - 'Olive green'. The birthstone of August and a pick on my Space-Inspired Names list. This shade of green is my absolute favourite, and the name is incredibly beautiful too. It's a good choice for Trendy with a Twist namers who want a variation of Olive.

Saffron - 'Orange-yellow'. I love the name Saffron and would use it with Saffy or Ronnie as a nickname. The colour itself is also stunning, reminiscent of sunrises and spices - read more about Saffron in my Food inspired list.

Sapphire - 'Blue'. A blue gemstone I also share in my Crystals, Rocks & Minerals list; Sapphire is an exquisite but soft name that perfectly replicates the calming blue colour and sparkling gem.

Scarlett - 'Red'. This vibrant, rich red colour is associated with both courage and love and would make a great choice for Timelessly Tasteful namers. The name Scarlett gained popularity after Scarlett O'Hara in *Gone With The Wind* and still has a glamorous and luxurious feel.

Violet - 'Purple'. This delicate purple flower also appears in my Flower and Disney lists and has been worn as a name for decades. The colour is a favourite of so many and Violet has a timeless appeal, with Lettie or Vivi as sweet nicknames.

BOYS

Azul - 'Blue'. With its Spanish meaning, this sky-blue colour always feels calming and positive and I love how trendy the name sounds. Pronounced Az-oul.

Cobalt - A blue shade that's also in demand as a mineral to power electric vehicles, I think it works really well as a name. With Coby being well-used, it's got that edge for Trendy with a Twist namers.

Cole - 'Victorious people'. The shade 'coal' is a rich black that makes me think of charcoal drawings, so it has creative flair as well as being a natural element. I would recommend switching the spelling to Cole rather than Coal to make it more wearable.

Indigo - A deep blue/purple, this colour has hopped firmly across into the name charts with the nickname Indie.

Mazarin - 'Dark blue'. A French word name for a deep blue colour, we recently welcomed baby Mazarin to our family in Sweden as a middle name, though he's named after the local almond cake. I adore the flowing, unique sound of Mazarin.

NEUTRAL

Blue - Blue is a gorgeous sounding name. The colour is associated with calmness, peace and trustworthiness, but it has an effervescence with its one-syllable charm.

Jade - 'Precious stone'. This green hue became a huge name hit that peaked in the nineties and then dropped out of style - maybe it was a victim of its own popularity. A baby Jade would today have a super-unique name that's as brilliant as the colour.

Navy - This deep blue is a trendy classic colour for both clothes and homes, and now it makes a stylish baby name as well.

MUTED COLOUR NAMES

Colour names can seem bright and bold, but if your personal palette is more in the pastels and softer tones, there are so many stunning options that will bring your style to life in your little one's name.

GIRLS

Blush - 'Pale pink'. A unique idea for a name that's hitting the charts off and on over the last few years. It's a feminine one-syllable name that beauty fans will adore.

Dusty - 'Sand coloured'. Rising in popularity is the cool name Dusty. It's impossible to ignore the link to Dusty Springfield and it's got a bit of cowboy cool, too. Dusty makes a unique and special moniker with a bit of hippy style.

Ivory - 'Pale white'. Ivory as a colour is that almost pearlescent white and we know it's a natural element from animals' tusks. With

Ivy being so popular, Ivory makes a great alternative for Stand Out & Shine appeal.

Lilac - 'Light purple'. Lily is such a popular girl's name, but it's Lilac that has that Trendy with a Twist moment. Lilac is a soft and floral colour, which would always be special to someone bearing this name.

Olive - This gorgeous muted green shade is so on-trend. Olive is a popular vintage name and the colour association really elevates it for me. A minimalist name that, like the colour, is super stylish.

Peach - Peach is one of those delicate colours we often see in nurseries for its calming effect. Peach is of course a fruit that is known for being so sweet, making it also a term of endearment - your sweet Peach. Peaches with an 's' ending might also tempt you, depending on your surname. If you love Peach but aren't a Stand Out & Shine namer, you can always try pairing it in the middle spot. See my Mastering the Middle Name feature for tips (see page 198).

BOYS

Bruno - 'Brown'. German Bruno is beginning to have its resurgence. With the strong 'o' ending and 'brown clothes vibe' bringing a bit of seventies retro to our wardrobes, Bruno is perfect for Trendy with a Twist namers. See my Earth Tones names list for more colour names (see page 121).

Gray - 'Grey'. Minimalist grey gets spelt with an 'a' here and if you prefer you can lengthen it to Grayson. Gray feels urban and modern, smart and creative.

Rusty - 'Ruddy'. Rusty is a really fun vintage name. It feels ready for a revival, overtaking its namesake Russell. A daring name with that ruddy red colour association.

Slate - 'Grey-green'. An Anglo-Saxon occupational name for someone who worked with this form of clay and rock, Slate is an arresting name idea. You could also do Slater.

Tanner - 'Leather maker'. This tan brown is such a popular pantone for our homes and in fashion. The name feels just as warm and rich. It would make an excellent choice for a Stand Out & Shine namer.

NEUTRAL

Ash - 'Happy'. What an upbeat name that also suggests a dark grey colour. I love how simple Ash is, yet it still has loads of character. The ash tree is a symbol of protection - you can find more tree names with powerful meanings in my Tree Names list (see page 24).

Hunter - One of the fastest-rising names a few years ago, this strong choice is amazing for girls and boys. Hunter green is a popular calming shade, which softens the sound of this name.

Sandy - 'Sand coloured'. Sandy has come full circle from a retro girl's name short for Sandra, to a beachy boho name with a lot of laidback charm.

GILDED NAMES

Adorning your baby with a luxe name inspired by all things sparkling and shiny is such a special place to find an option that is effervescent and luminous. I've chosen names in this list that bring that twinkle to the eye and that spark of joy to life and I love them all.

GIRLS

Arianell - A Welsh name meaning 'silver'. Pronounced Arry-A-Nell, Saint Arianell was a member of the Welsh royal family, so it's steeped in history and full of sparkle. Arianwen is an alternative with the same meaning.

Fidda - 'One who is like silver'. This Arabic girl name was given to women of high class and wealth. It's a glamorous Stand Out & Shine name.

Iskra - 'To sparkle'. This Slavic name meaning 'to spark' or 'sparkle' would be so special for the bright spark in your life. Iskra is so unique and stylish, very in vogue and truly memorable.

Naja - 'Silver hands'. In Greenlandic, Naja also means 'a boy's younger sister' which would make a great name if you're having a daughter after a son. The meaning of 'silver hands' feels very spiritual and I adore the gentle sound of this name.

Simay - 'Glitter moon'. A stunning Turkish name, the glitter moon is a wonderful icon and one that could be very dear to your heart. Simay has that exotic, intoxicating sound, perfect for a name so sparkly.

Tindra - 'To dazzle or sparkle'. This Scandinavian name has the most joyful meaning with a playful sound. Tindra in Nordic folklore was the name for someone who was touched by the celestial realm, so that magical charm.

Vega - 'Falling star'. Vega means 'stooping eagle' and also 'falling star', as it's the name of the brightest star in the constellation Lyra. Names starting with 'V' populate the top of the charts and Vega makes a cool and edgy choice. See more about Vega and names with a similar style in my Star Names list (see page 61).

Zahira - 'Luminous'. To shine bright is a wonderful reason to choose Arabic name Zahira. A name that glows on the page, Zahira is a beauty.

BOYS

Argo - 'Glistening'. Argo has one of the coolest name histories. Argo comes both from Argus, a giant with 100 eyes, and from the name of the infamous ship that took Jason and the Argonauts on their quest to find the Golden Fleece. An iconic name.

Aurelio - 'Golden one'. From Latin word *aurum*, which literally means gold, Aurelio was bestowed upon the elite in ancient Roman times and still makes a gorgeous name today. This soft name is interesting while being quite easy to say and spell, so it's a high hitter for me.

Elidor - 'Steel'. A Welsh boy name, meaning steel, Elidor has a modern romantic hero essence which I really like. Derived from a mythical monk and king named Elidur, this ancient name is a trendy modern pick.

Isambard - 'Bright iron'. A famous namesake is Isambard Kingdom Brunel who designed the Great Western Railways. I think it makes such a brave and edgy choice and as a Swindon girl, birthplace of the railways, it had to get a spot in this name guide.

Kessel - 'Coppersmith'. A boy's occupational name for a Coppersmith, Kessel sounds really on trend and I love the idea of these copper workers. The name is derived from a type of copper kettle, which lends the name a cosy charm all of its own. It sounds great as a first name for someone and I also discovered that 'Kessel' is a *Star Wars* planet, so it could be a fan fave, too.

Sterling - 'Silver'. The name Sterling means something that is of highest quality or value, like sterling silver. It makes for a grand yet playful boy name.

NEUTRAL

Emery - 'Industrious'. A huge name crush of mine for boys or girls, Emery is a dark-coloured substance used to polish surfaces, making them shine. With Emerson and Emily being such popular names, this twist will ensure that your baby is bound to shine brightly with their special name.

Golden - The great Goldie name rush has started and it has become a modern favourite. Gold will always be hard to reach which creates its value and I love using this precious metal as a name. It's got a retro vintage vibe that hits a lot of parent's criteria. Grab it while you can for your baby's name list.

Sindri - 'Sparkle'. Norse mythology has it that Sindri made Odin's ring, hence the meaning. Sindri feels right out of the realm of the fairies.

EARTH TONE NAMES

Where once beige was boring, you're now much more likely to see these shades adorning the walls of your friends' homes, babies' nurseries and fashionistas' wardrobes than ever before. If your home is a neutral heaven and you find calm in the minimal, then earth tones are especially gorgeous. The 'linen outfit of baby names', these all have understated cool.

GIRLS

Alba - 'White, light'. Alba comes from the Latin word *Albus*. It is also the Scottish Gaelic name for Scotland, making it a perfect pick if you have roots in Scotland.

Coco - 'Chocolate brown'. This is always fashionable for clothing, so could jump from your shopping bag to your name list. Well-known Coco Chanel gives it a glamour that makes it feel grown-up and playful all at once.

Golda - 'Gold'. If you enjoy this rich colour, Golda is a perfect pick for a vintage name that is so reminiscent of an era of glamour and opulence.

Hazel - 'Hazel tree'. A gentle auburn namesake that ticks vintage and colour name inspiration. This old-fashioned yet underused name is sure to stand out. Great for Timelessly Tasteful namers.

Maple - 'Maple tree'. A super sweet shade of brown that makes a wonderful alternative to Mabel. Maple is warm, endearing and so full of character.

Midori - The Japanese word for a green tone, Midori has a nature link being described as the colour of shoots and young leaves. The name sounds fashionable and stylish and I love Dory or Riri as nicknames.

Sienna - 'Orange-red'. Sienna is synonymous with the city in Italy, which was named after the iron-rich clay the buildings were made from. An enduringly stylish and bohemian name, Sienna is a modern classic.

Tawny - 'Pale orange-brown'. If your house is full of wicker and neutrals, I think this name would be perfect. It pops in and out of the charts but remains a rare choice that has so much style.

Xanthe - 'Golden'. It originated in Greek mythology as a female version of Xanthos. Xanthe was a water nymph with golden hair and the name has become well-known for its 'X' initial coupled with its elegant sound and meaning.

BOYS

Albion - 'White land'. Another name for Great Britain, just as Alba means Scotland, Albion was the ancient name for Great Briton. The root word for both was taken from the word for 'white', potentially inspired by the chalky cliffs. Albion makes a great twist on classic Albert and carries that ancient background with it.

Dune - 'Sand hill'. The sandy colour tone of dunes makes for a distinctive boy name. Lovers of the beach will be drawn to Dune and it's got that surfer-type style and confidence.

Obsidian - 'Volcanic glass'. A type of glass, you'll find a lot of paint colours called Obsidian, as it's so trendy. The volcanic glass is formed when lava cools quickly; what child wouldn't love that meaning? It's getting used more in recent years, possibly as an alternative to Oliver and Oscar higher up the charts, and Dion would make a great nickname.

Sable - 'Black'. This is the name of a lovely little mammal with dark, pretty fur. I love how the name sounds romantic and intriguing, and I adore the dark colour meaning for any of you whose wardrobe is 90 per cent black.

Tanwyn - 'White fire'. Welsh showstopper Tanwyn has such a powerful meaning with its cool-toned paleness of the white paired with the heat of the fire - a real modern hero of a name.

NEUTRAL

Copper - 'Metal of Cyprus'. The colour copper puts me right into the downstairs of *Downtown Abbey* with a big copper kettle, or upstairs in a luxury freestanding copper bath. It's a beautiful tone for clothes and copper-colour hair is trending, too. It comes from the occupational name for a maker of cups, buckets and tubs so if you love to craft, Copper could be for you.

Forest - 'Woodland'. My favourite shade of green. The name forest literally spells 'for rest', making it such a peaceful and calming choice. A forest has 60–100 per cent tree canopy cover compared to the woods, so surround yourself with soothing, rich colours that evoke the forest. It's a great pick for girls with the nickname Estee.

Ochre - 'Deep yellow'. Pronounced 'Oak-Er', I love this shade of earthy yellow. It's a tone reminiscent of the setting sun and the name really gives it the edge as a trendy unique choice. See my Crystals, Rocks & Minerals Names section, where I've also included Ochre, for more inspiration (page 75).

Roux - 'Russet brown'. More often used in the middle spot as a complementary one-syllable name, it's an all-time favourite of mine. Roux even *looks* nice as a word and it has a simplicity of sound that is by no means ordinary. The colour is rich and warm, just like the name.

NAME GAMES

I love a games night, so have created some super fun games to play when you're cutting down a long list of names you like and are trying to decide on 'the one'.

How fun would a Baby Name Dinner Party with all your best friends be? If you're part of a couple, a cosy Name Games Night In would get the ideas flowing, or grab the person you know who is most name obsessed, and they will be thrilled to come over with a bag full of snacks and throw themselves into helping.

I hope these game ideas bring you loads of fun, as naming a baby can sometimes end up as deep chats across the dinner table or snatched texts throughout the day when your mind is on other things. Sitting down and making it fun and light-hearted helps break the back of the conversation without it feeling like you're auditioning and judging names. A game will encourage the 'Yes' moments and these shared activities and honest chats will help the best names rise to the top.

Here's some game ideas.

HIGHER OR LOWER

Best for deciding from a long list of your favourite names

Players: 2 players

Objective of the game: To whittle down a long list of names to one.

The Rules: Write down all the names on your name list on a piece of paper, cut them up into individual pieces and pop them into a bowl. Player A pulls out a name and places it on the table, then pulls out a second name. Player B has to say if the second name is 'higher or lower' in their opinion than the first name. If it's 'higher' - i.e. they like it more - it replaces the first name which then gets put aside. Player A pulls out another name and Player B keeps going - is that 'higher or lower' in their opinion than the first? Keep rejecting all the lower names until you're left with just one.

Once you have just one name left on the table, jot it down. Then Swap! Put all the names back in the bowl and Player A becomes the chooser.

You can play again using the same name bowl and see how many times the same name rises to the top. You now have a winning name!

RENAME GAME

Best for finding new names you haven't thought of

Players: 2 players min

Objective of the game: To get inspired with names that 'suit you'.

The Rules: Rather than asking for baby name ideas, ask your friends, family or partner to rename YOU. Collect their answers on bits of paper or via text if you can't all get together and read out all the names, one-by-one, to your naming partner, giving your opinion.

If you're naming as a couple, ask them to do this for both of you. If you're having a baby with an opposite gender to you or to both of you, ask friends what name would suit you if you were a boy or girl or ask for gender-neutral gems.

Pick your favourite names from their suggestions to add to your name list.

HONESTY BOX

Best for getting to the hard truths

Players: 2-4 players

Objective of the game: Getting some really honest name opinions that help shape the criteria you have for your own baby name.

The Rules: Write down all the names of the kids in your life already; your friends' babies, colleagues' children, your nieces and nephews' names, neighbours and acquaintances' kids. Ideally people you both know so you each have a stronger opinion. Put the names in an 'honesty box' (and in this moment of honesty, I know you're going for the bottom drawer and grabbing the mixing bowl right now). Draw out one name at a time and both give your real, brutally honest opinion on the name. Do you like it? Is it boring to you? Were you surprised when you heard the name because you really didn't expect it? And discuss, why is that? Could it be one you wish you'd thought of? Is it really cool and daring? Does it suit the parents and why?

We're often very polite about other people's baby names and I struggle to articulate at times the reasons that I don't like certain picks; but I do enjoy getting brutally honest within a circle of trust - and it's illuminating.

One of my best friends picked a girl name I find dull. No, that's not honest, I find it really ugly because it's an eighties mum type of name and is also quite harsh sounding. So, from that I learnt that I like soft and feminine girl names. I gravitate towards modern names, so I edited my own name list accordingly.

I also know a friend who picked a place name for his baby. But I found it so cringe as it really didn't suit that person - they don't live near the location and it's famous for being a music, rock 'n roll type of city, and this friend doesn't reflect that in their life. Although I like the name on paper, it's just not for them. So, *my* criteria includes only considering a place name if it is of personal relevance - no matter how much I love it on paper.

These are things I've never said out loud before and I'm hoping they don't recognize themselves in the descriptions, but I did enjoy dishing the dirt to you.

CHART TOPPER

Best for comparing and whittling down your names

Players: 2 players - either play as a couple or with your chosen naming bestie.

Objective of the game: Finding your own personal chart topper

The Rules: Write your name list down on two sheets of paper. Count how many names there are, and your individual task is to number them like the name popularity lists or the music charts, with one being your favourite from the list down to the bottom being your least favourite.

Reveal where each name ranked for you both. Then add up their 'score'. The lowest score wins, as it's your personal chart topper.

It may be that you ranked it in different spots; but it's your joint first place name. Jot the name down and keep it on your baby name list for when baby arrives. It could be a hit that grows on you, even if it's not your immediate number one.

If you've played one or all these games, I know you'll have discovered some great contenders for your Baby Name. Jot only the top names on your personal name list and if you're early in the process, come back to these pages if you need to redo them to make a final decision. I've also included a Name Infographic on page 329 for you to take a final quiz if you get stuck after your baby has arrived. It's based on all the criteria you need the name to meet if you're still wavering. Head to that page if or when you need it.

VIRTUES

Meanings are powerful when it comes to finding your perfect name. In this section of the guide, I've pulled together virtues – a belief or character trait. These range from your values and wish for their life, to being a name that can somehow make sense of the often-difficult road to parenthood that doesn't always get discussed. I speak to parents every day who want a name meaning 'warrior' or 'strength' for their NICU baby in neo-natal intensive care, or a name that somehow brings to life how longed for this precious child has been. I love names with meanings like 'cheerful' and 'happiness'. Each one is listed in this guide, and I know you'll find some joy reading these lists and picking your favourites.

CLASSIC VIRTUE NAMES

Classic virtue names like Hope, Joy and Grace stem from the Puritans. The Puritans were protestants who created the trend for using the virtues they wanted their children to embody as their name. During the sixteenth and seventeenth centuries, the Puritans moved from England to America, which saw Virtue names boom during this period. I've delved into quite a few passenger lists from ships to find these names. A lot of them were made up of two words; Fear God, Love Joy, Make Peace, Hope Still and a very popular Puritan name was Truelove. Today we prefer one Virtue name. Some of these words are still in use today and some like Blythe, meaning carefree, have dropped out of popular usage so make a more discreet virtue pick. This is one of my favourite categories, as my niece's middle name is Loveday. Born on Valentine's Day, it was just right for her. My sister's name Naomi means 'pleasantness', something she truly embodied. Let's see which ones you love.

GIRLS

Anya - 'Grace'. Originally Anya derived from Anna, so it's an elegant and creative twist on a classic that will always Stand Out & Shine.

Arabella - 'Prayerful'. Arabella is such a refined, everlasting classic name. I love how gentle but grand it sounds. Perfect for those that love a beautiful sounding name or Timelessly Tasteful namers.

Charity - 'Christian love'. Its original meaning of 'Christian love' now means 'to volunteer' or 'an organization'. Southern Belle vibes make this super-trendy and it's really underused compared to some others, so you'll have a real gem. Any thrifting fans will love this name.

Cher - 'Dear one'. From the French *cherie* - so endearing. Cher has become an iconic name taken from the superstar of the same name. It gives me a lot of Baby Name Envy, as I think it's such a vibrant, loveable and minimalist name that packs a lot of boho style in it's simple and chic sound.

Constance - 'Steadfast'. Connie is higher in the charts now, but I adore how vintage Constance is. It's the first name of Lady Chatterley from D.H. Lawrence's *Lady Chatterley's Lover* and to add to the culture, Mozart and Oscar Wilde both had wives called Constance. Meaning to be strong and steady, Constanza is the elegant Spanish variant.

Credence - 'Confidence and integrity'. Credence is an old English word for someone who has integrity in their beliefs. It would be a bold name, but it sounds gorgeous and like it belongs among some of our more common vintage names.

Felicity - 'Happiness'. Sometimes translated as meaning 'happiness at home', maybe due to the 'city' ending, I think this is a beautiful choice for a girl.

Gloria - 'To praise'. I recently heard this used with its nickname Glow and fell in love. Gloria is way overdue it's revival.

Honour - One of the most famous puritan names, I love how pretty this is together with its meaning of upholding your beliefs and having integrity. You can also use Honora and Honoria.

Joy - This just couldn't be lovelier. I know a lot of people using this in the middle spot, but I adore it as a first name, ticking the vintage, boho and virtue trends.

Liberty - 'Freedom'. Libby and Bertie make great nicknames and Liberty is one of those names that always feels modern. It hasn't peaked in a decade and I think it's such a special meaning to bestow on your little adventurer.

Mercy - 'Compassion'. Mercy as a name brings that personality trait right to the fore. It's a vintage puritan name and as a Virtue name is beginning to make a comeback. Mercy makes a beautiful Stand Out & Shine name.

Naomi - 'Pleasantness'. My sister was named Naomi, my parents chose it in honour of Naomi James, the first woman to sail around the world single-handedly in 1978. Which, knowing my mum's canoeing skills, was a stretch of their imagination, but Naomi truly owned the meaning of pleasantness. As a sister, I was very envious of her fashionable name and she lived up to its meaning as the kindest and nicest person you'd hope to meet. This name has Best Friend Energy, just like her.

Pandora - 'All gifted'. Pandora feels upper class and sweet all at once - it stands out without being overly complex. Stunning and stylish.

Patience - 'Enduring'. Created by the Puritans who instilled values they believed in via their children's names, Patience sounds delightful as a word name. I really like the idea of retro and playful Patty as a nickname.

Phaedra - 'Bright'. Pronounced Fay-Dra this ancient Greek name makes a trendy alternative to Phoebe. Names meaning 'light' always tell a story of the light of your life and if you want a more interesting name that isn't hard to say, Phaedra is a wonderful choice.

Prudence - 'Good sense'. Pru gives me such Baby Name Envy as it's such a trendy vintage nickname for Prudence. It feels right out of a novel and would suit a little girl her whole life.

Reverie - 'Daydream'. One of my guilty pleasure names meaning 'a dream-like state'. So boho for your little daydream of a child. Whimsical and meaningful, Reverie is a second-look name that could add a lot of soul to your name list.

Saachi - 'Truth teller'. This shot to the top of my name crush list as soon as I found it. Pronounced Sar-Chee it just oozes cool to me and the meaning gives it that depth you get from a Virtue name.

Selah - 'To pause, to praise'. You'd see this word throughout the bible, inviting the reader to pause and pray. Pronounced Say-Luh - what a gem.

Sheridan - 'The searcher'. This Irish surname makes such a trendy first name with a beautiful spiritual meaning. For those who love exploring, soul searching and are always curious, Sheridan would fit into your family perfectly.

Sybil - 'Prophetess, oracle'. Once an occupational name, the Sybils were prophetesses in ancient Greece. They were assigned to holy places and were thought to predict what was going to happen in the future. Sybil is a quirky vintage pick with a meaning I predict will make it hit a lot of name lists.

Verity - 'Truth'. The most gorgeous virtue, using the 'V' at the beginning makes it stand out. A well-known name, but one that hasn't reached top spots, for me Verity sounds like a vintage literary heroine as well as a modern urban fashionista.

Whimsy - 'Fanciful'. I think Whimsy is so special if you're brave enough for this gorgeous word name. The traditional long form is Winsome, which I've had on my guilty pleasure name list for a few years.

BOYS

Aymes/Ames - 'Good friend'. From the French *ami*, it also sounds like someone with aims and goals, so a double virtue. With James being so popular, I love switching it up to Aymes.

Bravery - 'Courageous behaviour'. The noun for courage and valour was registered as a name in past centuries. I also came across the name Braveheart on the passenger list from boats leaving to go to America, likely from Scotland, where Robert the Bruce was nicknamed Braveheart. There he was fighting for Scottish independence and I think it is beautiful for babies showing so much courage. Perhaps a brave middle spot, see my Mastering the Middle Name feature for tips (see page 198).

Cybi - 'Victory'. This is the name of a sixth century Welsh saint and a Cornish nobleman - son of Salomon, known as King of Cornwall. Pronounced Cub-ey, it's a lovely off-beat Virtue name.

Darius - 'Possessing goodness'. The Persian meaning of Darius will bring a lot of love to this name - it has a sense of holding what is good dear to them. A thoughtful and caring connotation that is sweet for a baby boy.

Ernest/Earnest - 'Serious'. Taken from the old German word *ernust*. This adorable literary name gets a lot of love when I add it to lists. It comes with cute Ernie as a nickname and brings to mind Ernest Hemingway or Oscar Wilde's *The Importance of being Earnest*. With or without the 'a' it's a stylish and classic pick.

Ezra - 'To help'. Ezra is a distinctive Hebrew boy name with the 'z' adding some edginess. We always look for the helpers in any community and the name perfectly suits parents with values of care and kindness.

Liam - 'Guardian'. This popular boy name has a meaning that evokes someone who takes care of those around them and guards their own personality and passions with equal vigour. The guardian of your love, my nephew is called Liam, and he embodies all the qualities of this strong boy name.

Maverick - 'Unconventional and independent'. This name is climbing up the popularity charts despite it feeling quite daring. People love the three-syllable sound and the cheeky spark of personality it brings.

Muhammad - 'Praiseworthy'. Muhammad from the verb 'hamada', meaning praiseworthy, was the founder of Islam and the name is one of the most popular boy names in the world. The Quran was said to have been revealed by God through the angel Gabriel to Muhammad. An enduringly popular name, Muhammad will always be a top choice.

Noble - A truly wearable modern Virtue name that makes me think of the American bookstore. It means 'aristocratic' and having fine morals and it was also the name of a gold coin in use many years ago.

Saint - 'Holy'. A saint is an exemplary model and this title name has become a modern first name which is minimalist but full of character.

NEUTRAL

Amity - 'Friendship'. The most captivating name, Amity sounds gorgeous, and friendship is such a core value for so many of us, especially the relationship between siblings.

Blythe - 'Carefree'. The name Blythe sounds amazing when paired with a traditional name. Try it next to the others on your name list - its meaning is evocative of what we all want to bring to our babies' childhoods.

Harbour - 'A shelter'. I adore this Virtue name; you can also harbour feelings towards someone, which doubles down on its meaning and makes me love it even more.

Haven - 'A place of safety'. With Eva and Ava and Evan being so traditional, Haven is such a wearable Virtue name. Your pledge to them of such a cosy, safe space in a name is a gift - this name is so poetic and I adore it.

Hero - 'Brave defender'. Admired for courage, outstanding achievements, or noble qualities, this Virtue name is so trendy.

Journey - Derived via Old French from the Latin *diurnus* meaning 'of the day', we now use the word journey not just for travel, but also to describe a series of personal experiences. Life isn't about getting to the end, it's about the small moments, taking the good and the bad and this has become such a popular modern virtue name.

Promise - 'A pledge or vow'. Such a lovely word name that's getting use for both boys and girls.

Sage - 'Wise'. Sage hits so many trends - the colour, the virtue, the herb. Smudging or saging your house is said to clear it of any bad energy so it's a stunning one-syllable name with beautiful associations.

Serenity - 'A state of calm'. Serenity feels like calm after a turbulent time, which may express a feeling you'd love for your new baby.

True - 'Genuine'. For your true love, a real vintage gem that's making its way back into the popularity charts. Truly also adds a pretty ending.

Valour - 'Bold'. We don't often use the noun valour but we're familiar with it, which makes it really wearable as a name.

SANSKRIT & SPIRITUAL NAMES

Sanskrit names are very spiritual, as they are the sacred language of Hinduism and Hindi philosophy, plus the texts of Buddhism. Today these beautiful Virtue names are gaining so much popularity as modern parents move to a more spiritual way of living. The names are rich with deep power and meaning and if you belong to the religion or feel deeply aligned with the teachings, then it's an inspiring place to look for a name.

GIRLS

Anjali - 'Divine offering'. Used as a given name, Anjali is also a greeting - Anjali Mudra is the symbol of pressing two hands together.

Damini - 'Lightning'. From the Sanskrit word for Lightening, Damini is energetic and impactful just like its meaning.

Indu - 'Moon'. I love how special this Hindu name is. The Moon Cycles are often followed to get balance and harmony in life and Indu really evokes that spiritual side.

Tula - 'Balance'. A Sanskrit term used in yoga for getting things in balance. The name is so pretty, and the meaning really highlights the value of harmony.

Veda - 'Knowledge'. Pronounced as Vay-Da, the Veda's are one of the oldest scriptures. Some parents choose the alternative spelling of Veyda to make the pronunciation clear.

BOYS

Ajay - 'Invincible'. Pronounced A-Jay (not Ay-Jay), the meaning of being invincible brings a sense of strength and resilience to this trendy pick.

Ashwin - 'Horse tamer'. Also connected to the Lunar calendar, Ashwin begins when the Sun enters Virgo and the new moon after the Autumn equinox.

Bardo - 'The state between death and rebirth'. There are six Bardos in the Buddhist writings and these describe a journey through transitional states, with life constantly shifting and evolving, which makes for such a meaningful name.

Ravi - 'Sun'. Your little boy will be your son-shine and Ravi encapsulates that in a really on-trend name.

Rishi - 'Seer'. In Hindi a Rishi is the name for a sage or someone who can see or hear divine knowledge. A meaningful name for an old soul.

NEUTRAL

Asmi - 'I am'. A unique name with such a strong and confident meaning. It also means 'nature's beauty' which is a gorgeous sentiment for your baby.

Bodhi - 'Enlightenment'. Buddha is said to have gained enlightenment sitting under the Bodhi tree. The heart-shaped leaves of this sacred symbol are still celebrated.

Rohan - 'Ascending'. Rohan is a striking name that means 'ascending to high points' and 'a life of good deeds'. Pronounced Row-Han or Ro-an with a silent 'h', the strong 'o' is a solid favourite in modern names.

Zen - 'Meditation'. The state of calm makes a bold and dynamic name choice for Stand Out & Shine namers.

STORY-TELLING NAMES

Names with positive and powerful meanings can take us from 'like' to 'love', and for many people a meaning can tell a story; either of how their baby arrived in their life or a character and feeling they see them embodying. I loved Fredrik for my first baby more because it meant 'peaceful ruler'. I liked to imagine the big brother I never had and knew he would become - a kind and positive force who fully embodies the name's meaning. I adore Beatrice even more knowing it means 'she who brings happiness'. These names all have upbeat, joyous connotations that will be so personal to you and your own life experiences. Why not commemorate the story that brought you to parenthood plus the dreams and values you have for your child in a name?

GIRLS

Aine - 'Always and forever'. The meaning makes this such a gem of a name, and it has travelled a lot, picking up different meanings depending on the translation. In Japan the name Aine translates as two words meaning 'love' and 'green'. In Arabic it means 'one with beautiful eyes'. Wherever she travels, she can't go wrong on positive meanings. Pronunciations differ, but the Scandinavian I-Na is predominant.

Aisling - 'Dream or vision'. The enchanting meaning comes from a genre of Irish language poetry that was called 'aisling'. Pronounced Ash-Lin, it's such an elegant and striking name.

Alessia - 'Defender'. With its other meaning of 'truth teller', Italian Alessia has got real strength behind this lyrical and lively name.

Allegra - 'Cheerful or lively'. With musical links to 'allegro', this sparkling name means to play music or dance in an upbeat and bright way.

Beatrice - 'She who brings happiness'. The perfect name meaning and one of the most beloved British baby names.

Bonnie - 'Pretty'. This Scottish name has a modern vibe, and the benefit of being a strong name in its own right and not a nickname or short form for anything else.

Danica - 'Morning star'. In ancient Slavic mythology, Danica was the Sun's younger sister; a day star that was often worshipped at daybreak.

Esperanza - 'Hope and expectation'. This Spanish name has the most wonderful meaning for a much longed for baby. Modern sounding, but still a classic, I think this will hit a lot of sweet spots.

Evangeline - 'Bringer of good news'. What an amazing meaning, full of happiness at your new arrival and all the good she will spread in the world.

Farrah - 'Joy, happiness'. Farrah is both a Gaelic surname and Arabic first name. In both it translates to this bright and lively meaning of bringing joy and happiness into the world.

Fiadh - 'Wild'. I adore the meaning of this Irish girl name which is hugely popular in Ireland. The personality trait of being untamed and wildly free is appealing, but it also translates as 'deer', which the name rhymes with - pronounced Fee-Ah.

Gioia - 'Joy'. Italian for Joy, pronounced Joy-a. A cheerful and bright name, Gioia brings a twist to vintage Joy and a loving nod to George.

Iridessa - 'Fairy of the sun and light'. This name was invented by Disney, but I love how happy and upbeat it is, with a fairylike soft sound.

Irisa - 'Rainbow'. Iris was the mythological goddess of the rainbow and a messenger between the gods and humans, and this longer form of the name, Irisa, has so much potential.

Joyce - 'Joyous'. Joyce is such a throwback vintage name - traditionally a masculine name, now it's seen primarily on the girl's list. A character in *Stranger Things* and the surname of famous writer James Joyce, it has a vintage, quirky twang you don't get with Joy (one of my favourites as well). I'd be popping it on my list.

Jubilee - 'Rejoicing'. From the Old French word *jubileu,* it's a word that makes a fun and quirky name choice.

Kiki - 'Double happiness'. In Greek it also means 'Sunday's child', and 'having a Kiki' means to get together for chit-chat or gossip.

Laetitia - 'Joy'. The Roman goddess of celebrations brought us this playful name, perfect for bringing the joy to every little moment in life.

Lois - 'Most beautiful'. Lois has effortless style. It's got a rich etymology from the Greek verb *loion,* meaning 'best' or 'most beautiful' and it also appears in Hebrew, meaning 'lion'. Both catch my eye, but mostly I am drawn to the city-cool-mixed-with-minimalist-style that Lois encapsulates.

Novelli - 'New'. What better meaning for your new life with a newborn. It's a very pretty name that can be traced back to Venice and it brings Italian beauty and joy in its sound.

Oriana - 'Sunrise'. I adore the warmth and joy in this girl's name that evokes the feeling of starting each day afresh.

Simcha - 'Joy, festivity'. This Hebrew name is so celebratory. It translates as a gathering to celebrate and brings that same vibrancy and warmth.

BOYS

Ahmed - 'Highly praised'. A glorious meaning, Ahmed is a top pick of a name that should go straight to the top of your list.

Amias - 'Loved'. A French name in origin, Amias is traditionally pronounced with a silent 's', Ah-mi-a. A male form of Amy with the same appealing meaning.

Asher - 'Happiness'. Asher is a biblical name, so has a classic backdrop, but sounds really trendy for a baby boy. Happiness is the most important thing we want for our children and of course they are at the centre of our own joy, so picking the name Asher will always be a reminder of this.

Asho - 'Pure of heart'. Asho is unique, and I love the 'o' sound at the end for boys. It's a great name if you're after something easy to pronounce but stands out as extra special. Made for Trendy with a Twist namers.

Austin - 'Majestic'. A powerful Latin name with a grand and special meaning, 'majestic' or 'greatest' stamps this name out for your pride and joy.

Aziz - 'Respected'. A traditional Arabic name, Aziz means to be respected, cherished and powerful.

Beau - 'Beautiful'. A French boy name, this one-syllable gem is so stylish. It's a minimalist name with maximum impact.

Benne - 'Blessed'. An Anglo-Saxon name that became popular in Ireland and Scotland, it's a modern twist on Benjamin with such a special meaning.

Callahan - 'Bright headed'. An Irish surname, Callahan would be ideal for a bright and bubbly little boy. It sounds great as a first name, with its strong 'C' making this longer boy name seem punchy.

Cullen - 'Handsome'. A place name in Scotland and an Irish surname, Cullen has a fresh, modern style.

Felix - 'Happy, lucky'. Felix totally works for those with traditional tastes, but it's also trendy. It was in use as a first name in the Roman era and it was given to those who were lucky or successful. Today it feels just as fresh and upbeat with its cool 'x' ending.

Gilbert - 'Bright pledge'. A bright promise for the future ahead, Gil is a very cool nickname. Gilbert makes a quirky vintage pick.

Idris - 'Studious or enthusiastic leader'. Idris has Welsh and Arabic roots and in Arabic the name means to be studious and a smart leader. In Welsh it translates as 'enthusiastic leader'. Both these meanings set your little boy up for life.

Isaac - 'To laugh'. This meaning makes me think of childhood giggles, and it's the best feeling when you make your baby laugh for the first time. The meaning has significance too for a long-awaited child; when it was prophesized in the Bible that Sarah would have a second son, she laughed in disbelief. It's got a lot of style and substance.

Jayden - 'Thankful'. I love this meaning and it's one of the reasons to choose Jayden. It's also reminiscent of songbird Jay, which would be a perfect nickname. Read more about Jay in my Bird Names list (see page 98).

Kenzo - This Japanese word means 'strong' and 'healthy'. Kenzo is both cute and stylish for your baby boy.

Luke - 'Light giving'. Lucian, Luca and Lucas all share this lovely meaning that beams out happy vibes.

Neriah - 'Lamp of God'. Neriah is a Hebrew baby name, similar to more popular Noah. It's a beautiful sounding name that brings light with its religious meaning.

Tate - 'Cheerful'. An old Norse word meaning 'to be cheerful', Tate is just as upbeat and complements its meaning well with its one-syllable zip.

Winston - 'Joyful stone'. An Anglo-Saxon name made most famous by Winston Churchill, whose mother's maiden name was Winston and was passed on as his first name. This traditional name would be an adorable vintage choice. It's also the middle name of John Lennon if any music fans need convincing.

Yusuf - 'God increases'. A flowing Arabic name with this lovely message of an abundance of love and blessings.

NEUTRAL

Bliss - 'Intense happiness'. Bliss as a first name is eye-catching and the sentiment makes it doubly appealing.

Eden - 'Place of pleasure'. Eden is a true gender-neutral gem. I love the meaning taken from the Garden of Eden, a place of paradise and pleasure. It feels earthy and warm.

Salem - 'Complete'. How stunning is the meaning of being 'complete' or 'perfect'? Salem has been quietly gaining popularity in recent years and the meaning makes it a heart-warming choice.

NAMES MEANING 'LOVED'

One universal feeling as parents is how much we want our little ones to feel loved. There's no warmer sentiment or bigger feeling and you're already pouring that love into picking their name, which makes it so special. As you imagine your world with them in it, it's our adoration for them which will outshine anything else,

so pop a heart next to all the names you love in this section and know your baby is already so truly lucky to have you.

GIRLS

Amabel - 'Loving'. I remember first discovering the name Amabel with Ama as a short form and really being drawn to jot it down. I wanted to share it here as it's so distinctive. From the Latin word *amabilis*, meaning loving, came this sparkly name with such a special meaning.

Amy - 'Beloved'. Amy, from the French *amie*, is an understated, very loveable name. Its simplicity may mean it gets overlooked, but I think it's got a chic elegance and sweet nature, making it perfect for a Timelessly Tasteful namer.

Cora - 'Heart'. Cora is a very graceful name that has a gentle, old-worldly feel. Its meaning of 'heart' or 'daughter' in some translations gives it a simple elegance loaded with feeling.

Esme - 'Loved'. The name Esme is French in origin and has that unique sound that makes it special. It's classic enough to suit Timelessly Tasteful namers as well as those Trendy with a Twist parents.

Maeve - 'Intoxicating'. You'll be fully intoxicated by your little baby and could name her after this Irish queen to show how all-consuming your love is for her.

Nayeli - 'I love you'. I'm bowled over by how original this name is, literally meaning 'I love you'. Pronounced Ny-Ellie the name is from the Zapotec language, spoken by the indigenous people of southwestern Mexico.

BOYS

Caleb - 'Wholehearted'. To love with your whole heart is the perfect expression of what it feels like to become a parent. Caleb is a charismatic biblical name that sometimes translates as 'dog' (see my Animal Name list on page 97). This comes from Caleb's wholehearted Virtue meaning, with its links to loyalty and devotion.

David - 'Beloved'. A classic British staple, everyone knows a Dave. David has maybe been a victim of its own success, overlooked as a bit every day, but it's such a unique sounding name. Its heartwarming meaning of 'beloved' gives Timelessly Tasteful namers even more reason to choose it.

Kaipo - 'Sweetheart'. Wow, I love this name. Mainly used in Hawaii, if you adore Kai but feel it's too popular then Kaipo could be your little sweetheart's name.

Lennon - 'Sweetheart'. Lennon has it all - a special meaning, the nickname Lenny that is trendy and fun and John Lennon brings the music vibes - all reasons to give this name a big tick.

Osian - 'Little deer'. Celtic classic Osian, meaning little fawn or deer, has a charming other meaning of 'dear'. In Welsh it's pronounced O-Shan.

Rasmus - 'Beloved'. The patron saint of sailors, Rasmus is an unforgettable name with a heartfelt meaning. It sounds rugged and adventurous while having such a soft centre.

NEUTRAL

Caradoc - 'Beloved'. I have always loved the name Caradoc. It feels like a period drama name from Regency times, but it is in fact much more ancient, recorded as a name in Wales as far back as the Middle Ages. It's special, a blend of the romantic with strong sounds.

Corwinn - 'Heart's friend'. Irish name Corwinn really expresses that love and connection between two hearts. Traditionally a male name, I adore the sound of Corwinn for any gender.

Loveday - 'A day filled with love'. My sister chose Loveday for her daughter's middle name, as it was once widely used in the

Cotswolds where they lived. It's a first name that moved to a surname and was particular to Cornwall for a few decades as well. Our Lottie Loveday ended up being born early on Valentine's Day and Naomi always said she jinxed that.

NAMES MEANING 'STRENGTH'

Having a name meaning strength brings that extra courage and fighting spirit that we all need at times into a big piece of your baby's identity. It could be that you as their parent have needed strength to bring them into your world, perhaps they are a preemie and though delicate are remarkably strong. All these names celebrate the strength within.

GIRLS

Aoife - 'Warrior princess'. Aoife is pronounced Ee-Fa and is one of the most travelled Irish names. It also translates as 'radiance'. In Irish mythology she was a warrior princess and I love the sentiment, it feels like she tells a story.

Bridget - 'Power and strength'. Classic and always cool, Bridget packs a punch with its meaning. It's also such a sweet name for a little girl and will grow beautifully with them, too.

Matilda - 'Mighty in battle'. This gorgeous girl name is timeless. Had my first baby been a girl we were going to go with Matilda. I favoured its vintage style but it feels modern with Tilly or Tilda as nicknames.

Trudy - 'Universal strength'. A short form of Gertrude, this gorgeous name hasn't had its revival in the popularity lists, but I feel it is coming. The nickname True is a bonus, while this name gives such a strong and free vibe to a child who could take on anything.

Valerie - 'Healthy and strong'. Valerie is one of those untouched vintage names that I just adore; it gives me huge Baby Name Envy and ticks all the boxes as a stylish, vintage gem that is Trendy with a Twist gold.

BOYS

Anders - 'Strong and courageous'. The Scandinavian variant of Andrew has that nice 's' ending which blends so well with most surnames, a twist on a classic for Trendy with a Twist namers.

Aziel - 'God is my strength'. The name Aziel, pronounced Az-E-El with three syllables would be a cool pick. Strength comes in so many ways and often we or our child have to show a lot of it.

Callen - 'Brave'. A Gaelic boy name, Callen means 'brave' or 'powerful in battle'. Pronounced Cal-An to rhyme with Alan, it's a refreshing and inviting name.

Ethan - 'Strong and enduring'. I've always felt the name Ethan is successful at connecting brave namers with more traditional namers, as it has a unique sound. Ethan is relatively new in popularity but feels like a classic. Strength and endurance are often a part of our story into parenthood where we overcome challenges with so much love, and Ethan is a great name to recognize those qualities.

Fernando - 'Bold journey'. Also meaning adventurer, this is one of several names that encapsulate this spirit (see the Travel Names list on page 187 for more ideas). I adore how empowering Fernando is as a name.

Koa - 'Valiant'. A Hawaiian name given to those who show bravery, Koa is also the name of the native Koa tree, which is an important part of Hawaiian culture as a symbol of warrior spirit.

NEUTRAL

Clancy - 'Warrior'. Traditionally an Irish surname, I like the idea of Clancy as a fresh and edgy first name, bringing that warrior spirit.

Marceau - 'Little warrior'. The meaning and name both have my heart. Traditionally a male name from the God of War Mars, I feel Marceau is so special it would make a striking name for any gender.

Peyton - 'Fighting man's estate'. Peyton shows up in historical records as dating back to the thirteenth century where it's believed to have originally been a place name. Peyton is a characterful name, and if your baby has shown some fight, it would be a wonderful way to honour that.

MEANINGFUL MATCHES

How to find names with meanings that match your own

Do you know what your name means? I'm continuously shocked when a grown-up asks me this - as 'Princess-God is Gracious' aka 'Sarah-Jayne', I made my name my whole personality for quite a while as child. The study of name meanings is called onomatology. As you can see throughout *Baby Name Envy*, the name meanings often come from root words in Latin, Greek or Hebrew, which were sometimes linked to a place, character trait or occupation. So, Sarah, meaning 'princess', is derived from the Hebrew word *Sar* meaning 'chief' or 'prince'. Jayne, meaning 'God is Gracious', derives from the ancient Hebrew word for God in the Bible *ja:weɪ*, which became *Yahweh* and eventually translated into modern-day names John and Jane. Our names have been on quite a journey, and that's why I love looking at meanings.

I see so many people who really match their name meaning. In my own children, Freddie means 'peaceful ruler' and he's certainly a gentle soul, but he must be in control. The Scandic version of Finn means 'little blonde soldier', which tipped it into our top spot as a cute pairing.

Our surnames have fascinating meanings, too. Surnames were the last naming convention to be invented that we still carry to this day and were there to link us in identity to our family. Like Johnson - spoiler alert, his dad was called John. Or by occupation, Smith, Clark, Taylor. In comparison, our first names often describe a dwelling - Stanley meaning 'Stone by a field', which helped our ancestors distinguish each other.

My full surname is Ljungstrom (Strum online, as it doesn't travel well. My maiden surname was Whitcher, which comes with a bit of negative witch trial history, meaning I was thrilled to spell out Ljungstrom forever). Ljungstrom means 'heather stream' - a Ljung is a beautiful purple heather which grows by the lakes, and I love it so much, but it's maybe why Henrik didn't want another flower name for our children, which totally went over my head when picking.

Looking at your name meaning plus your surname is a great place to start a baby name search. It's a fun way to match sibling names too via their meaning - grab a pen and notepad and let's explore it for you.

How to find a meaningful match

A simple Google search will tell you what your name means. Check your first name and surname, as well as your partner's if you're naming as a couple.

As you go through *Baby Name Envy*, jot down names that have the same meaning as yours. If you like the name, it's often a way to feel that bond to your baby by sharing a name meaning. A mum named Grace may love baby Anya, meaning 'grace'. David means 'love', so a child called Lennon would be really special, with its meaning of 'sweetheart'.

♥ COUPLE BLEND-UP

If you are working on baby names with a partner, it's fun to try blending your name meanings together and see if they have a crossover. This is my favourite thing to do when I'm working with clients. My sister Naomi's name means 'pleasant' and her husband Lee's name means 'wood clearing', so Summer was a lovely name for their first daughter, as their names have that nature, sunny vibe. Looking at names in this way may surprise you with a strong idea you haven't thought of. Have fun doing this together, especially if the name chat feels one-sided. It's a really creative way to explore ideas and I've always found that if it has a meaningful link, it is more likely to stick.

♥ PAIR BY MEANING

If you already have children, it's so nice to pick names that link together somehow. Phoebe meaning 'moon' connects well with sister Seren, meaning 'star'. Issac, meaning 'to laugh', pairs well with brother Asher, meaning 'happiness'. There are so many wonderful ways to link siblings, and they will love that bond. There are more ideas for sibling naming in my Tips For Blending Sibling Names feature (see page 309).

PASSIONS

You light up most when talking about your passions, and that's why it's a wonderful area to explore when choosing a baby name. Our passions and interests make up so much of our identity and are the things we enjoy most in life. They inspire envy too – we don't want to miss out on what we're most passionate about – and you'll always be so proud of a name prompted by something special and personal to you. Our passions are often how we meet our partners too – two Disney fans lock eyes across a Mickey Mouse pancake and the rest, as they say, is history. My husband and I both love reading and I adored the name Finn on sight, with its playful Huckleberry Finn literary vibe. Foodies who cook every night and always know the best restaurants will be drawn to the Food-inspired names, and travel fanatics – I have you covered with Wanderlust, Place and even Mythical Places names.

LITERARY NAMES

Reading is a huge passion for so many people. It's something my husband and I get absorbed in. I can spend hours picking my next book and I enjoy reading the same stories I loved as a little girl to my own kids. Snuggling up in my mum's bed with my sister reading *Famous Five* must be one of my core memories. I also remember my teenage sister smuggling me a copy of Judy Bloom's *Forever*. I have never been able to walk past a book shop without going in for a browse. It's no surprise that I read English Literature and Philosophy at uni, but it is a huge surprise I got the opportunity to write my own book - and on baby names, my dream topic! I hope you love my picks for literary names. I invite you to choose your own favourite books and check out character names for personal inspiration, but here are some great reminders of the classics to get you started.

GIRLS

Aibileen - 'Land of meadows'. Inspired by *The Help* by Kathryn Stockett, Aibileen is such a pretty option for a little girl with its nature meaning.

Alice - 'Noble'. The tea party birthdays will be legendary if you choose this classic name from *Alice's Adventures in Wonderland* by Lewis Carroll. Timelessly Tasteful namers will love this one.

Arrietty - 'Lion star'. Inspired by *The Borrowers* by Mary Norton, in the story of small people who live in the walls of houses, the daughter in the clock family is called Arrietty.

Arwen - 'Noble maiden'. From the iconic *Lord of The Rings* by J.R.R. Tolkien. Arwen is a Welsh name and has that fanciful sound of a great fantasy literary name.

Avonlea - 'Woodland river'. The infamous fictitious village in Prince Edward Island, Canada, where *Anne of Green Gables* written by Lucy Maud Montgomery is set.

Celie - 'Heaven'. With its heavenly meaning, Celie was also the lead character in *The Colour Purple* by Alice Walker.

Emira - 'Princess'. A more contemporary read, in *Such A Fun Age* by Kiley Reid, Emira is a Slavic name which also means 'leader'.

Estella - 'Star'. The flawed but beautiful lead alongside Pip in Charles Dickens' *Great Expectations*. Estella has simple sounds that when combined create such a flowing name that's full of whimsy.

Heidi - 'Noble one'. The Swiss book *Heidi* by Johanna Spyri is one of the biggest—selling books of all time, and the name took off in popularity after its release.

Josephine - 'God will increase'. The full name of literary favourite Jo March in *Little Women* by Louisa May Alcott.

Juliet - 'Youthful'. A tragic Shakespeare heroine and a timeless name, Juliet was on my name list when I was expecting Freddie. Timelessly Tasteful for my husband, but romantic and literary for me, Juliet being the heroine from iconic *Romeo and Juliet* ticked both our boxes.

Luna - 'Moon'. The standout name from the *Harry Potter* series by J.K. Rowling. Luna is a modern name that boomed after the character in the book. Mystical and soulful, Luna is an instant fave.

Madeline - 'Tower'. The wildly popular children's book *Madeline* was created by Ludwig Bemelmans and will forever give the name Madeline a place in so many hearts.

Marianne - 'Grace'. Marianne from Jane Austen's *Sense and Sensibility* is a wonderful character, free-spirited and encompassing the 'sensibility' part of the book's title. See more about Marianne in my Regency list (see page 230).

Nancy - 'Grace'. The childhood favourite series of *Nancy Drew* books written by a collective of authors under the pseudonym Carolyn Keene features a teenage sleuth named Nancy. I also think of Nancy in Dicken *Oliver Twist*. It's a vintage name that feels gutsy and spirited thanks to its literary heritage.

Ophelia - 'Help'. A very beautiful Shakespearean name from *Hamlet* that's become fashionable, and works as an alternative to popular Olivia. Ophelia is enduringly pretty; see my Four Syllable Names list if you love long names.

Queenie - 'Queen'. From old English word *cwen,* meaning woman, Queenie was my Gran's name, though she dropped it and went by the fashionable name of the time Sandra. I can still remember first hearing her real name and thinking how much it suited her. Hopefully it's due it's revival after the hit novel *Queenie* by Candice Carty-Williams.

Rosaline - 'Lovely rose'. One of Shakespeare's favourites, Rosaline appears in *As You Like It.* Romeo's first girlfriend is also called Rosaline, who he is lamenting at the beginning of *Romeo and Juliet.*

Tess - 'Harvest'. This name sounds so vintage and is almost certainly underused - from *Tess of The D'Urbervilles* by Thomas Hardy, it has such star quality with its one-syllable punch.

Wendy - 'Friend'. It's often said that the name Wendy was invented by J.M Barrie for the book *Peter Pan,* which is almost true. He chose it in honour of a friend's daughter who tragically died of meningitis when she was five. Her name was Margaret and she used to call Barrie her 'fwendy-wendy'. The story of the children lost in the night is a parable of child death and Wendy was named in her honour.

Zuleika - 'Brilliant beauty'. Zuleika is the protagonist in *The Emperor's Babe* by Booker Prize winner Bernadine Evaristo.

BOYS

Atticus - 'Rugged coast'. Atticus is the protagonist from *To Kill a Mockingbird* by Harper Lee. One of my 'names that got away', I liked it for its literary allusions, but it's also newly popular so it felt really ownable for a little boy today with bags of style.

Banquo - 'Fair'. Banquo was made infamous in Shakepeare's *Macbeth*; the name is as dramatic as the play but not so well-known. It would make an edgy and grand name for a Stand Out & Shine namer.

Benvolio - 'Well-wisher'. Appearing in *Romeo and Juliet,* Benvolio is a bold, characterful name always associated with Shakespeare. It would be a Stand Out & Shine name for any literary fans.

Caspian - 'White'. *Prince Caspian* is one of *The Chronicles of Narnia* series by C.S. Lewis, and the name also references the sea between Asia and Europe. Caspian is a great Trendy with a Twist name - it's not complex, it sounds familiar but is still quite unusual. If you love literature or adore travel and the sea, Caspian could be for you.

Dorian - 'Gift'. *The Picture of Dorian Gray* is a great read, and I love the name meaning 'gift'. Perhaps that's why Oscar Wilde chose it, as Dorian Gray's picture is a gift and a curse. Pronounced Dorr-ian, it's an ancient Greek name from a tribe called The Dorians. Steeped in history with a classic book link, I think Dorian is cool and exciting.

Edward - 'Wealthy guard'. Edward Cullen in *Twilight* brings edge to this classic British name. It's a perfect Timelessly Tasteful name with nicknames Ed and Eddie.

Finn - 'Fair'. I chose this for our son, as I love how playful and outdoorsy it feels, with connections to the book *The Adventures of Huckleberry Finn*. In Scandinavian it can mean 'little blonde soldier', which sold it for me. It's such a soulful name and brings to mind a boy who loves to play and laugh, which fits my Finn perfectly.

Gilbert - 'Bright pledge'. So many people have a soft spot for this name after Gilbert Blythe from the *Anne of Green Gables* series by L.M. Montgomery. It's such a distinctive name - the strong 'G' can be divisive and sounds harsh to some, but I adore Gilbert. It's got a bit of that 'bright pledge' twinkle in its eye and would sound so adorable for a baby. Bertie or Gil would make modern nicknames, though I'd lovingly go with Bert.

Harpo - 'Harp player'. This character name from *The Colour Purple* by Alice Walker is a great male alternative to popular Harper.

Holden - 'Deep valley'. Anglo-Saxon name Holden is the first name of the lead character Holden Caulfield in *The Catcher in the Rye*. Holden has a contemporary style and if you love the book, it's a top name choice for a little boy.

Jarvis - 'Servant spear'. Appearing in Charles Dickens' *A Tale of Two Cities*, Jarvis is now so trendy. Names ending in 's' always flow well into surnames, and it's slightly quirky, but not unusual.

Lysander - 'Liberator'. From Shakespeare's *Midsummer Night's Dream*, Lysander has that unmistakable literary heritage and I really love the powerful meaning mixed with what is a gentle sounding name.

Okonkwo - 'Man born on Nkwo day'. This Igbo name is the famed lead character of *Things Fall Apart* by Chinua Achebe. Nkwo is the name of one of the four (market) days of the Igbo four-day week.

Oliver - 'Peace'. Endlessly popular, the name Oliver brings to mind the little boy in Charles Dickens, classic novel *Oliver Twist*.

Orlando - 'Fame of the land'. A name from Shakespeare's *As You Like It*, Orlando makes a great Trendy with a Twist name. It's a variation of the name Roland, which has that classic name heritage you can't ignore. Orlando is also a great option for Disney fans in honour of Disney World's location. To me it's fashionable and special without trying too hard.

Park - 'Enclosure'. I absolutely love the young adult book *Elinor & Park* by Rainbow Rowell, and Park is a popular Korean name. We're more familiar with Parker, but Park is a Stand Out & Shine name.

Robinson - 'Son of Robert'. A strong literary nod to *Robinson Crusoe* by Daniel Defoe, it is a name that gives a sense of adventure.

Sawyer - 'Woodcutter'. I had Sawyer on my name list for Finn, as I really liked how joyful it felt with *The Adventures of Tom Sawyer* as a literary nod. An occupational nature name with a playful side, Sawyer is one to consider.

Sebastian - 'Revered'. A favourite of Shakespeare, the name Sebastian has Greek origins, and Sebastians appear in *The Tempest, Twelfth Night* and *Two Gentlemen of Verona*. Sebastian is one of the longer boy names that have become more mainstream, and I also think Seb makes a perfect nickname. See my Four-Syllable Names list for long boy names (see page 263).

Watson - 'Son of Walter'. Sherlock's sidekick makes a strong first name, as it's a bit unexpected and quirky. Immediately reminiscent of the Sherlock Holmes detective novels, if you're a fan I'd jot Watson on your list as a daring first or meaningful middle name.

NEUTRAL

Darcy - 'Dark-haired'. Mr Darcy is widely known from Jane Austen's *Pride and Prejudice*. With its dark-haired meaning, it's a gender-neutral gem. Darcy works as a beautiful, elegant and proud name for any gender.

Darrell - 'Darling'. Such a brilliant name from Enid Blyton's *Mallory Towers*, in which Darrell was the female protagonist. A true gender-neutral gem, Darrell is still unusual, so would make a lovely name choice if you're after something classic that hasn't come back into style. I'm cheesy, so would probably make a bid for calling them Darrell Darling, using the meaning as a middle name. My Timelessly Tasteful namer Henrik would perhaps be flicking to the 'Veto Tax Hack' section right now.

Ellis - 'Kind'. Ellis Bell was Emily Brontë's pen name, which she chose as a gender-neutral name. Using a gender-neutral name today serves the same purpose for many people who don't wish their gender to precede them when meeting people or affect how they are treated. Ellis offers the best of all worlds - it's literary, historical and stylish.

Gatsby - 'Companion'. From *The Great Gatsby,* it's such a cool idea to take the surname of Jay Gatsby and bring that roaring twenties literary icon into your baby's name. I've taken the meaning from the character's 'real' name Gatz, a German surname meaning 'companion'.

Hero - 'Defender'. Inspired by Shakespeare's *Much Ado About Nothing,* any literary fans will enjoy the name Hero. The name is a bold statement as it's such a familiar word - but I wouldn't let that put you off - for Stand Out & Shine namers, Hero is iconic.

Scout - 'To listen'. From *To Kill a Mockingbird,* the name Scout is a lot of fun. It would really suit a playful family who love to get outside, and the meaning of 'to listen' also feels really mindful.

HARRY POTTER NAMES

For Harry Potter fans, I've delved deep into the world of Hogwarts. Rather than a list of character names, I'm the 'sorting hat' of Baby Names. The world created in the Harry Potter books lives in fans' hearts and each House at Hogwarts has its own mottos, colours, characters and animals. I adored the books and the rich world of characteristics from each house is where I've gone to get inspiration for names that bring the spirit of Potterdom to life. I hope you have fun and get creative to come up with your own ode to Harry Potter for your little muggle.

RAVENCLAW

Ravenclaws are known for having bright minds, being clever and academic. They are also spirited and can be eccentric, such as Luna Lovegood, one of the most beloved characters. Intuitive and creative, Ravenclaws love learning and are curious about the world around them. Ravenclaw colours are blue and bronze and their symbol is an eagle, celebrating their independence, boldness and linking to the House's element, air.

GIRLS

Dara - 'Pearl of wisdom'. In Aramaic the name meant 'marble' and Harry Potter sneaks into the Ravenclaw common room and finds a marble statue of Ravenclaw.

Ilma - 'Knowledge'. Meaning 'air' in Finnish and 'knowledge' in Arabic, Ilma brings all the qualities of the Ravenclaw. I love how light and soft the name is.

Rowena - 'Famous friend'. Welsh name Rowena celebrates the bright minds of the Ravenclaw house, meaning 'famous' or 'bright friend'. One of the founders of Hogwarts, Rowena Ravenclaw makes a perfect namesake for fans.

Saffi - 'Wisdom'. Ravenclaws are renowned for being clever and witty and Saffi is a Danish name that brings the spirit of the house to life.

BOYS

Arnie - 'Eagle ruler'. A super cool nickname for Arnold. Amongst Berties and Albies, I think Arnie is a quirkier pick that will give your baby boy some extra charm. The Ravenclaw symbol is an eagle.

Cato - 'Intelligent and all knowing'. In Roman history, Cato the elder was a Roman diplomat. The elder wand is the most powerful wand in Harry Potter. Find more Dark Academia names like Cato in my Goth Glam Names list (see page 294).

NEUTRAL

Gray - The Grey Lady is the ghost of the house, Rowena Ravenclaw's daughter who stole the diadem of wisdom and was killed by Baron. Gray with an 'a' feels prettier than Grey, which means to be neutral and balanced in colour psychology, matching the Ravenclaw personality. There's a whole Colour name list you'll love to visit next (see page 113).

HUFFLEPUFF

The most inclusive house, Hufflepuffs are very accepting of everyone and value hard work and dedication. The house colours are yellow and black, and the emblem is a badger which was on Helga Hufflepuff's cup and became one of the ways Voldemort held his soul. Hard workers, hence the name Hufflepuff, for the huffing and puffing they do, mainly in gardens and herbology.

GIRLS

Leala - 'Loyal'. A pretty French name, this is evocative of Lily Potter, Harry's mum. Hufflepuff's value loyalty highly so Leala feels perfect for this dedicated house.

Pomona - 'Fruit tree'. The teacher of herbology and head of the Hufflepuff House is fittingly called Pomona Sprout. Pomona was also the goddess of fruitful abundance.

Zizi - 'Sweetness'. Hebrew name Zizi stands out for all the right reasons. Meaning 'sweetness' it's friendly and open, just like the Hufflepuff house.

BOYS

Ames - 'Friend'. Ames is a Virtue name which links to James, Harry's father. The meaning of friend befits the people orientated Hufflepuffs.

Brock - 'Badger'. Earthy and outdoorsy, Brock gives a subtle nod to the Hufflepuff House emblem. Said to be the symbol for often being underestimated but tough.

Gil - 'Joy or happiness'. Gillyweed is what Harry takes to make sure he can breathe underwater. With a nod to the botanical world of *Harry Potter* and an upbeat and positive can-do meaning, Gil is a cool Harry Potter-inspired name.

NEUTRAL

Karmel - 'Garden'. Gender-neutral Karmel means orchard or garden, which would feel right at home with the passionate herbologists of Hufflepuff.

SLYTHERIN

The house of Slytherin is a cunning and clever house, and a Slytherin child has amazing ambitions and always reaches their goals. They take their time in situations and have a strong sense of self. The colour of Slytherin is a lovely green and a snake is their animal symbol.

GIRLS

Ebony - 'Dark black-wooded tree'. A mysterious name that I love, an ebony wand is the most common wand amongst Slytherins. You are considered non-conformist if you get this wand and hold fast to your beliefs.

Emerald - The Dark Mark is a skull made of Emerald stars. Voldemort's sign, The Dark Mark also appears as an emerald sign and tattoo for his supporters.

Merope - 'Mortal'. Merope is Voldemort's mother. In Greek mythology it means 'bee-eater bird' or 'sparkling face' - the face reminds me of Voldemort's disfigured face and interestingly Dumbledore means 'bumblebee', so a bee-eating bird was a great name idea.

BOYS

Conrad - 'Bold ruler'. This German name sounds stately and regal, bringing in the Slytherin's strong sense of self. It also looks great on the page spelt traditionally with a 'K' for Konrad.

Marvolo - 'Ill will'. Tom Marvolo Riddle is the name of he who should not be named and it's an anagram of 'I am Lord Voldemort'. Marvolo means 'I want to damage someone' - quite a dark literary gem.

Ophion - 'Serpent'. A serpent deity in mythology, Orphion makes a daring but trendy name with its mix of Oliver and Finn.

NEUTRAL

Quaid - 'Ruler of the army'. Irish moniker Quaid feels on the right side of grand and powerful for this house. It's a striking name that benefits from being so easy to say and spell.

GRYFFINDOR

Gryffindor is the house of the main characters in the Harry Potter series. A Gryffindor child is courageous and bravery is their key character trait. They are also kind but determined. The house colours are red and gold and the name Gryffindor translates as 'Griffin of gold'.

GIRLS

Emine - 'To be fearless'. I love this Arabic name meaning someone you can trust and believe in. Emine is a magnetic name.

Hermione - This unique name has now become world famous. It was said to be chosen as the author felt Hermione's studious parents would have picked this kind of complex baby name. It's from Greek mythology, the feminine form of Hermes, which also suits Hermione's role in the trio as advisor and messenger.

Otway - 'Beautiful heroine'. A lovely nod to Hermione, Otway is an Anglo-Saxon name with a few variations - Ottoway and Ottway. I enjoy its heroine vibe.

Ruby - Rubies are the stone of Gryffindor and the hourglass that counts the house points is full of little ruby stones. Also reminiscent of Rubeus Hagrid, which is a sweet link. There's lots more gemstone names in my Crystals, Rocks & Minerals list (see page 75).

Seraphina - 'Fiery one'. Gryffindor's element is fire, strongly associated with their house colours of gold and red. Whether arriving by the Floo Network into Diagon Alley, or creating magic using fire spell Incendio, Seraphina throws you right into the world of the Gryffindors.

BOYS

Altan - 'Red dawn'. With its meaning linked to the red colour of the house, this Turkish name is gallant and vibrant.

Barack - 'Lightening'. Arabic Barack has the dual meaning of 'lightening' and 'blessing', making it perfect for Potter fans.

Bolt - Harry's lightening scar gives the playful one-syllable name Bolt.

NEUTRAL

Hartley - 'Deer meadow'. Harry's Patronus is a stag. Hartley is evocative of having a courageous heart, something that defines the Gryffindors.

MUSIC NAMES

Music is what makes us feel more deeply and connect to what we're going through at different times of our life. We all have a special song, one that we may have danced to at our wedding or have loved since our childhood. If you pick a music-inspired name, it could come from a song, a singer, a band or an instrument. It's a hugely personal place to get name inspiration from. Take a moment to think of the songs and singers that mean something to you, then jot down their names and see if any resonate.

The word music comes from the 'art of the muses', who in mythology presided over music, song and dance. A muse is still a word we use for someone who inspires you, and this list is full of ideas.

INSTRUMENT NAMES

These names are perfect if you'd love your little one to play in a band or orchestra. Having an instrument name could be a huge inspiration.

GIRLS

Belle - 'Beautiful'. With its French meaning and allusions to the instrument itself, Belle keeps things simple while being extremely pretty.

Harper - 'Someone who plays the harp'. An occupational name, it burst onto the scene recently and is perfect if you're looking for a contemporary girl's name with a nod to classic music.

Musette - 'A small type of French bagpipe'. Musette could make such a fashionable, delicate name for a musical family.

Piper - 'Someone who plays the pipes'. I love this occupational girl's name. The bagpipes make it a traditional, lively name for Scottish families and anyone who enjoys music.

Viola - Larger than a violin, a viola makes a deeper sound and it's a pretty namesake, pronounced Vee-Oh-La and not Vy-Oh-La.

BOYS

Banjo - Probably my favourite name with a folksy vibe, Banjo is a cute name for a musical family.

Cornelius - 'Horn'. Roman surname Cornelius is so vintage it must be getting ready for a revival. It's a great name for brass players with its meaning of 'horn'. See Ready for Revival names for more quirky vintage ideas (page 202).

Drummer - With a rock band feel, this makes a great name for people who enjoy going to see live music and can picture their little one banging around on a drum kit one day.

Fife - 'A flute'. Fife is a Scottish place name and a flute-like instrument from medieval Europe. It makes a fun and upbeat baby name choice.

NEUTRAL

Timpani - 'Drum or strike'. Large kettle drums that are played in orchestras are called 'timpani'. With its Italian derivation, Timpani is a super-distinctive name that sounds really musical and modern.

SONG NAMES

For shower singers, opera lovers and musical theatre kids; I adore singing and have been in a few choirs and a fair few more karaoke booths. These names inspired by songs and singing are celebratory and so full of joy.

GIRLS

Allegra - 'Lively'. Allegra is so special, with its upbeat and cheerful three syllables taken from the tempo 'allegro'. The name has been used since the Roman era, so classic but exciting.

Aria - 'Song'. Pronounced Ah-Re-Uh and specifically referencing a solo in an opera, it's a popular girl's name. With a beautiful sound, it complements its musical meaning so well.

Cadence - 'The rhythm or flow of music'. Cadence comes from the Italian word *cadenza,* which referenced a decorative part of a musical piece. It's a vibrant name with sing-song overtones, pronounced Cay-dence.

Calliope - 'Beautiful voice'. Pronounced Cal-I-Oh-Pee. A firm favourite of the Baby Name Envy community, it's a complex but stunning name, hitting all the right notes if you love grand and striking names that turn heads.

Chantelle - 'To sing'. Chantelle derives from French word *chanter,* which means 'to sing'.

Harmony - 'Union'. Both a virtue of connection and perfect balance, Harmony's namesake is Greek goddess Harmonia whose gift was to bring people together with music.

Lerina - 'A song close to my heart'. A beautiful name for a girl that is softly feminine and powerful.

Lyric - 'Songlike'. A quirky name that feels poetic and romantic.

Melody - 'Singing'. Melody has been popular as a first name as far back as the 1940s and a melody in the ancient world derived from the Greek *melos,* meaning 'song', and *aeido,* meaning 'to sing'. It's a lovely idea to impart the joy of singing into your baby's name.

Shira - 'Singing'. Pretty Hebrew name Shira brings music, poetry and singing together into a name.

BOYS

Chanson - 'Song'. French Chanson gives trendy Sonny or Chance as nicknames and has a gorgeous lyrical meaning.

Lyron - 'My song and joy'. This is such a unique name with its impactful meaning. It's a heart-warming choice for a baby boy.

Ronen - 'Song'. A different spelling to Irish Ronan, Ronen means to sing a cheerful song. Of Hebrew origin, it's a classic with this spell-binding meaning for music lovers.

Zimri - 'My music, my praise'. Zimri brings the raising of voices together to life. A Hebrew name with a lovely sound, its meaning makes it such a striking name.

NEUTRAL

Leelo - 'Folk song'. Traditionally a female name from Estonia, Leelo has that boho feeling to it and I love its lyrical sound.

Morgan - 'Sea song'. Sailors' songs have a lot of stories, and Morgan brings those seafaring tidings to life.

Rhapsody - 'To sew songs together'. A word that could make a gorgeous name, meaning free-flowing music, and of course it's synonymous with the Queen song 'Bohemian Rhapsody' which is a head banger.

MUSIC ICONS

Music always tells a story, so think of which artists and songs are special to you. Do you have a favourite artist? What was the first dance at your wedding or is there a song you want to be 'your song' for your baby? I spent weeks picking personal songs for each of mine, which I'd sing them to sleep with; it's such a moving and meaningful theme to explore for baby name inspiration. Here

are some ideas of artists with amazing names to get your creative juices flowing.

GIRLS

Aretha - 'Virtue'. Synonymous with the great Aretha Franklin. Aretha embodies all those qualities we love in her music - soulful and powerful, it would make a wonderful choice for a little girl.

Demi - 'Half'. A musical name for modern singer Demi Lovato and a demisemiquaver musical note, this is a name full of glamour and elegance.

Etta - 'Ruler of the home'. Often picked by fans of Etta James. Originally a short form of Henrietta, it's become a crowd favourite in its own right.

Joni - 'God is gracious'. Joni became iconic because of Joni Mitchell and it has a retro seventies style that feels perfect for a Trendy with a Twist namer. It could also be spelt Joanie.

Joplin - 'Son of Job'. The surname of icon Janis Joplin. It's a biblical surname, but Joplin as a first name is fresh and exciting. It would be an amazing choice for music fans.

BOYS

Elvis - 'All-wise'. Having a resurgence, the name Elvis is interestingly banned from use in Sweden for being too iconic. But being associated with such an iconic singer anywhere else can't be a bad thing.

Freddie - 'Peaceful ruler'. A traditional English name with the Rock Royalty link to Freddie Mercury.

Harry - 'Powerful ruler'. Can Harry Styles keep this traditional name top of the charts? With the strength of its meaning, he certainly lives up to that as Pop Royalty, and this name would please Timelessly Tasteful namers everywhere.

Hendrix - 'Estate ruler'. An edgy and exciting boy's name and the surname of legendary Jimi Hendrix.

Jackson - 'Son of Jack'. This name boomed after Michael Jackson passed away and it's a more rock and roll variant of Jack.

Jagger - 'Cart'. A Jagger was an occupational name for someone who would carry and load horse carts. I love it as a first name and it fits in with so many names like Taylor and Miller, which were all once jobs and would make perfect sibling names for a Jagger.

Jimmy - 'Supplanter'. Jimmy Page and Jimi Hendrix make this a notable music hall of fame name. Short for James, Jimmy makes a great Trendy with a Twist name.

Lennon - 'Sweetheart'. A gorgeous Irish name with a glorious meaning and the surname of much-loved Beatle, John.

Miles - 'Soldier'. A fantastic one-syllable boy name for jazz fans of Miles Davis.

Otis - 'Wealthy'. Otis Redding, famous for soul music and rhythm and blues, gives this name a 1950s vibe which would be cute for a baby boy.

Wolfgang - 'Travelling wolf'. Mozart's first name Wolfgang is a German name that feels both classic and daring at the same time. Unusual, with a stellar musical heritage for your little boy.

NEUTRAL

Bowie - 'Yellow-haired'. The coolest name, honouring legend David Bowie. It has notes of classic Beau about it - very wearable but with an extra star quality.

Dusty - 'Brave warrior'. The name Dusty is a little bit cowboy but also picks up Dusty Springfield glamour. We had 'I Only Want to be with You' played at our wedding and me and my sister's karaoke song was 'Son of a Preacher Man'. Henrik was still too traditional for this name, but I wish I'd snuck it in the middle. Find more on Dusty in the Colour name list (see page 172).

Stevie - 'Crown'. Made hugely desirable by Stevie Nicks and Stevie Wonder. Stevie is a no-brainer if you love vintage names with a festival feel.

Taylor - 'To cut'. Swifties would love the name Taylor after superstar Taylor Swift. It has the original meaning of an occupational surname, but is now so associated with the megastar and would delight any little baby as they grow up.

DISNEY NAMES

The happiest place on earth and the movies that make childhood - what a genre to search for a name in. Disney is a real cultural touchstone for so many couples. It's incredible when you look at the history - as a young boy Walt Disney started his career drawing funny animations in a flip book for his sister to cheer her up, and then for other boys in his army barracks. He founded Disney Studios with his brother and I love that support and relationship with his sibling. What's special about the names in the movies is that many of them came from adaptations of old fairy tales. Passed on in word form as moral lessons, they are quite a dark read, but today they form a series of films that we enjoy whatever our age and never go out of style. I've picked my favourites and done some delving into the history of the tales. It's not all princesses and princes - there are so many stories to be heard in these names.

GIRLS

Aurora/Briar Rose - Both names for Sleeping Beauty. In the original Brother's Grimm tale, she's known as Briar Rose after the thorny bush surrounding her sleeping place for 100 years. The tale was made into a world-famous ballet where she was called Aurora, a name gaining so much use in recent years. Aurora was the Roman goddess of the Dawn. In the Disney movie both names are used - Aurora as her Princess name chosen by her parents and Briar Rose when she's in hiding with the fairies.

Belle - 'Beautiful'. *Beauty and the Beast* is a classic tale of learning to love beyond the surface. It's one of the oldest tales passed on as a story in many different cultures as far back as *Cupid and Psyche,* a myth from ancient Rome. The Disney movie was rewritten from scratch after the original felt too dark, and Belle was written as a more feminist character, based on Jo March in *Little Women*.

Cleo - 'To celebrate'. A subtle Disney nod to Cleo, the little fish in the film *Pinocchio*. Dickie Jones voiced Pinocchio when he was12 years old and he's one of the only child voices in the franchise.

Daisy - Daisy Duck is Donald's girlfriend. Find more on Daisy in my Flower Names list on page 17.

Esmerelda - 'Emerald'. Spanish name Esmerelda features in *The Hunchback of Notre Dame*. Meaning 'emerald', it feels just right for a magical fairy tale babe.

Flora, Fauna and Merryweather - The delightful fairies who look after Sleeping Beauty when Maleficent puts the curse on her as a baby.

Meg - 'Pearl'. Appearing in *Hercules,* this character is not a Disney Princess, as she's not royal, but I love the strong and short name which matches a feisty character.

Minnie - 'Will or desire'. Used often as a fun first name by celebrities, Mickey Mouse's sweetheart's name makes a gorgeous name for your youngest or a cute nickname for an Amelia.

Moana - 'Sea'. A stunning name that gained global popularity after the release of the Disney film. Find more Water Names in the list on page 88.

Nala - From *The Lion King,* Nala is a Swahili name meaning 'queen' or 'lion'.

Sally - 'Princess'. A ragdoll in the darker spooky Disney movie *The Nightmare Before Christmas,* she's kind and sensitive. The name's meaning has been out of style for a while and could be due a revival.

Snow - Taken from *Snow White,* the name Snow is picking up in popularity just behind Winter, which has already flown up the charts.

Tiana - 'Princess'. A perfectly chosen name from *The Princess and the Frog* story.

Willow - Grandmother Willow appears in *Pocahontas* as a wise advisor, and it would make a pretty choice for your little girl.

BOYS

Archimedes - The owl in *The Sword in The Stone* is so expressive and he's Merlin's sidekick. Named after the Greek scientist of the same name, it would be a really daring pick.

Bruno - 'Brown'. 'We Don't Talk About Bruno' from *Encanto* is Disney's biggest-selling song to date from the film *Encanto,* hitting the Number One spot. Only 'A Whole New World' by Aladdin did the same in 1993. A handsome and on-trend name, see my Colours name list for more on Bruno and other colour options (page 114).

Buzz - Buzz Lightyear in the *Toy Story* movies is named after the second man to walk on the moon, and Buzz translates as meaning 'village in the woods', which has a nice feel.

Chip - Such a hipster-cool name and the cutest character from *Beauty and the Beast.* As a cup he has a chip on his lid and when he turns into a boy, he has a chip on his tooth. There's also Chip from Chip and Dale in the Disney cartoon world to add to the cuteness.

Cubby - One of the most famous Lost Boys from *Peter Pan,* the name has the baby animal trend. Teddy is so wearable, so why not Cubby?

Flynn - 'Ruddy'. The lead character in *Tangled* alongside Rapunzel, Flynn has a charming twinkle in its eye. I love it for Trendy with a Twist namers.

Gus - 'Exalted'. Gus was the name of one of Cinderella's sidekick mice. Its meaning perfectly matches his own transformation to a beautiful horse.

Maui - 'Trickster god'. The wildly popular character in *Moana* and a god name that hits two trends. Maui was the trickster god in Polynesian mythology who one of the Hawaiian islands was named after. A great alternative to a Maverick, think of all the reasons to holiday in Hawaii.

Mickey - The iconic mascot of Disney, he was almost called 'Mortimer Mouse' until Walt Disney's wife Lillian suggested 'Mickey' sounded better for one of the first personality animated characters in the world. Originally Walt Disney also voiced Mickey. Now it's a fun, vintage nickname for Michael that feels so wearable.

Oaken - 'Oak tree'. Oaken's trading post is a great moment of light relief in the movie *Frozen*, and I adore it as a name. In Oaken's shop there's a hidden plush Mickey on the shelves, which Disney are famous for doing in their movies.

Oswald - Oswald the Lucky Rabbit preceded Mickey Mouse as Walt Disney's first creation under Universal Pictures. When producer Charles Mintz couldn't pay more for Disney's animation time, Walt left and dreamt up a new character, Mickey Mouse, and produced the cartoon himself.

Walt - 'Power of the army'. Walter Elias Disney is the animator and original voice of Mickey Mouse, and the vintage name Walter is having a comeback. Calling your baby Walt is a subtle nod to the magic of Disney - curl up and watch the films with your family over and over again. I've sometimes felt I co-parent with Elsa from

Frozen; such is the influence she's had over my kids as they sit in front of the TV while I quickly get the dinner on. I'm always grateful Disney exists to add a little magic to their days.

NEUTRAL

Ariel - 'Lion of god'. From *The Little Mermaid,* Ariel is traditionally a male name. It was picked for the mermaid princess and many believe it is a nod to the magical sprite in Shakespeare's *The Tempest*. However, I love the fan theory that it's because she dreams of a life in the air, not under water.

Bambi - 'Child'. Based on the book *Bambi, A Life in the Woods* by Felix Salten, published in 1923, the cute deer has made its way into the name world. Taken from the Italian *bambino,* which means child, it skews towards the feminine. However, Bambi is actually a male deer so it works for any gender. If you love *Bambi* go for it, it's a charming name.

Remy - 'Oarsman'. Remy is the cute chef rat in *Ratatouille* and has become so popular, flying up both the boy and girl charts. It's informal but not a 'nickname' name and has the elegance of so many French names.

FOOD NAMES

Do you love nothing more than getting creative in the kitchen? Is your favourite thing to watch on TV a cooking or baking show, and is picking herbs, spices and ingredients top of your love language? I know so many people who relax with a good cookbook. Food brings people together and as a name consultant I always say that, just like a chef, there's always a new, fresh or classic idea when it comes to helping pick a baby name. Just like flowers, food has inspired names for centuries. From spices like Saffron to herbs like Basil. Here are my ideas for foodie names.

GIRLS

Anise - 'Spice'. What a stunning name, especially with the Star Anise spice reference which adds even more sparkle to it.

Bree - 'High or noble'. For those of us who cannot behave ourselves around cheese, you could honour Brie with the name spelling version Bree. Brie is known as the Queen of Cheeses in its home region of France.

Cherry - Both the fruit and the beautiful cherry blossom symbolizing 'new beginnings' make this an adorable name idea.

Clementine - 'Calm'. Derived from the goddess Clemency. The clementine fruit was named after a person called Clement who found them in an orphanage he worked in and began to propagate. Clementine has boomed for girls, and why not try Clement for a boy?

Clove - An aromatic spice, Clove would make a trendy and interesting name. It's also beautiful with the word 'love' in it.

Dulce - 'Sweet'. Pronounced Dul-See, this two-syllable Italian word has become a popular girl's name. It has an old-school feel with European flair.

Ginger - The spice (and Spice Girl) Ginger has a glamorous old Hollywood feel. It would make a fun and playful middle name.

Honey - 'Nectar'. A lovely term of endearment, as it's synonymous with being sweet. Honey has been gaining a lot of use as a girl's name and I really love it for Stand Out & Shine namers.

Maple - 'Maple tree'. Maple trees are a vibrant tree that are famed for making syrup. Similar in sound to vintage Mabel, Maple feels more traditional than it is, making it a brilliant name pick with a touch of foodie fun.

Nori - 'Ocean moss'. The seaweed used to make sushi is a fun, food-inspired name that is super-wearable for a little girl.

Pepper - 'Spice'. It's such a playful name and I think if you're brave enough, you'll get a lot of compliments for Pepper. It could make a good nickname for longer form Penelope or even Juniper.

Rosemary - 'Dew of the sea'. A garden herb that has been commonly used as a popular girl's name for many years, Rosemary has fallen out of favour recently, but it's such an elegant and traditional name, it would make a lovely choice for a modern little girl.

Saffron - 'Yellow flower'. Used to make the spice, it's a luxury ingredient because it takes a lot of effort to harvest. Saffron is linked with purity and some religious people wear saffron robes to represent that. A lovely foodie alternative to Sophie.

Zamora - 'Wild olives'. The meaning has put this the top of my trendy girl names list. It's a stunner that takes me straight to the olive groves. Zamora is also the name of a beautiful city in Spain and *amora* means love in Spanish, too. So many reasons to name your little love Zamora.

BOYS

Basil - 'King'. This herb is part of the mint family, giving it a fresh zing. Basil is fast becoming vintage gold where it's been languishing in 'vintage old' status for a few decades. Bas is a trendy nickname, making Basil a perhaps unexpected but brilliant pick for Trendy with a Twist namers.

Baker - 'To dry by heat'. An occupational surname, baking is such a popular hobby and the 'surname as first name' trend make this a cute idea for a baby name.

Dion - 'God of wine'. A trip to the vineyard, dapper Dion has all the style of sipping on that cold glass of wine. From Dionysus the God of Wine and Revelry, Dion is a great name for your tiny entertainer.

Fraser - 'Strawberry'. From the French *fraise,* it's just the sweetest name meaning for a traditional but not common boy name.

Herbie - 'Illustrious warrior'. Taken from the long name Herbert. This is a fantastic alternative to Freddie or Albie, with such a kitchen garden association.

Rye - 'King'. The name of a grain used to make bread and whiskey. I love it for any gender, and it's got the literary nod to *The Catcher in the Rye* too.

NEUTRAL

Mai Kana - 'Come and eat'. A Fijian phrase that makes a really pretty word name and has such a welcoming meaning.

Miller - 'One who grinds grain'. I adore this gender-neutral name, and for a subtle foodie nod it could be a stylish pick.

Sage - 'Wise'. A very spiritual herb used for 'smudging' your house to clear negative energy and to add flavour to your food. It's one of my favourite foodie names that gives me a lot of Baby Name Envy - sweet, simple and stunning.

ART NAMES

Passion names are all about what you love; what you really enjoy creating and what stimulates your mind. Art is such a huge force. As a mum of three little ones, I'm in my PVA glue era, but I've pulled some gorgeous name inspiration from the world of art, crafts and creativity for you. I've always been a creative person, a blank piece of paper is a joy to me, and if you're the same, these names could leap out at you.

GIRLS

Aislin - 'Dream or vision'. I adore the idea of using a name meaning 'to have vision' for a creative family.

Avenlee - 'Creative'. I love this rare gem of a name that is both whimsical and beautiful with the most special meaning for a life you created.

Brigit - 'Exalted one'. From Brighid, the Celtic goddess of fire, poetry, and wisdom. Brigit would suit Timelessly Tasteful namers with its familiar classic sound.

Cleotha - 'Artist'. A lovely long form of popular Cleo with elegant 'tha' at the end which makes it feel more classic.

Frida - Mexican artist Frida Kahlo's self-portrait is one of the world's most recognizable images, and it is such a pretty but powerful name for your little work of art.

Madonna - 'My lady'. This iconic name resonant of the subject of so many paintings would make a great name for a brave and creative soul.

Minerva - Minerva was goddess of handicraft, making this the ideal name for those who love crafting.

Mona - 'Noble or aristocratic'. Inspired by one of the world's most iconic paintings the 'Mona Lisa', here's a sweet option with sophisticated connotations.

Penelope - 'Weaver'. If you love crochet and handmaking garments, this name weaves all those passions into your baby girl's name.

BOYS

Adwin - 'Artist'. Adwin is a Ghanaian name meaning 'artist' and it relates to all kinds of art; it's such a celebration of being creative.

Banksy - The invented name of secret street artist Banksy is starting to appear in the name charts. A quirky and fun baby name.

David - 'Beloved'. Michelangelo's iconic statue in Florence would make a statuesque namesake and please Timelessly Tasteful namers with its classic charm.

Dali - 'Drawn towards god'. The surname of artist Salvador Dali makes such a creative name idea; it reminds me of the word 'darling', which makes me want to list it even more.

Matisse - 'Gift of God'. Taken from the name Matthew and the surname of the infamous French painter Henri Matisse, it's a name that explodes with colour.

Pablo - 'Little'. The Spanish form of the name Paul, Pablo is so on trend with its 'o' ending. Pablo Picasso took his mother's maiden name to shrug off associations with his original family who were famous glovemakers, and then he went on to create over 50,000 works of art.

Saatchi - 'Watchmaker'. I recommend this name a lot, as I think makes a fantastic first name, and for an artistic family it's a great link to the famous gallery. Spelt Saachi in Japanese, it also means 'happiness'.

Tate - 'Cheerful'. The famous Tate art galleries were named after nineteenth-century sugar magnate Henry Tate, of Tate & Lyle Sugars, who himself founded the galleries. It's a bright one-syllable name with a whole lot of charm.

Vincent - 'To conquer'. Van Gogh and his genius makes this name an art lover's dream and Vinnie would make a cute nickname.

NEUTRAL

Emin - 'Truth'. What a great name meaning and a super-wearable and stylish name after the irrepressible Tracey Emin.

Monet - The Impressionist style of Claude Monet is very romantic and iconic. Monet would make such a creative and individualist name idea.

Paisley - 'Church'. Paisley has always been a name crush of mine. Its meaning of 'church' surprised me, but it's also a place name in Scotland which was the home of textile makers of the distinctive paisley-patterned garments and homeware. Conjuring up the feather-shaped pattern based on a pinecone, the name Paisley lends itself to an artistic family.

Winslow - 'Friend's hill'. Winslow Homer was a nineteenth-century landscape artist. It's a bohemian name with a nature-inspired meaning, perfect as an arty moniker. Check out my Bohemian Names list if you love this style of name (see page 301).

FILM NAMES

Do you say 'movie' or 'film'? A movie was a huge culture change when moving pictures were invented and film was the actual medium for recording them. We all love to chat about our favourite movie, and they hold deep memories, from first dates, childhood classics, films you watch to cheer yourself up and even some that are life-changing. I famously watched *The Sound of Music* every day for about a year when I was a little girl, it's one of my family's favourite stories about me. I even watched it in labour, then called my baby Fredrik, like the oldest von Trapp boy. I totally didn't make the link at the time. Here's some ideas from the world of film.

GIRLS

Annie - 'Grace'. The musical remake of the same name is one of our family favourites, and Annie is also one of the twins in *Parent Trap* as well as *Sleepless in Seattle*'s leading lady.

Carmen - 'Garden'. I adore the name Carmen. In the 1954 movie of the same name, Carmen Jones was played by Dorothy Dandridge. It led to her becoming the first African American to earn a Oscar nomination for Best Performance by an Actress in a Leading Role.

Cher - 'Beloved'. The actress and singer makes this name iconic and the character Cher in the movie *Clueless* is a classic. The name is fun and wearable and will always make people smile.

Dorothy - 'Gift of God'. A glorious name that hasn't managed to retain the high spots of some other vintage gems. In *The Wiz*'s Diana Ross and *The Wizard Of Oz*'s Judy Garland, the character of Dorothy is iconic. Singing 'Somewhere Over the Rainbow' as her lullaby would be so adorable.

Journey - 'Passage'. *Jingle Jangle: A Christmas Journey* is a modern Christmas classic, and I adore the main character's name Journey.

Jovie - 'Joyful'. Christmas movies could be such a special place to find a baby name if you enjoy that time of year. Our all-time favourite family watches are always at Christmas time and the name Jovie from *Elf* has my heart. Trendy with a Twist namers will like how it sounds like Josie.

Leia - 'Weary'. The meaning might make your smile if you've got a non-sleeping newborn or are preparing for baby life, but the *Star Wars* princess vibes are gorgeous.

Rita - 'Pearl'. *Sister Act 2: Back in the Habit* could have been your teenage favourite film, as it was mine. It puts the nineties name, on-trend Rita firmly into a current and cool name list. 'Oh, Happy Day' when it comes to announcing such a classic throwback name with such a shiny and precious meaning.

Shuri - 'Village'. Such a strong name with a powerful meaning we all know it takes a village to raise a child and I like bringing that meaning to a name. Also, it's the name of the lead engineer and princess in the movie *Black Panther*, so it's a great pick.

Vada - 'Knowledge'. Pronounced Vey-Duh, the name sprung onto our screens in the iconic movie *My Girl*. If you love the song, it's also a great crossover. The screenplay was originally called *Born Jaundiced* - which just cements the point on names being so important - ha ha!

Wednesday - 'Woden'. The day of the week was named 'Woden's Day'. Woden was chief of the Anglo-Saxon gods, god of war and battle. Wednesday Addams has shot it back to popularity and her name was chosen after the rhyme 'Wednesday's child is full of woe'. A brave goth-glam name idea, which Harry Potter fans may know is the name of actor Rupert Grint's daughter.

BOYS

Elliott - 'Brave'. The letter connections to *E.T.* were no coincidence, and Elliott works brilliantly for a modern baby boy.

Ellis - 'Kind, benevolent'. Rated one of the best movies of all time *The Shawshank Redemption* introduced us to Ellis Boyd 'Red' Redding.

Frederick - 'Peaceful ruler'. I chose the name Fredrik, spelt the Swedish way, for my first baby boy. He always goes by Freddie and sometimes Fred, which I think is very cool for a teen. Freddie came with his own name; I looked at him in the delivery room ready to go with my first choice Oskar, and out of my mouth popped the words, 'Hello Freddie'. The baby who made me a mother. I didn't even make the link between insisting between contractions at home that Henrik went out to buy a DVD of my favourite movie *The Sound of Music* for me to watch. The oldest Von Trapp makes a great namesake, and to this day Freddie loves it when I sing songs from the movie to him and dress him in lederhosen. I've included that to see if he reads his mum's baby name book . . .

Inigo - 'Fiery'. *The Princess Bride* is a cult classic, originally a book. But it's the infamous line 'My name is Inigo Montoya' that has made the name Inigo legendary.

Jack - 'God is gracious'. From Jack Dawson in *Titanic* to Captain Jack Sparrow in *Pirates of the Caribbean,* whichever is more your vibe, the name has star quality that means it's never gone out of fashion.

Marty - 'Descendant of Mars'. A derivative of Martin, the name Marty, from the beloved film *Back To The Future,* sends your baby straight to retro kitsch cool.

Rocky - 'Rock or rest'. Nailing both the nature vibe and an iconic movie character, the name Rocky is strong and outdoorsy.

Vito - 'Life'. Not to be confused with 'veto', saying 'no', this popular Italian name is known everywhere and inspired by *The Godfather.*

NEUTRAL

Indiana - 'Land of the Indians'. A place name, Indiana received its name because the state was largely possessed by native tribes. It was chosen for character Indiana Jones after Spielberg's pet dog Indiana. There is an in-joke mentioned in the movie series when Jones' father reveals he actually called his son Henry and their dog Indiana, but the explorer pinched the dog's name. The name is popular nowadays, with nickname Indie being even higher up the charts.

Jules - 'Youthful'. Gender neutral Jules was made iconic in the film *Pulp Fiction*. An action-packed, fun and lively name perfect for movie fans.

Ripley - 'Clearing in the woods'. From iconic movie character Ellen Ripley in *Alien,* the name Ripley is definitely in the Hollywood Hall Of Fame and I love it as a first name. It's distinct but gentle in sound.

PICKING YOUR FILM-INSPIRED NAME

If watching films is one of your favourite pastimes, you'll find lots of inspiration for baby names amongst the characters. Use the following questions below to discover some baby name gems:

- Which movie character's name always stood out to you when you were younger? I used to love Madison in the film *Splash* and Shelby from *Steel Magnolias*. Jot down those names that stood out for you and consider whether you would list any for your baby?
- Do you have a movie moment together or a date or story you feel expresses something about you as a couple? Don't just look at the names of the characters in the movie - pay attention to the actors and directors too and there could be a name that really stands out.
- Next time you're watching a movie, wait until the very end and read all the names in the closing credits. It's a wonderful place to find name ideas that also links to what you love.
- If your passion is movies, there's also some fun ways to bring the world of film into your baby's name. How about Oscar, named after the awards, Edison after the inventor of the kinetoscope (an early form of moving picture) or Lumi in honour of the Lumière brothers creators of the first projected film.
- Golden Age Hollywood surnames are always fresh for a meaningful middle name inspired by a love of cinema; Monroe, Garland, Gable or Olivier - there's so many to choose from.

TRAVEL

Picking a name based on a place is a very ancient way of naming. It originally helped people locate each other by having a name that literally meant the place where they dwell. It was an identity signaller – who you are and where you came from. It's the meaning of a lot of names you'll have heard of: Stanley means 'stony field', which was used to refer to people who came from stony meadows. Chester means 'walled town', Beverley means 'beaver stream', and George means 'farmer'.

It's also fun to look at more specific places and not just countries and cities. Is there a special restaurant you love or a landmark that you treasure? There may be a famous person linked to the city or town – that could also make a wonderful name.

Here I've listed place names and names inspired by a love of travel – something I know is of really high value for so many of us who want our little ones to see the world. Let's explore some travel-inspired names together.

PLACE NAMES

Countries and cities have long been borrowed as baby names. I think it's best to use a place you have a personal connection to or have visited, so there's that special story to add meaning to a name. Here's some ideas from around the world that I love, to give you some inspiration.

GIRLS

Bali - 'Strength'. Bali is one of the 18,000 islands that make up the Indonesian Archipelago and it is most certainly on many bucket lists as a dream destination. It's a jaw-droppingly beautiful name - so elegant and unique in sound. The nickname for the main island in the peninsula is Island of the Gods, and I love the idea of bringing that piece of paradise into your baby name.

Erin - 'Ireland'. Éire was the name of the goddess who was the personification of the island in Irish mythology. It was later modernized to Erin.

Eivissa - The name for the island Ibiza in Catalan, Eivissa is a gentle and bohemian name that complements the hippy heritage of the island. Stand Out & Shine namers should grab this one while they can.

Florence - 'To blossom'. I love the Latin verb *floreo,* meaning 'I blossom/I flower/I flourish'. It adds so much to this pretty name. Florence is a name that became more popular here after Florence Nightingale (who was born in Florence). Great for Timelessly Tasteful namers.

Ireland - 'Isle of the woods'. Ireland was named after Éire, the goddess of abundance. I really like Ireland as a name and it would make a fun middle spot or daring first name.

Sahara - 'Desert'. The Sahara is a huge desert in Africa, one of the hottest places in the world and as big as China - it's such an exotic, grand and iconic name.

Topanga - 'Where the mountain meets the sea'. Topanga is in California and seems to be a really boho area full of artists and the stunning Topanga canyon. What a varied and awe-inspiring meaning for a beautiful three-syllable name.

Vienna - 'Forest stream'. The name Vienna seems to be having its moment - after the popularity of Sienna, perhaps. It has similar sounds to the more classic Olivia as well. The city is known as 'The City of Music' because there have been more famous composers living there than anywhere else. It has also been called 'The City of Dreams' because it was the home of Sigmund Freud, a famous psychoanalyst.

BOYS

Kingston - 'Kings town'. Iconic Jamaican city or a British town in Surrey, Kingston is urban and regal as a name. It feels fresh but not unusual, which makes it a brilliant name pick.

Loxley - 'Lynx glade'. Loxley is a village and river name in Yorkshire, England, famous for being the purported birthplace of Robin Hood who was also known as Robin of Loxley. I really love how this name has that hero swagger but is so gentle and truly unforgettable.

Oslo - 'Meadow of gods'. The capital of Norway is a name I see on lots of lists. With similarities to Otto, it's a very cool name. Nickname Ossie works well too, and the meaning elevates it for me.

Oxford - 'Where the ox cross'. A ford is a shallow crossing where cattle would cross, giving the city its name. Synonymous with the university, Oxford has always been a prestigious city that's popular with tourists. My sister lived in Oxford for a long time, and I adored exploring the city with her, hanging out at the covered market and sitting in the university gardens. Steeped in history, how distinct would this be as a name?

Scottie - 'Scotland'. Scottie has such a trendy sound, literally meaning from Scotland. A fashionable alternative to classic Scott, it's lovely if you have roots in the country.

Santiago - Santiago is a version of 'James', which came from Saint James, a place named in honour of where the Saint was said to have been buried. It's been incredibly popular in recent years as a first name. Santi is a cute nickname, or even Saint if you don't want to commit to the full name.

NEUTRAL

Berlin - 'Bear'. The 'Ber-' at the beginning sounds like the German word Bär (bear) and a bear appears in the coat of arms of the city and represents chivalry. Some historians say the name Berlin was created for the area when it was marshy land, but now it's a contemporary city filled with culture and history and would make a great name for your baby.

Bristol - 'Place by the bridge'. Named after the bridge that was built over the River Avon, now known as a vibrant place with lots of soul, it's one of my favourite cities for vintage shopping and vegan eateries.

Bronx - This area of New York City was named after the Bronx River, which was named after a Swede, Jonas Bronck. It makes an exciting and interesting name for Stand Out & Shine namers.

Camden - 'Valley with fields'. Camden town in North London is famous for its market and music scene. Its vast, nature-filled meaning is quite different from the bustling artistic district, but the name is laid-back and stylish, just like the place.

Devon - 'Deep valley'. A beautiful county, Devon is a relatively well-known first name. It's very pretty to say and the county is one of our most beloved. It was the first place people settled after the last ice age and with its coastline, gorgeous hillsides and rural villages, it's a lovely namesake.

Kyoto - 'Capital'. The cultural capital of Japan. Kyoto is an energetic and spirited name and with three syllables, it's quite lyrical in sound. If you're a huge fan of Japan, Kyoto could be a fitting name.

Nairobi - 'Cool water'. The largest city in Kenya is named after the river that runs through it. Pronounced Ny-Ro-Bee, it sounds so sleek and sophisticated as a name and would definitely be a contender.

Rio - 'River of January'. A world-famous river, but Rio also means 'place of the cherry blossoms' in Japan. See the Minimalist names list (page 259) for more like Rio that pack a lot of style into a pared-back name.

Somerset - 'Land of the summer people'. The county of Somerset has such a beautiful and fitting name. Bath is the most famous city in Somerset, but the shoreline is equally gorgeous. Glastonbury takes place here each summer, lending the name an air of rock and roll, and it really is a place for the sunshine.

THE 'MEET-CUTE' NAME

If I'm helping a couple name their baby, I always ask them how they met, and where. It has inspired a lot of very meaningful baby names. My husband and I met in Canterbury while we were at university, and I wish someone had given me this tip when naming our babies. Although, we did eventually list Marlowe after Christopher Marlowe. Our joint university halls were Elliot Halls, after T.S. Elliot - a name ruined by association for me, sadly, by a particularly mean boy at school (why do they always have the best names?). I worked at the Saffron Café, and Henrik and I would sneak in little dates during my shifts. Saffron would have made a sweet name for my little girl, I wish I'd thought of it at the time - I would have adored to tell her that story. Be as creative as you like - it would make a lovely evening as a couple, creating a list of names for your baby in this way.

Jot down the name of these meet-cute places and experiences and see if any inspire a name. It will always be packed with personal meaning.

- Street names: It could be the one you grew up on or where you live now. One couple I worked with met on Carnaby Street in London and loved the name Carnaby as a sweet nod.
- Engagement or marriage places: If you're in a couple, lots of people love to bring in the place where they got engaged or married. My sister got engaged in Rhodes and loved it as a middle name idea. Did your wedding venue have a special name? I even named a baby after a wedding champagne - Ayala.
- Special moments: Capturing your highlights in a list could spark a name idea, whether that be a character in the movie you watched on your first date, a place name from the town where you first met or somewhere you went on holiday together. What about a landmark like Liberty if you loved New York or Devon if it's your happy place together.

WANDERLUST NAMES

Wanderlust is all about that desire to travel and I've picked names that bring that escapism and passion to life in their meaning. If you're always watching travel shows and love nothing more than planning an itinerary for a mini break, these names could all make it onto your list.

GIRLS

Asra - 'To travel at night'. Nighttime drives to grandparents, that late night rush to hospital to give birth, the meaning is so evocative, and Asra is such a romantic name for lovers of road trips.

Saoirse - 'Freedom'. Pronounced Sur-sha, the meaning of 'freedom' is such a strong and empowering one. Saoirse is an Irish name and it feels like it brings the Irish countryside to life.

Shelby - 'Place where willows grow'. Willow is already such a popular name, but Shelby has a vintage vibe and an appealing sense of sounding like an imaginary seaside town. A little Shelby would honour the name Michelle and take you and your daughter straight to the beach.

Wanda - 'Wanderer'. Wanda is a vintage name with a whimsical meaning. It's so underused but has bags of vintage cool, a wonderful choice for a Stand Out & Shine parents.

BOYS

Axis - 'Imaginary line around which the world rotates'. Once every day, the earth spins on its axis. Axis is a fantastic quirkier take on the already-established name Atlas, and where Alex is traditional, Axis is super-wearable. Of course, your world will revolve around your baby boy, so it hits straight to the heart.

Ferdinand - 'Journey'. Your baby is your wildest adventure and the name Ferdinand is just adorable. A wonderful choice to mark the journey you've been through to get to parenthood and the one you'll go on with your baby boy.

Kymani - 'Adventurous traveller'. What a stunning African name. Bob Marley chose Ky-Mani for his son, pronounced Ki-mani.

Peregrine - 'Traveller'. If you want an elaborate name for your son, go with Peregrine, a stately boy's name of Latin origin taken from the name Peregrinus. Another Old English meaning of the name is 'someone living near a pear tree.' It's the perfect pick for parents smitten by wanderlust.

Rasalas - 'The northern star of the lion's head'. Your guiding light, I love this gorgeous sounding name with such powerful meaning. See Space & Star names for more ideas (page 55).

Travers - 'Crossroads'. An English and French name, Travers was an occupational name for a gatherer of tolls. It's a fantastic twist on Travis, and it feels super-whimsical for your crossroad of life into parenthood. Perfect for Trendy with a Twist namers.

Tripp - 'Journey'. This also means 'three' or 'third', which could be a sweet name for your first baby if you're becoming a trio or he's your third born. A Trippe was also the name for a travelling dancer, which I now want to bring back as my own spiritual name. It's a fun word name if you love to travel, but it sounds complete as a cool boy name in its own right.

Wolfgang - 'Travelling wolf'. Wolfgang has fallen out of style in recent decades but with its evocative meaning of both the powerful animal combined with '-gang'. meaning path or to travel, I think it makes a brilliant pick.

NEUTRAL

Meridien - 'Pleasant valley'. Meridien is a surname, but for travel lovers it has the link to the imaginary semicircle on the earth's surface that reaches from top to bottom, like the arch of an atlas.

I think it makes an incredibly unique name for adventurous globe trotters.

Scout - 'To listen'. A scout was an occupational name for someone who gathers information, which translates so well to the idea of scouting for locations and travelling the world before we introduce our baby to it.

Suede - 'From Sweden'. A bit of a twist on the Wanderlust list, the material suede comes from a French term 'gants de Suède' which means 'gloves from Sweden'. A quirky nod to the Nordic country.

MYTHICAL PLACE NAMES

Not all famous places really exist in the world. I researched mythical places and there are so many amazing names which would be incredible for a baby. Realms that exist in fables and fairy tales and paradise gardens which feel totally magical. Here's some stunning names packed full of wonder and vibrant stories.

GIRLS

Annwyn - 'The otherworld in Welsh mythology'. Abundance, food, delights and eternal youth - Annwyn was a paradise place. Names ending 'wyn' sound traditional and romantic.

Arcadia - 'Peace, unspoilt'. An unspoilt paradise feels perfect for your newbie. Named after an ancient Greek tribe, Arcadia in mythology was also a wilderness paradise. The name flows beautifully, ending in the 'ia' which is so popular.

Avalon 'Isle of Apples'. This mythical place is where Arthur pulled the sword from the stone. The name is stunning as is its evocative meaning, with short form Ava being a lovely variation.

Lyonesse - This Cornish place is famous because it's where Tristan dwelled in *Tristan and Isolde*, the classic Arthurian legend.

Pronounced Lay-on-ee-se, I love the nod to our English female football team, too.

Zezura - 'Oasis of little birds'. This is the name of a famed oasis in the Sahara desert. The legend tells that it's where the king and queen of Zezura are sleeping, guarded by giants. Zezura is a trendy and stunning name.

BOYS

Finias - In Irish mythology there were four mythical cities and one was called Finias. A great long form version for the ever-popular Finn and Trendy with a Twist namers could spell it Phineas.

Kitezh - An invisible city from Russian folklore full of treasures, God made the city invisible to protect it from invaders. The name Kitezh really works and it's certainly got a wonderful story to tell.

Olympus - Home of the gods and namesake of the Olympic Games. With Olivia and Oliver being so popular, this is a great Stand Out & Shine alternative.

Summerland - In Paganism Summerland was the term for the afterlife. It's a pastoral and calm, tranquil place and would make a trendy middle spot name.

NEUTRAL

Atlantis - The lost continent of Atlantis was originally mentioned by Greek philosopher Plato as the ultimate utopia. Atlantis was said to have sunk into the ocean. It's a grand sounding name but one that most people will have heard of and it feels fun and interesting as a name for your baby.

Elysian/Elysienne - The Elysian Fields in Greek mythology are where heroes are buried, and where good people go when they pass on. A paradise field, a truly perfect idyllic idea for a special baby name.

Nirvana - 'Transcendent'. To be in a state of nirvana is to be truly happy, transcending any pain. The band of the same name may make the name less, or more appealing depending on your style, but I adore it as a name in its own right.

MASTERING THE MIDDLE NAME

Middle names can sometimes get overlooked in the hunt for a great name, but it's the absolute best spot for getting creative, elevating the flow and character of the full name and showing some personality. In the nineties, the UK collectively seemed to agree that every girl would have the middle name Louise - there must have been something in the hospital tea. James clung on for a while for boys as the epitome of middle-of-the-road middle names. The middle spot had become like the salad draw at the bottom of the fridge, where good intentions go to die.

However, I'm now calling all 'Brave Middle Namers' to unite in agreement on the fact that when you find that ideal middle name it unlocks the next level in loving your baby's full name.

How many middle names are too many? You can register as many middle names as you want, but I believe two is a good limit. It gives you space for a brave pick plus a family nod. Or why not try a mix of long and short names that work with your surname.

Here are my different ways to master the middle:

- Opposites attract. I love the juxtaposition of a differently styled first and middle name to make a name feel unique and special. Like pairing pretty Willow with gender-neutral Scout. Or vintage Reggie with modern Cove. Olivia Sage, Percival Jax, Reverie Rose, Arlo Ernest, the list is endless. Try out mixing opposite styles, especially if the style quiz showed you that as a couple combo you differ. If you're a Stand Out & Shine namer and your partner is Trendy with a Twist or Timelessly Tasteful, you'll delight in how much it changes the feel of the overall name.
- Do you have a guilty pleasure name? Guilty pleasure names are the ones you love but are too scared to admit to, as

you're worried it's a bit 'out there' or weird. Like that weird guilty crush you don't think anyone else will 'get' (I've seen the way you look at Simon Cowell). Believe that you have great taste and do not doubt yourself, as I promise you might regret not using it. If your inner Stand Out & Shine is bursting to get out, here's the place to follow it. My daughter is called Evelina Blossom - Blossom was a firm veto from Timelessly Tasteful Henrik. But with her Scandi version of Evelyn as a first name, I loved the flow of Blossom in the middle spot, it being a Stand Out & Shine floral name that worked perfectly.

- Is there a family member or loved one you want to honour? This could be their space, at the very heart of your child's name - yes, that did make me laugh writing it, but I'm sticking to my PR spin about the middle being the heartbeat for those family faves (if, and only if, you yourself really want to use it). Don't be pressured into it by anyone else in the family, as this is your baby to name. We 100 per cent wanted David in there, after my younger cousin who is so special to me. Henrik and I were really happy to give our firstborn the name Fredrik David. If you don't adore your family name/s, look at my Create Your Own 'Tribute Name' Guide (page 212). I do kind of wish I'd gone with Davey for a more Trendy with a Twist take on David, which feels a little more us.
- If none of these feels like you, then play to your name style. If you're a Timelessly Tasteful namer, then find the perfect era pairing to really cement the look and feel of the name. Grace, Rose, Arthur and George make timeless and tasteful picks that pair with so many names. Are you Trendy with a Twist? Then Jax, Everett, Rosalie and Maeve complement a

lot of the classics and add that bit of edge. For Stand Out & Shines, Jago is a fresh take on James and Lux could be the new Louise.

Get creative and enjoy a second spin of Baby Name Envy for the B-side of your baby's name. It's often where the true gems lie. I also recommend playing one of my name games, like Chart Topper (see page 127), to find a really complementary name that you'll love forever.

VINTAGE

Just like sifting through the rails at a vintage shop, you will find absolute treasures by exploring decades-old name-registration lists. Names come in and out of style and different time periods have their revivals – a name that once felt outdated like Mabel or Stanley can suddenly turn into vintage gold when viewed with fresh eyes.

'Dad' names, 'grandad' names and 'great grandparent' names are beloved for a good reason – we don't have associations with older names and they become brand-new again while retaining their status as a classic. Just like an amazing vintage coat I recently found at the charity shop – it's totally wearable, a one-off no one else will have and it's lived a long life and stood the test of time. Let's dust it off and give it its day on the runway (by which I mean the school run, ha ha).

Have a look back at your own family tree for some vintage gems. We found Freddie on both sides of the family which was one of the reasons we listed it. Add the ones you like most to your baby name list and do a little research into the background of the name.

Let's delve into the racks of my 'vintage name store' (which I'll be over here overthinking an imaginary name for) and

help you sift through for that perfect piece. Welcome to the Moniker Market Vintage Kilo Sale (I'll keep thinking) . . .

READY FOR REVIVAL NAMES

Rare but rising, these vintage names were once common but fell out of style. Now having their retro revival, I think they're all simply gorgeous.

GIRLS

Alma - 'Soul'. The River Alma inspired this name back in 1854 after the Battle of Alma. Its meaning of 'soul' feels like it has depth, and Alma connects on a lot of levels.

Constance - 'Steadfast'. With cute nickname Connie, Constance is a Virtue name which sounds so stylish, yet remains unshowy.

Doris - 'Gift'. A sea nymph in Greek mythology and part of the Dorian tribe; I associate it with singer Doris Day. Doris is a quirky pick these days, but is a stunning sounding name with bags of vintage elegance and charm.

Edith - 'Wealth'. An Anglo-Saxon name, Edith looks and sounds beautiful. While old-school, it's become very fashionable with its strong, stylish, laid-back elegance.

Edna - 'Rejuvenation'. Taken from the same word as Eden, it's not quite rejuvenated yet, but is just getting old enough to become new again.

Gladys - 'Princess'. This Welsh name comes from Gwladys, a Royal in the sixth century. It's a hugely well-known name but isn't used often, making it perfect for an overdue revival.

Hyacinth - 'Purple'. This stunning flower name got plucked out of popular use, but it has beautiful colour to it and sounds elegant and gentle. Cici would be a fun modern nickname.

Joyce - 'Joyous'. From 'rejoice', I love the name Joy, but adore how Joyce adds an even more vintage feel to such a happy name.

Marjorie - 'Pearl'. Margot has been the unexpected rising vintage gem of recent years, so I'd be so tempted to jump back to Marjorie. Also said to be inspired by the spice, marjoram is traditionally used to make wreaths of wedding flowers. Aphrodite used to wear a garland of marjoram as it was linked to love - and I do love it.

Maud - 'Powerful battler'. A variation of Matilda, which has stayed a popular classic, Maud has faded out but could do a Maeve-style fashion comeback. Similar sounding to Audrey, it's perhaps a polarizing name that you'll either love or hate.

Mavis - 'Songbird'. With echoes of a lot of our most popular girl names, Mavis is becoming popular again. It's a charming name which always makes me smile and the songbird meaning is a stunning namesake for a cheerful and perhaps unexpected name pick.

Mildred - 'Gentle strength'. Mildred has been sat at the back of the vintage name wardrobe since the end of the 1920s and is ready for a dust-off. It's definitely a love-it-or-hate-it kind of name, but I think it oozes cool, as it's still a little offbeat. Millie is a popular nickname and Midge was its traditional but playful short form used in the twenties.

Myrtle - 'Evergreen'. Popular in the nineteenth century, I can totally get behind a revival of Myrtle, pronounced Mur-Tle. Most well-known nowadays Moaning Myrtle in the *Harry Potter* series (see my full Harry Potter Names list on page 160) the character may not have helped this pretty botanical name with its comeback. I think it's got the charm of a Victorian botanical poster or vintage skirt - when paired with a modern staple, it's full to the brim of unique style. Try mixing and matching it with more common names on your list.

Nancy - 'Grace'. Nancy was originally a pet form for Anne but grew in popularity. Nancy is a spirited name with a lot of main character energy.

Nettie - 'Grace'. Nettie is a vintage nickname for Jeanette or Annette that sounds lovely in its own right. Nettie would stand out among the more popular 'ie' ending names and has a really old-school sound right out of a storybook.

Norah - 'Light'. This stunning name feels so modern for a vibrant baby girl. With its alternative meaning of honour taken from Honora, Norah is stylish and simple but totally unforgettable.

Opal - 'Jewel'. Most popular around the beginning of the 1900s, Opal is such a strong and vibrant name.

Phyllis - 'Greenery'. Phyllis was a more common name up until the end of the 1950s, with a nature meaning and its gentle sounds. Phyllis would make a brilliant vintage revival choice.

Tabitha - 'Gazelle'. Such a gorgeous name, Tabitha dates back in history to a biblical figure who was given the name as she had the grace and beauty of a gazelle. It immediately makes me think of a quilted blanket and linen dress and I would list this if you wanted an underused vintage classic.

BOYS

Adrian - 'From Hadria'. I love this northern Italian name. Understated but cool, Adrian is a great pick and will please Timelessly Tasteful namers.

Basil - 'King'. Once the ruler of the Byzantine Empire, I think Basil is an adorable, offbeat vintage name with echoes of the fragrant herb basil that was used in perfume for royals.

Bernard - 'Strong as a bear'. Saint Bernard, the patron saint of the alps and skiers, oversaw a monastery in the mountains and when people went on pilgrimages to Rome, they often stopped there. Alpine Spaniels were kept at the monastery, now known as St Bernards, as they were amazing rescue dogs who would find pilgrims and restore them with whiskey, which they had in a jar around their neck.

Cecil - 'Blind'. The names Cecil and Cecelia could 'blind' you with love for this pretty option. It just makes me smile so much with its cute quirkiness. It's traditional but daring - two styles that would combine beautifully.

Charles - 'Free man'. Charles feels quite formal now we're more used to seeing Charlie atop the charts, but it's got that quintessential classic vintage vibe about it. A British staple, Charles is an eternally popular name that Timelessly Tasteful namers will adore.

Clive - 'Cliff'. Clive was nearly extinct for a while but it's very handsome and modern sounding if you take a fresh look at it.

Edwin - 'Rich friend'. The English form of Odin and the first name of Buzz Aldrin (the second man to set foot on the Moon), I think Edwin is so bang on-trend and overdue a comeback. We love names ending in 'win' and Edward has been a pillar of vintage boy names for years, so why not give it a twist? Nicknames like Teddy and Ned work.

Ernest - 'Serious'. Vintage gem Ernest is a variation of the adjective earnest. It gets a great reaction, as it's such a sweet throwback. It's one we've all heard of, but still remains a rare pick. With the nickname Ernie, Ernest is seriously ready for revival.

Frank - 'Free man'. The Germanic Frank tribe gave this name popularity - you had to be an elder in the Frank tribe to be able to give opinions, which is where the phrase 'to be frank' came from. It's a down-to-earth, happy sounding name that works just as well for a baby as a teen and grown-up.

Grover - 'Grove of trees'. In 1884 Stephen Grover Cleveland became president of the United States and made this a classic vintage American moniker.

Hector - 'To have or to hold'. What a gorgeous meaning your little one would have if their name was associated with the Greek legend of Hector the warrior and Sir Hector, knight of the Round Table in Arthurian legend. The name is steadily rising but not trending, which is a good trajectory for getting a name that won't suddenly boom.

Hugo - 'Heart or spirit'. With the popular 'o' ending, Hugo is a classic boy's name that will always warm your heart. I think of it as spirited and loving, so it's one that really matches its meaning. In recent history the name was reserved for the upper classes in the UK, but like Arthur it's now a popular name across the playground.

Percival - 'Pierce the valley'. A knight of the Round Table in Arthurian legend and Albus Dumbledore's middle name in *Harry Potter*, it's not yet made its comeback. The nickname Percy started a slow but steady boost up the charts in 2010 after being unranked in 2001. You could go with Perry, meaning 'pear tree', as a short form.

Ralph - 'Wolf'. The name Ralph came over with the Vikings and maybe that Scandi cool is where its new popularity is coming from. A simple, understated name, you might list Ralph if you're after a less obvious vintage boy name. I also love Rafe and Raul which are more modern variations.

Rupert - 'Bright fame'. With roots name Robert, Rupert is a lively but laid-back name that has the plus points of not being obviously nicknamed, which some parents really like. It's friendly and warm, with the meaning bright.

Travis - 'To cross'. Travis is a French name in origin, someone who would work collecting tolls for people to cross a boundary or bridge. It's a name that is registered as far back as the fourteenth century in England and works just as well today with the special 'v' sound.

Walter - 'Power of the army'. The name Walter is just on the right side of vintage gold after many years of being out of style. Worn by many poets, creatives and adventurers, Walter is an upbeat choice that is bound to gain a lot of envious compliments.

Wilbur - 'Brilliant'. Wilbur, meaning bright or wilful, also translates as 'wild boar', which gives it a bit of edge. Overshadowed by William, Wilbur feels like a quirkier choice.

Wilfred - 'Desiring peace'. The name Wilfred has had a big leap from being basically extinct in the nineties to parents picking it back up in the 2000s. The nickname Wilf is a twist on the popular' Will. From William to Wilfred to . . . Wilbur perhaps? If William is a tailored suit, Wilfred is a mod jacket from the sixties - smart but cool.

Winston - 'Joyful stone'. Dating back to the ninth century AD, Winston is steeped gravitas and feels quite iconic as a vintage name. I love the meaning with joy encapsulated. If you really like the idea of a nature-inspired name, then flick through my Nature names lists and as there are so many stunning ideas (see page 15).

NEUTRAL

Eugene/Eugenia - 'Well born'. There's something about Eugene and Eugenia that I just adore. Once so out-dated, they are now bang on-trend. Gene is popping up on loads of Trendy with a Twist name lists, it could be the one for you.

Francis/Frances - 'Free man'. A longer variation of Frank, Francis has dropped out of popularity in the last few decades but it's such a brilliant name. With a literary and old-school British feel, I also really like Frankie as a nickname, or Cece. It could be perfect for Trendy with a Twist namers, as there are so many options.

Sidney - 'Wide river meadow'. Sidney has been mainly used for girls recently and spelt like the Australian city, Sydney. However, it works for any gender, especially with cute Sid as a quirky nickname.

VINTAGE NAMES THAT HAVEN'T COME BACK

A lot of vintage names are either what I call Vintage Gold or Vintage Old, and these are gold. Barry is a celeb pick these days, Alan is now hipster, Agatha is trending. You may need to challenge yourself on a few of these, as they're achingly old-school, but that just means you're ahead of the curve and could be the one to bring back a classic.

GIRLS

Agatha - 'Good'. A third-century saint, the name Agatha became popular during the 1930s. The strong 'g' is a polarizing sound, but if you're after a vintage gold name that isn't frilly, then Agatha is your girl. I'd go with Gigi as the nickname, or pretty Thea.

Cecily - 'Blind'. This super-dainty name feels uber vintage. It's an aristocratic name that's dipped in popularity and I think would be such a cool choice for your baby girl. With trendy Cece, she'd be giving Baby Name Envy for sure. Whether honouring a loved one who is blind or loving the feeling of being blinded by love, it's a distinctive meaning.

Dovie - 'Peace'. I would be listing Dovie so quickly, a popular name throughout the 1940s, it dropped out of use but is turning heads lower down the charts. With similar sounding Evie being so well-loved, Dovie would be truly wearable.

Elvira - 'Truth'. Pronounced Ell-Vera, this Visigoth name is just a dream. With its sincere meaning I adore the sound and it's giving me serious Baby Name Envy.

Emmeline - 'Industrious'. If Emily has always been a guilty pleasure name but feels too obvious, then Emmeline is waiting in the wings. With game-changer Emmeline Pankhurst who organised the British suffragette movement, it feels soft but strong. Pronounced Emma-Leen.

Enid - 'Soul or life'. The meaning sells this to me, as well as the unique sound of the name Enid. A legendary beauty in Welsh after the Celtic goddess, it was once the highest compliment you could give a woman to call her 'a second Enid'.

Loretta - 'Laurel'. Popular in the 1950s, Loretta gives you pretty Etta as a nickname and modern Lo. It's got a real cottagecore vibe to it.

Phyllis - 'Greenery'. A vintage botanical girl name that's been unranked for years, it's got three big ticks from me. Totally unique, Phyllis has now moved from 'grumpy grandma' to 'vintage gem'. I can just imagine how adorable this would be on a little girl, gentle and unexpected - you can so pop that on your list.

Sally - 'Princess'. Taking an unfair dive in recent years, Sally is happy-go-lucky and would make a cool rare name.

Wilma - 'Protector'. I hear the name Wilma more often in Sweden and it always sounds really on-trend. It's picking up some use again after a bit of a hiatus from the charts and it truly feels happy and playful, the Mabel of its time.

BOYS

Arnold - 'Eagle power'. A medieval boy name that hasn't been flying high in recent years, so feels quite fresh. Arnie could be the new Archie.

Bernard - 'Brave as a bear'. Nickname Bernie and its cool meaning makes Bernard a big draw.

Cyril - 'Master'. Cyril sounds gentle but actually is a hugely revered name meaning 'lord' or 'master'. The name has been given to popes and saints but now languishes nearly out of use. One to resurrect on your list if you love a truly historic name with a distinct sound.

Earl - 'Nobleman'. Earl feels ripe for revival, as it's a popular title name like Saint, Prince or the particularly lovely vintage name Pearl. Earl is a rare minimalist pick.

Edgar - 'Wealthy spear'. A subtle twist on Edward or Edwin, Edgar just needs a little encouragement to get back up the charts. It reminds me of Noah with the strong 'g' of Hugo and it's working for me for your vintage boy's name list.

Floyd - 'Gray-haired'. With Finn and Flynn being popular, this Celtic vintage name feels daring but edgy, with music links to the legendary band Pink Floyd or to famous blues musician Floyd Council. List this for an off-the-chart hit.

Gilbert - 'Bright pledge'. I have a lot of love for the name Gilbert. It's not so different from Will or Bertie, which have remained popular, and has a charming countryside feel.

Graham - 'Grey home'. Originally a place name from Lincolnshire, Graham was a widely popular name right up until the late nineties when it dropped to almost being extinct. Grayson took off around the same time to perhaps replace it, but if you love a traditional name, Graham could be a unique pick for now.

Harold - 'Army ruler'. A strong name that's not risen from the vintage ashes just yet. Perhaps that's due to it not having so many nickname options, but it's a quirky choice.

Ivor - 'Bow warrior'. Ivor is so traditional around the UK, with the power of its warrior meaning complementing the strong sound of the name.

Lawrence - 'Bright'. Lawrence has travelled a lot as a name, primarily as a surname. Originally it appears to have Italian roots. The sound is delightful and I particularly like Lawrie as a short form.

Leonard - 'Lion's strength'. Leonard has roots as an Irish surname and Lenny would be such a cute nickname.

Milton - 'Mill town'. Once a traditional British name, Milton now gets minimal use. However, it ticks a lot of modern parents' criteria being a vintage name with a trendy sound.

Norman - 'North man'. The history of Norman is interesting, as it was originally the term for Vikings here in the UK. When the Vikings invaded, they called themselves 'naromenn', meaning 'Men from the North'. It's a massively quirky name that hasn't been in style for generations but could find a place in your heart.

Redvers - 'Place of rivers'. This Victorian boy name is totally extinct, and I adore it. It was a common military name after war hero Sir Redvers Buller who was awarded the Victoria Cross for his services during the Boer War. It took off as a name immediately after in his honour, then declined.

Reginald - 'Ruling with power'. From the root word Regina meaning 'queen', the name Reginald has started its comeback, powered by cute nickname Reggie.

Richard - 'Strong ruler'. Peaking in the nineties, this kingly name hasn't remained popular alongside Edward, William and Henry. It's interesting to see Richard fall out of favour and to think of it as quite a daring pick.

Roland - 'Famous land'. In medieval England Roland was a beloved name after Charlemagne's nephew, who was famed for being eight foot tall. Roland inspired folk songs and poetry and the name took off. It's declined in popularity in the last few decades, so snap Roland up if you are drawn to it.

Ronald - 'Advice'. Ronnie has made a comeback from the 1920s name Ronald. A Harry Potter literary megastar, see my Harry Potter list (page 160) for more from the world of Hogwarts.

Trevor - 'Large homestead'. Trevor is of Welsh origin and was a highly sought-after name associated with someone who owned a lot of land. It's taken a dip over the past few decades in the UK, but is super well-known and has the trendy 'v' of ever-popular Oliver, so it could make a great alternative.

NEUTRAL

Bob/Bobby - 'Bright fame'. Bobby works for girls and boys, originating from classic Robert. Bobby has come back for boys more than girls to-date, but it's always been on my radar for Trendy with a Twist namers, as it feels individual and spirited.

Geri/Jerry - 'Rules with spear'. For Geraldine or Jeremy, Jerry is such a throwback pick but it really works amongst the other vintage nicknames that have remained at the top of the charts. I'd be listing it for a short and sweet gem.

Patrick - 'Noble'. The patron saint of Ireland, Patrick has always been traditionally a male name; however, lately I've heard it on a couple of girls and think it could make a brilliant gender-neutral name. Pat and Patti are nice, and Paddy was always the Irish nickname, which is super-sweet. Consider Patrick in a new way and put it on your list.

CREATE YOUR OWN 'TRIBUTE NAME'

TIPS FOR HONOURING A LOVED ONE

When it comes to considering Vintage names for your baby, it may be that you have someone in your family who you want to honour. Passing on family names is a gorgeous tradition - but the names are not always as lovely as the sentiment behind it.

That's why I often help people come up with what we call a 'Tribute Name' - a 'this name is inspired by a real person but rewritten for a modern audicnce' vibe. Here's my method for creating your own bespoke name, in your style, that still works as a tribute. Everyone's happy; these make gorgeous middle name spots or a first name that is full of meaning.

Working with One Name:

- Switch up the ending - the most common way to modernize an older name is to simply keep the first prominent letters. David could become Davis or Davey. Emily could be Emmeline, Emory or Emerson.
- Take the key sounds of the name - what sound do you love in the name? This is a great way to create more options. For example, Lauren can become Audra, Aurelia or Aubrey using the pretty 'au'. Henry could be Enzo or Rhys, taking just a part of the original and adding some flair.
- Look into the name in different countries and variations. A great example is John, which is often cited as a name people want to tribute. The name has been changed many times across the globe to Shaun, Ivan, Evan, Jonas, Johan.
- I'm sure you've thought of using a nickname as a tribute and it's also fun to try switching genders for more inspiration.

Sandra becomes Sandy for a boy, Albert becomes Bertie for a girl.

- If you have two people you want to honour, you can blend names together. For example, Naomi and Lee can become Miley or Millie, Lina or Emmeline, Alena or Amalia, Liam or Leon, Miller or Milan, Lennon or Niall.

CAN HONOURING A LOVED ONE WITH A NAME GO WRONG?

I once had a dilemma from a listener on the Baby Name Envy Podcast who made me consider the possibility that not everyone wants their name to be passed on.

A family rift had broken out when a baby was given the name of their aunt. The mum just loved the name and the family nod felt like an extra reason to use it. However, this aunt wasn't happy, as she instantly became Big Alice and baby was Little Alice. Neither felt nice - Big Alice was not happy with her new title and the baby's mum was frustrated that the family wanted to nickname her daughter Ally to differentiate. This story has stuck with me, unless you are comfortable with giving your baby a nickname or initial name (AJ for instance), then it could be worth sense checking.

VINTAGE NICKNAMES AS FIRST NAMES

If a longer vintage name sounds a bit too formal, there's so many nicknames that have now become more popular than the original. In this list I'm leading with the shorter, more playful nickname as the front runner, but I'll let you know where it came from. I often suggest this when couples are clashing, with one parent wanting a more traditional name and the other wanting more of a Stand Out & Shine name. It's a great way of meeting both criteria.

GIRLS

Cece - 'Blind'. A short form of Cecelia, I love all the Fifi, Gigi and Mimi tribe of nicknames, and Cece sounds super-stylish.

Coco - 'People of victory'. If it feels too much of a nickname, you could always go with with Collette or Nicole.

Effie - 'Well-spoken or pretty voice'. From long vintage name Euphemia, Effie is such a retro, romantic sounding girl name. It appears throughout literature and movies and always stands out.

Elsie - 'Pledged to God'. Our most popular nickname as first name, taken from Elizabeth. Elsie is lively and precious and has climbed ahead of other options, but all are lovely - Libby, Betty, Betsy, Beth, Eliza, Elspeth, there's so many ways to keep Elizabeth in the charts.

Emmy - 'Work'. I adore this nickname for Emmeline and it's a popular first name all by itself.

Evie - 'Life'. This is such a beautiful name with equally special meaning. Evie has taken over from its longer vintage name Evelyn. I used Scandinavian version Evelina and I never tire of saying or hearing her name.

Goldie - 'Made of gold'. Marigold with the nickname Goldie is so stunning. See more in my Gilded Names list if you're a magpie when it comes to sparkle (see page 118).

Hallie - 'Home ruler'. Another pretty nickname for Harriet.

Hattie - 'Home ruler'. From the same house as Harry, Harriet lends us this super-adorable nickname. I'm thinking bonnets, and I can't even pretend that I'm not.

Josie - 'God will increase'. Short for Josephine, Josie is as pretty as a Daisy and as vintage as a Rosie. It could be the perfect name and is so often overlooked - add it to your list.

Lola - 'Sorrow'. A short form of Dolores, which was a Spanish name for Mary, known as 'Our Lady of Sorrows'. Despite its sad meaning, Lola is such an upbeat name. It has vintage charm but sounds so modern.

Lottie - 'Free'. Taken from Charlotte, Lottie is lively and full of fun with its cheerful sound. My sister chose Lottie for her second daughter and of course, even with a 'nickname as first name', we added to it, calling her Lottie Lulu, or just Lulu. I love how it grows with her and she fully embodies the meaning of 'free', being the wild adorable child in our family.

May/Mae - A short form for Mary or Margaret, May is such a sweet name. The month is named after goddess of fertility Maia - more popularly spelt Maya, which is higher in the charts. But May is more often used as a double-barrel second with Lily-May, Daisy-May and Gracie-May all ranking.

Mimi - 'Industrious'. Mimi could be short for a few names, from Marilyn to Margot, but I chose the meaning based on it being short for Amelia, as I love the combination of the popular first name and short unique nickname. My sister Naomi's nickname was Mimi, as it's how I said her name when I was little - my children call her

Auntie Mimi I think she was very grateful for such a cool nickname, as she always got called 'Nay' by friends.

Nell - 'Shining light'. This one-syllable wonder is fashionable and understated. Originally a nickname for Helen, it's straight from a vintage book and will always sound original. Nellie is also very popular.

Norah - 'Light'. A very pretty vintage name taken from Eleanor. If you have Noah on your boy list, Nora or Norah with the 'h' should be on your girl name list. It's unique to say with the long vowel, Noor-Ah, and sounds very romantic because of it.

Peggy - 'Pearl'. Margaret is the name that keeps on giving when it comes to nicknames. Peggy is pleasingly vintage and heading up the charts hot on the heels of popular Pearl. Also, Margot, Marnie and Meg all come from Margaret, so go as rare as you want.

Penny - 'Weaver'. The vintage nickname for Penelope, Penny has so much character. I associate it with a lucky penny, which is such a sweet meaning for your baby.

Sadie - 'Princess'. The name Sadie is a nickname for Sarah, who knew? I love its indie cool vibes; you can't deny that Sadie's got character.

Tiggy - 'Worthy of one's parents'. Traditionally, Tiggy was short for the Greek name Antigone, pronounced with four syllables, Anne-Tig-Oh-Nee. Tiggy is so vibrant and spirited. If you prefer to keep it as a nickname, but aren't sold on Antigone, you could pick Tabitha or even Antonia if you wanted a more classic vibe.

Tilly - 'Mighty battle'. Taken from the ever-popular Matilda, Tilly is so feminine. Tilda would have been our name for Freddie had he been a girl, so that I could have used pet name Tilly. If you're not onboard with Tilly, check out Tiggy, above.

Trudy - 'Universal strength'. Short for Gertude, this has the loveliest name meaning. See my Virtues name lists for more like this (page 129).

Willa - 'Will or protection'. From Wilhelmina, Willa has been making it back onto the charts. A stylish, understated name, vintage Willa is a fresh pick from the archives.

Winnie - 'Fair one'. A new big hitter in the charts, the name Winnie is so fresh and modern while having many amazing long form ideas. I'd be listing it as traditional Winifred, which I'm loving lately - but she could also go by Freddy if she wanted. Or why not go modern with Winslow or Winslet, both place names.

BOYS

Albie - 'Noble'. Taken from Albert, Albie is extremely cool and fits right up there with the most timeless vintage names.

Archie - 'Brave'. Archibald could feel a bit of a mouthful for modern tastes, but we've kept the name's spirit with the popular nickname Archie.

Auggie - 'Great'. The longer form is Augustus, also increasingly popular in recent decades. Reminiscent of the month of August, it's a name filled with sunshine.

Dougie - 'Dark stream'. Such a trendy name with that slightly mysterious meaning, I think Dougie makes such a brilliant alternative to many of the more frequently heard nickname names.

Howie - 'High defender'. This nickname, taken from Howard, has a retro feel that people adore. It's a vintage name that is down to earth and fun.

Jonty - 'Gift of God'. An affectionate name for classic Jonathan, cheeky Jonty is gaining use all on its own merit.

Monty - 'Mountain'. Montgomery is such a strong name, just like it's meaning, and little Monty would certainly stand out among some of the more common nicknames.

Reggie - 'Mighty counsellor'. Reginald has made space for Reggie, which is so much less formal and a sweet pick with a grand meaning.

NEUTRAL

Bernie - 'Brave as a bear'. From Bernard and Bernadette, Bernie is still a lot less common than a lot of vintage names and I think it's full of character and confidence.

Ronnie - 'Advice'. From Ronald, Ronnie has quickly taken over as the preferred version of this vintage name. It's mainly used for boys, but also can be a short form of Veronica and works just as well as a cool girl name.

Teddy - 'God's gift'. Originally from Theodore or Theodora, it's also used as a short form for Edward. Teddy is never going out of style and it still sounds fashionable. It's stood the test of time since Theodore Roosevelt inspired the creation of the teddy bear, which is synonymous with childhood. This name will be the envy of all your friends when they come over for first cuddles with Teddy.

HACKS FOR WHEN YOU JUST CAN'T DECIDE ON A NAME

Here's three top hacks I've created to help solve some of the common questions we ask ourselves when deciding on that final baby name. These hacks are a super fun way to try out the names on your name list before baby arrives.

THE NAME TAG HACK – BEST FOR . . . WILL IT SUIT THEM AT ALL AGES?

If you're not sure whether the name you're picking is a little babyish or if it will suit them as a grown-up, try imagining it on your partner or yourself. If you can imagine your partner being introduced as a Wolfie or Jax, chances are it will suit your son. And similarly, if you would make a good Bess or Winnie, it will grow with your daughter. If the name on your fully grown selves suddenly seems a bit jarring, it might not be the one.

Picturing my husband as a Freddie made me love the name for our son. Try using the name out loud on each other and if you're having a baby by yourself, try out the hack below.

THE BABY VOICE HACK – BEST FOR . . . IS IT TOO SERIOUS FOR A BABY?

If you're worried your grand or vintage name choice sounds too serious or maybe a little old-fashioned for a baby, ask a friend or family member's child to say it. I loved hearing my own personal Baby Name List read by little ones. I was unsure about Hugo but it sounded so sweet when my niece said it. Do try it; it's so illuminating.

THE COFFEE CUP HACK – BEST FOR . . . IS IT TOO UNIQUE?

In *Baby Name Envy*, you can find names from unique to traditional and I always encourage people to stick within their style, but often people have that braver name on their name list and are worried about what other people will say.

Sometimes we hold back from those more daring names due worry that our child will constantly have to correct or respell their name. To check this out before you commit, I invented the coffee shop hack.

In the coffee shop they often ask for your name and write it on your cup; instead of your real name, give the barista the baby name. How do you feel saying it out loud? Did you have to spell it or repeat it? Did that bother you or not at all? It's a real-world litmus test that a lot of my clients have said they've loved.

HISTORY

There are some periods in history that had distinctive name styles and there are so many forgotten names to be rediscovered. I've picked the best names from some of our most iconic eras, from strong and interesting Anglo-Saxon names to the high-jinks of socialites in the roaring twenties. This section is essentially a baby name time machine, so let's go further back and dust off some perfect name picks.

ANGLO-SAXON NAMES

The Anglo-Saxons were a cultural group that inhabited a lot of early England and Scotland and spoke Old English. Anglo-Saxon names were Germanic in origin and used a lot of letters and sounds we don't use today, like Ælfred. Anglo-Saxon names were recorded, and we can still look back at them today and see where some became adapted into a more modern language which is why they make amazing, relevant names. I'm a firm believer that if it's phonetic and easily spelt, then a unique name works, which is why I've left out Aethelflaed, Hrafnlaug and Engilgund but have some other brilliant inspiration for you.

GIRLS

Aelswith - The wife of King Alfred the Great in Anglo-Saxon rule. Pronounced Ale-s-with. I love how bohemian the name sounds - it's romantic and charming and really denotes it's Anglo-Saxon heritage.

Alodia - 'Riches'. Similar in sound to Elodie, Saint Alodia was a Spanish saint, and the name dates to an ancient kingdom of the same name that inspired it.

Arleigh - 'From the meadow of the hare'. An alternative meaning for Arleigh is 'promise', which is so graceful. Arleigh immediately grabs attention for being so unique and its sound and flow make it truly special.

Domino - 'Belonging to the Lord'. I adore this Latin name which also has Greek heritage. A Domino was a black and white priests' cloak, which inspired the name of the game Dominoes. A Stand Out & Shine name, Domino has a historic feel that fits right into a modern playground.

Doretta - 'Gift from God'. If you like Etta, this Anglo-Saxon moniker could provide a long form that's ultra-vintage. It's so characterful,

Doretta just feels like someone with bags of energy and heaps of style. A true Stand Out & Shine name.

Eadlin - 'Princess'. Pronounced Eed-Lin. The strong 'd' is classic of Anglo-Saxon names, and it becomes a very grand and elegant name that really stands out for all the right reasons.

Elswyth - 'Elf from the willow trees'. Wow, if you love fantasy and nature-inspired names, then Elswyth is one of my favourites. So romantic and magical in feel, Elswyth gives me so much Baby Name Envy.

Fritha - 'Peace'. Fritha has a quirky style all of its own, and harks back to an era where so many 'th' sounds appeared in longer names. Fritha should shoot through time and onto your baby name list immediately.

BOYS

Dexter - 'Dyer'. Dexter is so modern and fresh sounding but dates to Anglo-Saxon Britain as the name for someone who worked dying fabrics. Today it's got an urban and edgy feel.

Holt - 'Son of the unspoiled forests'. With a colt being a baby horse, I wonder if that's where Holt comes from. A one-syllable, strong boy name, it's got a carefree feel with that outdoorsy meaning.

Kipp - 'From the pointed hill'. This sounds so modern but dates to the Anglo-Saxon era. It's also slang for a short nap or bed and makes a cute nickname for Charles.

Oslac - 'Curious'. With similarities to Oscar, Lucas and Jack, this is a strong boy name, and the meaning is so unique and perfect for your curious baby boy.

Sheply - 'From the sheep's meadow'. Sheply was an occupational surname and Shepherd is a fun name, but Sheply feels more wearable somehow. The Sheply family were a big clan in Yorkshire during the Anglo-Saxon times.

Torr - 'From the watch tower'. Tor is a high tower, the most famous being the Glastonbury Tor. Pronounced like the word 'tour', it's a strong one-syllable name with the mystical tor being a trendy namesake.

Wulfric - 'Wolf ruler'. Wulfric was an Anglo-Saxon nobleman and the name was highly popular. The idea of using Wulfric excites me; it's got trendy Wolfy as a nickname and sounds really modern.

NEUTRAL

Kin - 'Family'. Not technically an Anglo-Saxon personal name, but Kin is a word we still occasionally use today with a similar meaning and I think it makes such an amazing word name. A cool middle spot or minimalist first name, Kin takes a special place in the charts.

Leif - 'Heir'. Anglo-Saxon names were compound names made up of a prefix and suffix and Leif was a common prefix. Now mainly used in Scandinavia as a male name, pronounced Lay-f, it's a stylish one-syllable name with historic flair. The meaning is fun too.

Rune - 'Secret'. I absolutely adore the name Rune, pronounced Roon, though you can also go Runa if you prefer to take it to two syllables. The Anglo-Saxon runes were an alphabet, which was used to write messages. The name means 'secret' or 'mystery' in old German and people believed if you put the runes in the right order, they had magical powers. Whimsical word names are so popular, and Rune makes a brave first name or middle spot - see my Romantasy Names list for more like Rune (page 288).

ANCIENT ROMAN NAMES

In Rome they invented the name tradition we still stick to today, Tria Nomina. Romans invented the Praenomen 'personal name', Noman 'clan name' and Cognomen which was a 'given name' to some higher-ranking people based on a personal character trait or achievement. They used it to distinguish Romans from foreigners

and it's why we still see so many names meaning 'warrior', 'victor' or 'strong in battle'. Also, maybe less complimentary, names meaning 'bald' and 'chickpea nose'.

In ancient Roman times, parents would have eight days to name their baby. During this time they would check the baby for its survival potential and occasionally that led to the baby not getting a naming ceremony if they expected to wait for a healthier first son to be the father's namesake. There were only around 18 popular names because names were passed on in families, with male and female versions. Boys were given their father's name, then other male relatives' names in order of importance. Girls just had one name per family, usually the male name with an added 'ia' or 'illa' to denote what order they were born in. Julius Caesar's daughters were called Claudia premia, Claudia secondi and on.

There are some glorious names that I've sifted the history books to uncover and they feel really bold and very elegant and many have that Roman warrior grandness peppered in too.

GIRLS

Aelia - 'Sunshine'. Pronounced with a silent 'A', Aelia was traditionally pronounced 'Eelia'. The female form from the Roman god Helios who rode across the sky in a chariot to bring the Sun up.

Cloelia - 'Famous'. Cloelia sounds like a modern name. There's an incredible story of a Roman woman known only as Cloelia who was taken hostage during a Roman battle and escaped her captors by swimming across the Tiber, taking all the other female captives with her. The story adds a lot of girl power to stunning Cloelia.

Cornelia - 'Wise'. The first wife of Julius Caesar, to be called Cornelia was a very proud name as she was thought of as the ultimate Roman woman. Lia or Connie make modern nicknames for Cornelia and you can find more like Connie in the Vintage Nicknames as First Names list (see page 215).

Decima - 'Tenth'. Decima is a fascinating name, as it was widely used in Roman times but was also one of Roman mythology's 'Fates', who were personified as three women. Decima controlled your life span, so when it was said to be in the hands of fate - that's Decima. It's got a fashionable flair and would make a hip Stand Out & Shine name.

Helvia - 'Blonde hair'. Helvia was associated with the Sun in Roman times and the name feels truly modern in sound for a sandy-haired baby girl.

Tulla - 'Hill'. The feminine form of Tullus, Tullus Hostilius was the third king of Rome and made the name popular. Pronounced Too-Lah, it's sounds gorgeous and I can see it paired with a classic middle name. So simple and elegant.

Valeria - 'Strong'. From Valerius, a Roman saint and martyr, and pronounced Val-Air-Re-Uh, this is such a wearable name.

BOYS

Caesar - 'Hairy'. Julius Caesar has made us all familiar with the name, and although it means 'hairy', it was also used as a title for nobility going forward. It's a complex name in spelling, firmly related to the man who created the Roman Empire. A good pick for historians.

Cicero - 'Chickpea'. I remember the moment my first child whispered those three little words every mum wants to hear, 'I love hummus'. Maybe you've been looking for a way to bring this dip, let's call it mum catnip, into your baby's name. Cicero was very well-known in academic circles as the philosopher and politician prominent in Roman life. The name comes from one of his ancestor's cognomens, as he was said to have a cleft in the tip of his nose resembling a chickpea. Honestly, the most random of all facts in this name book, I had to include it. I can see why cognomens have gone out of style. But Cicero is stunning, and I love the link to the iconic thought leader if you were brave enough.

Magnus - 'Great'. Still rising in the charts due to the trend for strong ancient names. In Rome, Magnus was a name for great leaders.

Marcellus - 'Young warrior'. This name was given to young boys who were expected to go on to be warriors and display qualities of a protective nature. Marcellus is getting a lot more use again recently. It's a unique name and I love the sound.

Marcus - 'Dedicated to Mars'. The Roman god of war, Marcus was one of the most prominent names of the Roman era. It's still popular today around Europe and sounds a lot more gentle than his namesake.

Maurice - 'Dark-skinned'. Maurice has its roots in Saint Maurice, a third-century Roman soldier from Egypt. The French kept the spelling Maurice, whereas in Britain it became Morris, but Maurice is an elegant and effortlessly cool boy name.

Roman - 'From Rome'. A trendy name for modern parents, it's got a handsome vibe, and it also feels whimsical - to roam.

Tullius - 'One who leads'. Marcus Tullius Cicero is still studied today for his writing and ideas on politics and philosophy. Tully would make such a cute nickname.

NEUTRAL

Aquila - 'Eagle'. Also a constellation, an eagle was believed to carry thunderbolts through the air. Such a strong and powerful name.

Fausta - 'Fortunate'. In Ancient Rome, Faustus would have been the male version, but I think Fausta makes a great neutral name. With its meaning of 'fortunate', it has a nickname feel that's super quirky.

Jovian - 'Of Jupiter'. The name of a fourth-century Roman Emperor, Jovian makes a regal and space-related twist on a Roman name. See more of Jovian and other space names in my Space-Inspired Names list (page 56).

REGENCY NAMES

The Regency era only lasted nine years, between 1811-1820, a short period when King George III became unwell, so his eldest son George became Regent Prince. George IV was young and became the patron of new arts like painting and sculpture plus technology. It was a romantic and artistic time - author Jane Austen captured it in her writing on romance, wealth, fashion and the strict rules for high society.

It was an interesting time for names, as society was still incredibly formal. In public, people were referred to as Miss, Mr and Mrs, even between married couples, and only in private would they use their first names. Girls would then get a sweet family name, like Lizzie in *Pride and Prejudice*, but for men it was slightly different and considered affectionate to call them by their surname. I still see this playing out today sometimes, which is really fascinating. There's a whole list of 'surnames as first names' in this book that bring a touch of formal class to the modern era.

There were only around 300 names in circulation during the Regency era, meaning the population shared a lot of the same names. The tradition was to pass names on through the family, with the oldest child being named after the father's parents, the second being named after the mother's parents, then once that duty was fulfilled, parents were free to pick a more popular name from the era. Biblical, royal and saints' names were still in circulation, plus the Norman Conquest had introduced some French names to society. The trend for compound names like Sarah-Jayne started and the French and Italian variants sprinkled some romance onto established names, with Olive becoming Olivia and Alice becoming Alicia. It was its own exciting Baby Name Boom, you just needed to have a lot of babies to join in.

GIRLS

Ann - 'Favoured'. Ann was in the top 100 in the seventies but has largely been replaced by a newer version - Annie and Anna all overtook lovely Ann, and now it's rarely heard. If you love a minimalist aesthetic and understated cool, then Ann gives that.

Charlotte - 'Free man'. Charlotte is a variation of Charles and was in use during the regency era after being introduced by Queen Charlotte, mother of the Prince Regency. She was a German princess who had a love for gardening and she introduced the Christmas tree to Britain, bringing the first one to Windsor Castle. Lottie, Lotta and Charlie are all great nicknames, and even Arlo for that more gender-neutral spin would be a cool way to modernize traditional Charlotte.

Eleanor - 'Light-hearted or shining light'. The name Eleanor came over from France during the Regency period and is still such a coveted name for parents looking for something pretty and traditional.

Elizabeth - 'God is my oath'. Elizabeth is classic and elegant, plus very royal. There are so many variations too, Elspeth, Eliza and Libby are my favourites.

Hannah - 'Grace'. One of my preferred traditional girl names, Hannah has such a lovely modern sound, it's incredible to think it was this popular in the Regency era. There's lots of notable nineties Hannah's when the name was really on-trend, and it would make a great pairing to any vintage name.

Hester - 'Star'. Hester is a quintessential Regency name, with adventurer and traveller Lady Hester Stanhope being a notable society figure at the time. Hester takes me back to the Regency halls and if you love a rare vintage name, it has that historic feel.

Lucy - 'Light bringer'. Lucy has the appeal of a nickname, but it's complete already and just as playful. The meaning comes from 'lux', meaning 'to shine', which has become a popular modern name all of itself. I have a soft spot for Lucy from *The Lion, The Witch and The Wardrobe* and from the iconic retro TV show *I Love Lucy*. It's always felt like a spirited name, which is why I'm sure it's used so much in songs and character names.

Marianne - 'Grace or sea of bitterness'. All the variations for Mary have one meaning of sorrow or bitterness. Marianne is the French variation and pronunciation can change to Mary-Anne but should be Marry-Anne. From Marianne Dashwood in *Sense and Sensibility* to Marianne Sheridan in book sensation *Normal People*, it's got main character energy, as we'd say these days, but feels bookish and thoughtful.

Martha - 'Lady'. The meaning is quite interesting, as Martha always seems to be the name of the maid in a regency drama. With Margot and Mabel rocketing up the charts, I think Martha will be having a popularity surge.

Mary - 'Beloved'. I adore the name Mary, and it was number one for decades. Still one of the most globally used names, it's got such regency charm that surprisingly it is now a rarer pick in the UK.

Miriam - 'Wished-for child'. A variant of Mary that's fallen out of use, but it has a quintessentially vintage feel.

Ruth - 'Friend'. What a gorgeous meaning, a little friend for life. Ruth is a great pick for Timelessly Tasteful namers who also love a minimalist name.

Sarah - 'Princess'. Sarah held onto its top 100 spot until 2017, but it has slowly slid to, let's say, a more unique spot on the popularity lists. Another British classic, Sarah is a bit like the Dave of baby names, we all know at least one. And I say this as a Sarah-Jayne. It's an ancient name, soft and pretty, which has led to its popularity and with no obvious nicknames, it doesn't get shortened.

BOYS

Abraham - 'Father of multitudes'. A rarer Regency name but a name that has travelled globally due to its religious roots. If it feels a bit grand for a baby, Abe is a super-sweet nickname that fits in with other modern picks.

Albion - 'White land'. One of the earliest names for Great Britain, it's thought to be named after the White Cliffs of Dover, which many people would have seen when arriving to the island.

Augustus - 'Majestic'. The middle name of the prince Regent and a modern royal name to this day, it's a quirky vintage boy name that has a sunny side.

Carew - 'Chariot'. I discovered this name on a Regency name list and love its romantic vibe that harks back to the Regency era. A traditional Welsh name, it sounds so modern yet is a real vintage gem.

Duncan - 'Dark-haired warrior'. The Scottish name Duncan is very handsome, and I can see a Regency era romantic hero perfectly suiting the name. It remained a favourite through the nineties but has fallen out of our top lists since, so it would be a rare pick for a romantic throwback name.

Ewan - 'Born from the Yew tree'. A gorgeous Scottish name that appears in Regency name listings. The nature meaning is lovely, with a Yew tree symbolizing rebirth and everlasting life.

John - 'God is gracious'. John sounds very normcore, but such a hugely favoured name around the world. The A-list celebrity whose star has only started to wane since the nineties, being overtaken in popularity by one of it's nicknames, Jack. It started as a saint's name and rode the tide of being passed down generation to generation. It has also sparked a lot of variations - Evan, Sean, Ian and more. A modern twist would be to use Jonny, which has that playful 'nickname as first name' vibe. If you want to honour a John, Jonah and Johan also add a bit of cool.

Joseph - 'He shall add'. An enduringly popular biblical name, Joseph was a well-loved pick during the Regency era.

Samuel - 'God has heard' Samuel Taylor Coleridge was a hugely popular poet writing in the Regency era. He was called the founder of the Romantic movement, believing in the power of beauty, nature, imagination and 'individualism', a new social thought about the power of the individual. A great namesake and Sam is still a laidback nickname.

Thomas - 'Twin'. I really like the name Thomas, it's got a lovely sound and great meaning as well. Tom and Tommy do some heavy lifting in the nickname department too. A classic for a reason.

NEUTRAL

Landau - 'Carriage'. A Landau is the name of the two-seater horse-drawn carriages popular during the Regency era to ride and be seen in. The original show-off's ride, the Landau was a luxury item with a fold-down hood so the passenger could enjoy being seen out and about in their finery. It's the perfect pick for historians and vehicle-lovers, but the sound jumps out at me; pronounced Lan-dow, it's such a find.

Spencer - 'Steward'. Spencer was a dominant surname during Regency times when the Earl-Spencers were a family of note. The very short female jackets worn at the time were called a Spencer Jacket after the earl. Traditionally a male name, Spencer is being registered for girls as well and has that regal nod, making it a perfect period piece.

Trousseau - 'Little bundle'. For Regency buffs, Trousseau makes a fascinating name. With its French meaning, every bride in the Regency era would collect a trousseau, a collection of the items she would wear during her wedding. I adore the sound with virtuous

'True' and a hint of 'Beau' - I'd use it as a brave middle name with a classic first name.

VICTORIAN NAMES

The Victorian era was the reigning decades of Queen Victoria, from 1837 until her death in 1901. Victorians loved names with meaning, and there was a really exciting baby name boom at the time. This could be due to the name approvals coming mainly from christening priests up until the Reformation, who loosened their strict christening rule that names had to be from the Bible. Older upper classes were shocked by a new popularity in what they called 'Romantic Names'. The new wave of names was thought to be inspired by the penny papers of the time, cheaper tabloid-style papers and books. Steam printing had made literature much more accessible, and names were being inspired by popular stories, meaning that the naming pool grew rapidly. The Victorian hipsters did us lots of name favours.

GIRLS

Adelaide - 'Noble'. Adelaide feels like such a modern girl name, but it was the middle name of Queen Victoria and Prince Albert's first daughter, who was named Victoria Adelaide after Queen Adelaide, Victoria's aunt. Queen Adelaide was renowned for her kindness and the Australian city was named after her. A truly gorgeous name with royal history, city vibes and the pretty 'a' and 'l' sounds we see all over the charts used in a refreshing way.

Alderose - 'Old rose'. A compound name used for Victorian baby girls makes such a special choice. It would be the perfect quirky middle name update for classic Rose.

Beatrice - 'Bringer of joy'. The name Beatrice seemed to trend with Victorians due to their love of Shakespeare - the name from *Much Ado About Nothing* took off, particularly as it was one of Queen

Victoria's daughter's names. A beautifully traditional name for Timelessly Tasteful namers that never loses popularity.

Clara - 'Bright or famous'. A romanticized version of Claire, the name Clara has that star quality and vintage beauty. Clara Novello might have popularized the name during the Victorian era, a famous soprano singer who sang for royalty and was the mother of Ivor Novello, the Welsh talent.

Dora - 'Gift'. The name Dora sprung into pop culture after the character in Charles Dickens' *David Copperfield*. Pronounced Door-a, I really enjoy that it sounds a bit like 'adorable' and has a strong but sweet character to it.

Dulcinea - 'Sweet'. The shortened Dulcie is a real vintage find. Taken from a French word for 'sweet', it was adapted throughout Victorian times to add the longer more romantic 'ea' ending.

Ellen - 'Light' The short form of Eleanor was a top name during the Victorian era.

Emma - 'Whole'. A loveable and elegant name, Emma's meaning of 'whole' or 'universal' is grand but beautiful in its simplicity. Emma will always be a stunning name choice for Timelessly Tasteful parents.

Ethel - 'Noble'. The name Ethel was one of the trending names of the era, used in two popular novels of the decade. It hasn't had its revival yet; but one person's dated name is another's hipster pick.

Euphemia - 'Well-spoken'. Pronounced You-Fee-Mia, the name was really popular during Victorian times, especially in Scotland. Effie is gaining its stride amongst the other vintage nicknames and the long form is so gorgeous.

Gladys - 'Princess'. One romantic name that soared during the Victorian era was Gladys, which I think is just on the right side of quirky-vintage. It's playful and unexpected. Although fighting extinction, it could fit a lot of your criteria if you're seeking a literary, vintage vibe.

Hazel - 'Reconciliation'. In the Victorian language of flowers - see my Flowers list (page 17) for more on the fascinating way Victorians communicated with flowers - Hazel was a symbol for reconciliation. They also registered names like Hazeltine and Hazeltina. Hazel brings to life that comfort of nature and warm autumn tones - a stylish choice with real beauty.

Ida - 'Hardworking'. Ida is a graceful, stunning name, famed during the Victorian era for the comic opera *Princess Ida*, which told the story of a princess who set up a women-only university and taught that women were superior to men. The opera was a huge hit, and the name soared.

Jane - 'God is gracious'. Inspired by the names Joan and Virginia came the lovely Jane. Jane Austen did gain popularity at the end of the Victorian era, but the name was already a popular girl's name passed on from the Regency era, when Jane was alive and writing. Jane has suffered a bit for being a 'plain' and simple one-syllable name that lost out to more romanticized names over the years. As half a Jane myself, Sarah-Jayne, I do like how classic the name is. Like Ann and Ruth, Jane has its place on a vintage name list.

Louisa - 'Famous warrior'. Louisa was a top name of the time. My theory around the much-debated phenomenon of why so many millennial women have the middle name Louise is how well it blends with sounds in popular first names. It's pretty 'L' sound and long vowel middle add a sparkle that parents everywhere collectively agree hits the spot. Louisa has that same ability to blend well and add some gorgeous gentle sounds to anything it's paired with.

Maud - 'Powerful in battle'. A short form of Matilda. Maud has been out of style for decades, perhaps lacking softness. However, I love a strong female name and it's time to bring back Maud. I'd use it as a sweet one-syllable middle name if you've chosen a very feminine first name. For Stand Out & Shine namers, Maud is a big tick.

Victoria - 'Victory'. The Roman goddess who became the namesake for Queen Victoria. Queen Victoria's full name was Alexandrina Victoria, but she changed it to Victoria when she took the throne. Some say it was to make a stand against her parents or to be distinct as the first Queen Victoria. We likely all know a Victoria, and Vicky was a nineties classroom staple, but don't let that put you off this gorgeous name. A bit of Posh Spice and a pinch of the Roman goddess of victory are the only ingredients needed for a strong girl name.

Winifred - 'Blessed peace or friend of peace'. The Victorians loved the whimsical nature of the name Winifred and it's a truly vintage gem, dating back even earlier. It's an anglicized version of Welsh Gwenfrewi and the story of Saint Winifred is tragic but also magical and hopeful. Beheaded by her suitor when she turned him down, she was resurrected and the place where her head fell became an important healing spring - St Winefride's Well is one of the oldest pilgrimage sites. A Welsh gem that has dropped out of the charts recently, but with Winnie ticking the vintage nickname trend and cool Freddy as an option, you would have a truly gorgeous name.

BOYS

Archibald - 'Bold'. This Scottish gem gained popularity in Victorian times and is a super-cute long form for Archie.

Arthur - 'Bear'. Queen Victoria used this cool boy's name for one of her sons. It stayed popular for decades and has recently soared up the charts again. A classic name for your baby bear. Artie is a massive selling point of the name Arthur for me, and Art would work so well for a laidback teen.

Barnabas - 'Son of Consolation'. Names ending in 's' flow so well as first or middle spots - my son's middle name is Barnaby and I love it. This name was an endearment name, historically given to people who displayed encouragement and ability to lift up those around them. It perfectly embodies my little Finn Barnaby Bo, and Barnabas is a real Trendy with a Twist name.

Benjamin - 'Son of my right hand or favourite son'. An incredibly likeable name, Ben is a classic, and Benji feels so sweet for when they are little. Your 'right hand man' is an adorable meaning from when leaders would have their second in command on their right, which was usually their strongest fighting hand. If you're a Timelessly Tasteful namer who prefers to keep things traditional with names like Jack or Felix, Benjamin should fit your list perfectly.

Emmanuel - 'God with us'. If you are drawn to long boy names like Sebastian and Nathaniel, then Emmanuel might be your vibe. Manuel is also a popular variation of this biblical name.

Harold - 'Army ruler'. The last Anglo-Saxon king of England was considered a vintage gem for hip Victorians and has literary kudos from Charles Dickens' *Bleak House*.

Henry - 'Home ruler'. This old German name was the name of many kings and was so popular that the phrase 'Tom, Dick and Harry' became slang for men in general. Harry is the colloquial version of Henry - both have stood the test of time, but Henry is more old-school and traditional. The Swedish version Henrik is my husband's name, with variations Enrique, Hendrick and Hendrix.

Herbert - 'Illustrious warrior'. Herbie and Bertie give Herbert a touch of modern edge.

Morris - 'Dark'. Morris seems to have travelled to the UK during the Norman Conquest, perhaps named after Saint Maurice. A hugely popular first name, it became a common surname as it passed through families and also gave us Morrison, son of Morris. It's a sweet and gentle Victorian name that fits into the 'surname as first name' trend.

Redvers - 'Place of rivers'. The name Redvers boomed in Victorian times after Sir Redvers Buller won the Victoria Cross, and was much celebrated at the time. The name would hit my list for sure - with its classic, vintage sound, it stands out among other whimsical nature names and ticks all the boxes for those who want to Stand Out & Shine.

Richard - 'Strong ruler'. Saint Richard is the patron saint of the poor and travellers. It's a name that has been passed through families and remained a nineties highflier when Ricky was the coolest guy on the cul-de-sac and Richard was the ultimate boy next door. It's taken a nosedive recently; Richard doesn't have as many useable nicknames as some others - yes, I'm blaming you Dick. But it will always be a classic if you're brave enough to go against the current grain.

Robert - 'Bright fame'. Robbie, Rob, Bob and Bobby have all been the backbone of British baby names, never far from a school register for decades. We all probably have associations with at least one Robert and they're all pretty cool guys. Timelessly Tasteful namers might want to take a second look at this one.

Sidney - 'Wide water meadow'. Sid has punk associations and vintage vibes, making it a trendy name that was popular in Victorian times and is just now having its comeback. Interestingly, it's also an anagram of 'Disney'.

Walter - 'Power of the army'. There were no royal Walters, but the name became popular as the Victorians enjoyed the work of Sir Walter Scott's many plays, songs and poetry. It's just edged back onto the right side of cool and makes a more unusual choice if you love William and Arthur.

NEUTRAL

Ephraim - 'Fruitful'. Biblical name Ephraim, pronounced Eff-Raym, was a romantic name loved by authors, including Dickens in the Victorian era. Traditionally male, the meaning gives bags of abundance and fertility and it works as an historic vibe name for any gender.

Florin - 'To flower'. A Florin was a coin in the Victorian era worth two shillings and one of the first coins to feature a monarch, the young Queen Victoria. The word florin was chosen for the coin due to it being the same size as a popular trade coin in Europe called *fiorino d'oro*. A truly stylish gender-neutral name - read more on Florin in my Summer Names list (see page 43).

Whitby - 'White farm'. Whitby in North Yorkshire was a popular holiday destination during Victorian times when the railway opened and it became a hotspot for the upper class to visit. Whitby still has many Victorian museums and links to iconic Victorian novel *Dracula* where Bram Stoker's dark tale tells of his infamous character alighting in Whitby. A brilliant Victorian-inspired name for Stand Out & Shine namers.

ROARING TWENTIES NAMES

World War One had ended in 1918 and ushered in an amazing decade of change and push-back from young people who were against the traditional roles of the Victorian times. The 1920s was the time of jazz, Art Deco and silent movies. The Suffragettes had paved the way for women to vote for the first time, and this explosion of girl power bought a huge fashion change. Flappers were teenage girls who thankfully ripped off the corsets and wore their hair in a bob. Knee-length skirts replaced longer dresses and makeup was piled on with the invention of metal lipstick containers and powder compacts. It was also an exciting time in the US when Black artists, musicians, sports stars and writers were gaining huge followings during the Harlem Renaissance. There was a cultural revival of African-American dance and music styles that were widely popular and celebrated Black life and art. The names were just as fun and spirited.

GIRLS

Ada - 'Noble'. Ada, pronounced Ay-Da, was one of the most popular names of the 1920s. A shortened form of Victorian Adelaide. This vintage gem soared up the charts as our fastest-rising girl name at the beginning of 2020 - it's firmly having its 100-year revival and is perfect if you're after that classic name with a bit of spice.

Audrey - 'Noble strength'. Similar in beauty to super-popular Olivia and Amelia, Audrey has a 1920s glam. Audrey Hepburn was born in the 1920s, though she wouldn't rise to fame until much later, but this name will never go out of style.

Baby - 'Sweetheart, newborn'. Teresa 'Baby' Jungman was the It girl of the 1920s. Part of the crowd of young aristocrats who threw the best parties, she was the unrequited love of Evelyn Waugh and inspired a lot of teens of the time. I love how she went by Baby, due to being the youngest of the family. The name has become a very rare and probably unadvisable first name, but we know nobody puts baby in a corner and perhaps it's right up your street.

Bessie - 'God is my oath'. Bessie Smith was a headliner and 'Queen of the Blues' during the 1920s. Bessie has that star quality - a variant of Elizabeth with the echo of a music icon behind it, the perfect name.

Betty - 'God is my oath'. The iconic Betty Boop was a cartoon character based on the fashion of the Flappers. The name Betty is a variant of Elizabeth and was a popular name for teens of the era, inspiring the character. Super-playful and outgoing.

Coco - 'Darling'. The origin of the name Coco is varied with some saying it comes from cocoa and some from Greek Kleio, but I like it being the French endearment word for 'darling'. Gabrielle 'Coco' Chanel was the fashion icon of the 1920s and is synonymous with the name. Today it stands out amongst other vintage gems and will always make you smile.

Evelyn - 'Life'. The name Evelyn has so many variations to its meaning. Broken down, it means 'life lake' but some branches of the name date back to Germanic gem Aveline, meaning either 'hazelnut' or 'bird'. Evelyn is one of the true unisex names. Notable author Evelyn Waugh married a woman named Evelyn. Evelina is my daughter's name, and both these names were considered lower class during Victorian times - undesirable 'romantic' names from novels that eventually boomed in popularity during the golden twenties and sound beautiful today.

Florence - 'Flourishing'. Florence Mills is known for her perfect flapper bob; a huge part of the Harlem Renaissance, her story is so uplifting. Due to her talent for comedy, she was dubbed in theatres 'the Queen of Happiness'.

Gloria - 'Glory'. Gloria Swanson reigns as one of the stars of 1920s cinema. With so many 'ia' ending names getting a lot of use, unusual Gloria would make a brilliant Trendy with a Twist name.

Josephine - 'Increases'. Josephine Baker was the Black dancer and performer who epitomized the 1920s scene in Paris, moving from America to perform across Paris. Her dances and costumes became iconic symbols of the roaring twenties. The first black actress to star in a silent movie, Josephine is a true trailblazer, spying on the Nazi's during performances in Paris and returning to America where she forced venues not to segregate audiences. The name meaning stands out and I adore nickname Josie and quirky Finn for a modern Josephine who will love the story of her famous namesake.

Loelia - 'Night'. It's hard to find a unique 'L' name for girls, as most are flying high in the charts, but 1920s aristocrat Loelia Lindsay is a fascinating namesake. Loelia was a true bohemian with a love for gardening and needlework and she was a writer for *Homes & Gardens* magazine. Married twice, once with Winston Churchill as best man, she was a leading lady of the 1920s and her name has star quality for any little girl today.

Sunday - 'Sun goddess'. Sunday Wilshin was a 1920s British actress who started out in the West End as a child and became an executive in film and radio. She was christened Sundae Mary, which is also a pretty spelling and name pairing. I adore the name Sunday and it feels full of the glamour and freedom of that time.

Zelda - 'Battle maid'. From Griselda, the name of F. Scott Fitzgerald's wife, who was known as the first American flapper.

Zita - 'Seeker'. Zita Jungman was a well-known socialite of the 1920s with a fantastic first name. The name is just so ready for revival, it's got that lovely Virtue meaning and is super unique.

Zora - 'Dawn'. Zora Neale Hurston was a leading writer during the Harlem Renaissance, writing short satires about her experiences as an African-American woman. Hurston would later go on to write the pivotal novel *Their Eyes Were Watching God*. Zora's Harlem apartment was a meeting place for change makers and artists of the 1920s, a truly inspiring and trail-blazing name to give your little girl.

BOYS

Anthony - 'Praiseworthy'. While Anthony hits the popularity lists, Tony was the street name made iconic by the mobsters in America in the 1920s.

Barry - 'Fair haired'. The name Barry, also spelt Barrie, was in high use in the 1920s. Originally a Gaelic name from the name Finbar, which I love the idea of using with the nickname Finn. It's a brave choice but could hit the high notes if you're after a retro name.

Bugsy - 'Crazy'. The mobster nickname for Benjamin Siegel was taken from the street term for someone a little . . . short tempered. While the mobster may not be a likely namesake, the name is so iconic from the movie *Bugsy Malone* set in the 1920s. I'd use it as a nickname for a name like Barnaby.

Cecil - 'Six'. Cecil Beaton was a truly cool photographer working for *Vogue* by the end of the 1920s after kicking up a storm in London with the fash pack of the time. He later became an actor and costume designer on Broadway. The name hasn't had its fashion comeback, but I personally think it's so cool.

Chaplin - 'Clergyman'. Charlie Chaplin was a leading man with many of his most iconic movies made in the 1920s. British-born Chaplin is said to have one of the most dramatic rags-to-riches stories ever, growing up in the workhouse and leaving school at 13 years old to pursue his career as an actor. He eventually founded United Artists and produced his own silent movies. The name will always be associated with his style.

Claude - 'Lame'. The meaning is shared with Claudia from Roman Emperor Claudius who had an unknown disability. Claude McKay was a prominent Jamaican-American writer in the 1920s and the name has that artistic vibe.

Daniel - 'God is my judge'. A classic name that was riding high in the 1920s, Danny makes a great nickname.

Duke - 'Leader'. Duke Ellington was the greatest jazz player of the era. With residencies at the iconic Cotton Club in Harlem, Duke created the sound of the decade that we still love. The name is very cool, perhaps more often a pet name, let's be honest, but these title names are having an upswing in the charts and you couldn't get a better namesake.

Gerald - 'Ruler of the spear'. Gerald has quite a strong and imposing name meaning for such a gentle sounding name. It's not been in vogue for a while - Jerry as a short form feels right out of the 1920s, but Gerald would make a classic, retro name choice for your little boy.

Langston - 'Tall man'. Langston Hughes was at the forefront of the Harlem Renaissance, writing about Black lives and reaching new audiences collaborating with the jazz musicians on the Harlem scene. The name Langston has great spirit and fits the 'surname as first name' trend with a game-changing namesake.

Louis - 'Famed warrior'. Pronounced Lou-Ee with a silent 's' at the end, renowned musician Louis Armstrong's career exploded in the 1920s bringing so many much-loved songs into the world. The name has so much history and Armstrong brings some musical edge to this vintage classic.

Terence - 'Soft, smooth'. What a brilliant name meaning for the perfect 1920s vibe for your little Terence.

Vincent - 'Prevailing'. Vincent has a real retro cool, and I defy anyone not to love cute nickname Vinnie for their baby boy.

NEUTRAL

Bailey - 'Berry clearing'. I've always really liked the name Bailey, it's got a nature feel and works as a delightful gender-neutral name. Mary Bailey was one of the greatest aviators of the 1920s the first woman to fly solo across the Irish Sea and completing so many record-breaking flights during the era. A lush namesake and Stand Out & Shine name.

Gatsby - 'Companion'. *The Great Gatsby* was published in 1925; set in Long Island, it's the quintessential 1920s tale. The lead character James Gatsby took his name from Gatz, meaning 'companion'. It makes such an edgy and literary cool name; I once heard it on a little girl and have never forgotten it.

Trilby - 'Sings with trills'. I absolutely love the meaning of Trilby. Trilby hats had become a favoured fashion choice in the 1920s and the name feels so of the era. It sounds upbeat as a name and would make a brilliant choice if you love 1920's style.

NINETIES NAMES

It was the era that gave us Nirvana, *Friends*, The Spice Girls and Harry Potter. If you wanted to access the internet it would take a while to get your modem started, but there was an explosion of influences, and everyone picked sides. It was the decade of grunge, hip hop, girl power and Brit pop and you couldn't like them all. I was lucky enough to grow up covering my walls with *Smash Hits* posters and watching MTV when I wanted to pretend I cared about anything other than if Take That might one day be performing at 'nappy night' in Cairo's nightclub Swindon.

Names had their own shake-up in the charts as parents were influenced by TV, travel and of course the world wide web. The nineties saw the start of 'fast fashion' names, some of which have almost become extinct today. But choosing a nineties name for your baby is on the rise, alongside checked shirts and velvet chokers, so get in there early for a fashion-forward nineties revival.

GIRLS

Amy - 'Beloved'. Amy gets overlooked when flicking through name lists, but stop and sit with it for a while. With its unfussy prettiness, if you're after a traditional and timeless name with a lovely meaning, list Amy.

Claire - 'Clear'. A staple through the eighties and nineties, this French name was super-in vogue. It's also got a spiritual side with a 'Clare' being someone who can see or hear clear messages from beyond our realm of consciousness. It's a stylish pick with special meaning if you love to explore spirituality.

Gemma - 'Precious jewel'. I see Gemma on a lot of name lists recently - it's got a classic style that gets a bit overlooked. See the Crystals, Rocks & Minerals list for more gemstone name ideas (page 75).

Hayley - 'Hay field'. Hayley was the girl next door in the nineties. It's since become less common, but with a lovely nature meaning, Hayley feels happy and fun.

Jessica - 'To behold'. Invented by Shakespeare, the name Jessica came from seemingly nowhere to dominate the playgrounds of the nineties. Jessie or Jess gave a bit of variety to the pretty name. If you can get past any associations you might have, the name is a fantastic three-syllable beauty.

Jodie - 'God will increase'. From Joseph came Jude and Jodie. Jodie is used for any gender, and I adore the strong 'o' sound.

Katie - 'Pure'. From the name Catherine, Katie or Kate feel like the quintessential girl next door names and Katie has stood the test of time for a reason. We all know a Katie and maybe overlook it for that reason, but it's a stunner.

Kelly - 'Bright-headed'. An old Celtic surname and frequent place name in Scotland, Kelly became the ultimate girl name in the nineties.

Kimberly - 'Royal fortress'. Kimberley was originally a place name in Old English before being given as a first name. It was always a unisex name but feels a lot more feminine nowadays. Sadly in decline since it's nineties heyday, Kimberly is a cool name with a strong meaning that's due a revival.

Kirsty - 'Follower of Christ'. A short form of Christopher, Christina, Kirsten and Kirsty are unexpected choices these days and Kirsty is nearly extinct. So, if you want a rare name, Kirsty could be perfect and I love Kit as a nickname.

Lauren - 'Laurel tree'. Lauren was a modern twist on Laura and the meaning is so pretty. In ancient Greek myths, palaces were made of Laurel trees and in Roman times, Laurel wreaths were worn as crowns to symbolize victory. The symbol carries on and it's why we use the term 'Poet Laureate'. The nineties girl-next-door could be a winning name with cute Ren as a nickname for your little one.

Natalie - 'Day of birth or Christmas'. From the Latin *Natale Domini* meaning 'Birth of the Lord', the names Natalie and Natalia were nineties classics.

Nicole - 'Victory'. The name Nicola and Nicole date back to ancient Greece and the God Nike. It's a great sporty choice if you want a vibrant classic that would now be unique.

Rebecca - 'To tie together'. Rebecca hit the top spot for the first time in the mid-nineties. Becky was a perky nickname that didn't feel as traditional as the other variants of the name passed on through the last few decades. But Bebe or Cece stand out as more modern nicknames for now.

Sophie - 'Wisdom'. You'll never tire of the name Sophie, it is a classic for a reason, a real beauty of a name with a soulful meaning to match.

Stephanie - 'Crown or garland'. Stephanos was the origin of feminine form Stephanie. The name was originally considered very aristocratic, then it boomed into popular use, peaking in the nineties. Nowadays it's less common for newborns, but would make a lovely choice if you're a Timelessly Tasteful namer.

Zoe - 'Life'. An elegant and strong name, Zoe has ancient Greek roots with its meaning, but became popular during the nineties. Today it still stands out with the lively 'Z' initial adding an edgy, fun feel.

BOYS

Adam - 'Earth'. Also translated as simply 'man' after the biblical first man. Adam is an eternal classic that never falls out of popularity.

Alexander - 'Defender or warrior'. Alexander the Great is a namesake worth having - the Greek King, tutored by Aristotle, who created one of the largest empires in history. With trendy Alex and Xander as nicknames, it's no wonder this name has remained popular.

Bradley - 'Broad meadow'. An Irish surname with an expansive nature meaning, it's now become a super-trendy first name.

Christopher - 'Bearer of Christ'. There were a lot of babies named Chris born in the nineties - it's a beautiful name that unfortunately has become a bit overlooked, but that does make it a rare gem for a newborn.

Daniel - 'God is my judge'. From the Old Testament, Daniel and its feminine counterpart Danielle would have been hard to dodge in a nineties maternity ward. Still in our top 100 names, Daniel is a traditional name with a very distinct sound that Timelessly Tasteful parents will love.

Jack - 'God is gracious'. From the name John, Jack became the less formal version that gives a perfect one-syllable, playful first name. Wildly popular, Jack was huge in the nineties and remains near the top end of the name charts.

James - 'Supplanter'. A strange name meaning, originally it also meant 'One who grabs the heel' from the biblical namesake Jacob who was born holding his twin's heel. It developed into meaning 'to follow' or 'supplant'. A gorgeous name that never goes out of style and has been adapted across the world. Iago in Welsh, Kimo in Hawaiian, Seamus in Irish, Giacomo in Italian. If you're honouring a James, you're in luck.

Joshua - 'The lord is salvation'. Joshua is a wonderful sounding name, with Josh feeling on the edgy side of traditional.

Jordan - 'To flow'. With its gorgeous meaning and the inevitable link to the river of the same name, Jordan sounds fresh and modern and full of nature.

Luke - 'Light-giving'. Biblical Luke was everywhere in the nineties, it's got a cool edginess to it, being short and strong in sound, and the meaning feels so powerful for a little one who will be the light of your life.

Matthew - 'Gift of God'. In the nineties, every friendship group had a Matt or two or three. Like Dave, it became a kind of 'everyman' name, but it's fallen out of popularity due to being so overused, which could be your sign to snap up this nineties trending name before your friends do.

Michael - 'Who is like God'. One of the archangels, Michael is a strong boy name that still gets a lot of use since its heyday in the nineties. Michael appears across many religions as Angel of Mercy. The name is endlessly nicknamed with Mike, Mikey, Micah and Mickey, so I'd pick your preferred one fast before his friends do.

Ryan - 'Little king'. This Irish surname has ancient roots but feels very modern, having become a bit of a pop culture staple.

NEUTRAL

Cameron - 'Crooked river'. Whether it's nineties star Cameron Diaz or James Cameron, director of the biggest grossing movie of the decade *Titanic*, Cameron was part of the culture and it's a shame it's fallen by the wayside as a name. I love that it gives you Ronnie as a nickname too, and it feels like a perfect gender-neutral gem.

Firby - 'Farm settlement'. If you want to be super-playful, it's fun to look at some of the icons of the nineties, like the Furby - an iconic electronic toy that sparked a craze when released in 1998. While it was so-called for looking like a ball of fur, the name existed as surname Firby way before. So, a classic name with a large dose of nineties nostalgia for those who want quirkiness with a big pinch of retro.

Levi - 'To join'. If you can't get enough of your Levi 501's, the nineties fashion staple was as big back then with the adverts being some of the most iconic of the decade. Levi was a popular name but dated a little. However, with the trendy 'v' sound and nineties revival in full swing, it could be your Stand Out & Shine name. Its meaning of 'to join' or 'connect' is extra special when thinking about your growing family.

WHEN TO SHARE YOUR BABY NAME

One big consideration many people overlook when it comes to picking a baby name is to share or not to share? It's totally personal, but it's worth considering the pros and cons of announcing your chosen name early, asking for opinions or going full secret squirrel.

I am always on the side of keeping your name secret until the baby is born. In my experience, when someone hears a name, they love to give their opinion on it, whether asked for or not. And even though logically you don't care that they sat next to a Felix at school, and he was horrible or that they know two dogs called Stella, a negative story can really dent your confidence in the name you've picked. Also, you could do a swerve once the baby arrives. I was so sure I was going with the name Oskar with my first baby, but then I just looked at him and knew he was Freddie - if I'd got the printed nursery plaque and personalized clothes, I may not have felt I could make that change. So, it's important to consider.

If you choose to keep it private and someone asks you the names you're considering, a polite, 'I'm still thinking about names' is all you need to give them. Then once they're here looking so adorable, people are far less likely to give a negative name comment, as unsurprisingly Felix from Heathside Primary Tadpole class 1996 suddenly doesn't spring to mind when they're gazing at your gorgeous newborn.

It's totally personal and I was lucky enough to know lots of expectant parents when I was choosing my firstborn's name. Some would refer to their bump or scan by the name they'd picked really early on and found it super bonding with their unborn child to be already using the name, rather than saying 'the baby'. I've also known people announce their baby's name to other expectant friends early doors to make sure they've laid claim to the name. Which could work but could also backfire, as for some, nothing makes a name more tempting than being told you can't use it. Read more about the true crime that is Baby Name Stealing on page 322.

If you want to try out a name to test pronunciation and spelling, you can always drop it into conversation. A friend of mine wanted to check if her foreign family would pronounce the name Neve properly; she had the genius idea of getting them to talk about the actress Neve Campbell who they promptly all called Nev, confirming her suspicion they didn't know it was a long 'e'. She opted for pretty Neeva instead.

Whichever approach feels most natural to you, do consider the pros and cons, and if you're naming as a couple, get on board together so neither of you let slip.

SOUNDS & SYLLABLES

Throughout this book you'll often hear me talk about the sound or flow of a name. That's incredibly important when creating a list of names you love. You may naturally fall into loving longer names with interesting sounds or gravitate to the shorter, one-syllable names which have a simplicity of style. If you have a long surname, you may want to balance it and vice versa. It also reflects your style – longer names are often louder and bolder with lots of consonants or can be whimsical and flowy, ending in extra vowels. Shorter names can be bold and punchy and give a laidback and unshowy vibe while still being gorgeous. Here I explore all sounds and syllables, so you can explore what most befits you and your babe.

MAXIMALIST NAMES

I'm a total maximalist. I love a pattern and if there's a pattern clash in an outfit that works in a way I wouldn't have thought of, I'm screenshotting that and recreating it. The aesthetic is sometimes called 'more is more' and it appears across art, interior design, fashion and music. To my tastes, a name with contrasting sounds and plenty of syllables is the catwalk of baby name style, and for those drawn to the longer, more complex names, this list has plenty to pick from.

GIRLS

Atarah - 'Crown'. Pronounced A-Tara, a lesser-known biblical name, it has bags of elegance and its strong sounds make it fit its regal meaning.

Amaryllis - 'To sparkle'. So well known as the flower, Ama means 'loveable' and this name has its own vibrancy and is achingly cool. So deserving of a spot on your name list, it will turn heads and so will she.

Angharad - 'Much loved'. This Welsh girl name pronounced Ann-Ha-Rad feels like a vintage blend of Ann and Harriet to me. So unique, Angharad was the partner of Percival in the legend of King Arthur. See the section on Names Meaning 'Loved' for more (page 143).

Cassiopeia - 'Cassia juice'. Cassia is similar to cinnamon, but the name is best known as a constellation formed by five great stars, so pretty. Pronounced Cassio-Pee-A, she was a Greek Goddess known for her beauty, so if you favour long girl names, then this should hit the spot. See Star Names for more similar constellation-inspired baby names.

Ceridwen - 'Poetry or song'. Ceridwen is a Welsh name and she was the goddess of poetry, inspiration and the cauldron of transfiguration. With its lyrical sound and meaning, it's pronounced Care-Id-Wen.

Delphinia - 'Dolphin'. Delphi is such a pretty nickname. It was a place the ancient Greeks considered the centre of the world. A stunning name for the little lady who will be at the centre of yours. Super-wearable, she's got style and doesn't follow the trends. A true Stand Out & Shine name choice.

Dorothea - 'Gift of God'. My lovely niece is called Summer Dorothea Rose, and we use all three names whenever we can. Dorothea is so stylish, the 'a' ending makes it sound more edgy than original Dorothy. To me it's got that hip style, perfect for a bright and vibrant maximalist aesthetic.

Eulalia - 'Well-spoken'. Pronounced You-Lay-Le-Ah. So maximalist, but soft with the 'l' sounds, it's the ideal name for this vibe.

Serendipity - 'Unexpected good fortune'. The poster girl for the hippy Virtue names, it's so long and special I had to include it here.

Theodosia - 'Divine gift'. The feminine form of Theodore, it's so pretty with its ending pronounced 'sha' vs 'seea'. Plus you get Teddi as a nickname, which I've always loved so much for girls.

BOYS

Abdullah - 'Servant of God'. An Arabic classic, enduringly popular Abdullah will never go out of style.

Aldemar - 'Nobleman'. Pronounced Al-De-Mar. This Hungarian name was a term of honour, to be esteemed or noble. I adore the flow of Aldemar - it hasn't been widely used, so feels unique and ideal if you have Hungarian roots.

Apollonia - 'Belonging to Apollo'. Apollonia was an ancient Greek trading city. It's such a grand name that matches the vibes of this historic city founded in 600 BC. I love how bold and fearless it is.

Aurelio/Aurelius - 'Golden'. The name of the Roman Emperor, Aurelius is an opulent and sleek baby name with a touch of glamour from its gold meaning.

Beauregard - 'A beautiful view'. An old French surname with a stunning meaning. Beau is such a popular short form and he will always be your most beautiful view.

Elijah - 'My God is Yahweh'. Elijah is such an interesting and attractive name to say and looks lovely on paper. In the bible Elijah was both a prophet and miracle worker, a classic name with a lot of charm.

Ezekiel - 'Strength of God'. One of my name crushes that's rising in use, Ezekiel is an Old Testament name adding a bit of hip to the charts. Pronounced Ee-Zee-Key-Ul, Zeke is the common nickname. If you love Noah, maybe bounce onto Ezekiel for biblical style that is much more unique.

Galileo - 'From Galilee'. The astronomer makes this name well-known, so maximalist, so bohemian - you're already singing when you hear this name.

Lysander - 'Liberator'. A Shakespeare character from *A Midsummer Night's Dream* and Luna Lovegood's son in the Harry Potter books. It's already familiar from the play and sounds sophisticated, but you could shorten it to Scandinavian Anders.

Maximus - 'Greatest'. The poster name for this list with its meaning of 'greatest'. Originally a title given to warriors and gladiators who were the biggest and the best, Maximus is such a fun and cool name.

Oleander - 'Evergreen tree'. I adore this maximalist twist on Oliver, pronounced Olly-Ander. The Oleander plant is poisonous, so it's got a bit of bite as well.

Ozias - 'Salvation'. This ancient name with spiritual meaning is a truly unique but really on-trend name for Stand Out & Shine namers.

Phineas - 'Bronze-coloured'. Pronounced Finn-E-As, Hebrew Phineus has multiple meanings, 'serpent's mouth' included. A noteworthy name, I have a little Finn myself, but Phineas gives me a lot of Baby Name Envy.

Zephaniah - 'God has hidden'. An Old Testament boy name, Zephaniah feels so trendy with it's awesome 'Z beginning. I love the sound of this four-syllable name, Zeff-en-eye-ah - it's both gorgeous and grand.

NEUTRAL

Calico - 'Multicoloured'. Calico is a type of fabric that is often printed with bright colours and patterns. For artistic flair and a bold statement, the name Calico sounds spot-on for a colourful unisex name.

Prisma - 'Prism'. Prisma isn't historically a name, but a Latin word for a prism we know reflects light into a multicoloured rainbow. It's an illumination and gives that maximalist style of bright colours all wrapped up in an eye-catching name.

Tintin - 'Bells ringing'. I know a Swedish Tintin and as soon as I heard it I loved with how adventurous and daring it was. Synonymous with the comic book character, the word originates from maximalist 'tintinnabulation' - which means 'the sound of bells ringing'. I love how loud it is as a meaning and name.

MINIMALIST NAMES

The love of simple forms and function is known to help us relax, think and clear a cluttered mind, plus it has an extreme beauty. My husband is Swedish and he's a to-the-core minimalist. A minimalist

name uses less syllables and simple sounds which create a laid-back elegance and are never dull. This name guide has a perfect blend of interest and simplicity. See what names spring out at you here. They're not just one-syllable names, but are elegant, timeless and understated with that pared-back cool.

GIRLS

Alma - 'Soul'. Spanish Alma is vintage without being retro and so stylish. It has a simplicity but makes an impact with its beautiful meaning.

Anais - 'Merciful' Pronounced A-Nay, the 's' is silent, but some parents choose to use it. It's a name that has bags of style and feels like it belongs in a high-end store. If that's where you're shopping for a name, I'll ring it up for you.

Cosima - 'Beauty in order'. The name Cosima seems to sum up the minimalist trend in its meaning - the beauty of everything being functional and in its place. It's a long name with every syllable short and sweet.

Emma - 'Whole'. A timeless classic, Emma oozes pared-back style. Never out of fashion, Emma is an investment piece for Timelessly Tasteful namers.

Eve - 'Source of life'. This stunningly simple name seems to get less recognition than loads of more complex biblical variations of it. A charming classic.

Faye - 'Fairy'. The name Faye is simple, chic and timeless. Its meaning of 'fairy' is one that a lot of parents will love for their little baby, but in Old French it also means 'loyalty', which is equally lovely. A bit of a forgotten gem.

Isla - 'Island'. A Scottish name originally referring to the beauty of Scotland, Isla is a charming and spirited name that's sweetly elegant and simple too.

Lena - 'Light'. Pronounced Lee-Nah, this gentle girl name doesn't fade into the background but draws attention. I adore 'L' names, as they always sound soft and whimsical and Lena makes a unique pick.

Naomi - 'Pleasant'. Super-stylish and gaining popularity, it's got high-fashion kudos and is a biblical name that suits a lifestyle of simple elegance.

BOYS

Arlo - 'Fortified hill'. Arlo is a trendy short name that nonetheless has a lovely flow to it and makes a really cool nature-inspired name.

Beau - 'Beauty'. If you love a minimalist style and find beauty in simplicity, Beau feels like the perfect name. A French boy name, it works for girls too.

Eli - 'Elevated'. I love the uplifting meaning of Eli, and it really is a special name for being so straight forward. Pronounced Ee-Ly, it's a perfect example of how much impact a minimalist name can have.

Elon - 'Oak tree'. Short, sweet simplicity with that lovely nature meaning and appealing sound.

Fife - 'Pipe'. A Scottish place name, but also the name of a medieval flute. I love the sounds and it perfectly balances a longer surname. Folky and gentle, see more instrument names in my Music list (page 166).

Joel - 'Lord'. Joel is a one-syllable name that looks so pretty on paper. It's soft to say like Noah, and it's not fussy. My gorgeous nephew is called Joel and he's full of character and love - an understated name that will always be treasured.

Jude - 'Praised'. Jude's one-syllable style is so strong. It has a fashionable fresh vibe despite it being an ancient name.

Keir - 'Dark'. Irish Keir packs a punch with its characterful meaning and strong sound.

Oscar - 'God's spear'. Oscar is an adorable name that will grow with your son, with the lovely Ossie as a short form. Its literary link to Oscar Wilde is a bonus, plus if you love the world of film, it's got the cute nod to the Oscars (allegedly after a remark that the statue looked like someone's Uncle Oscar). I was 100 per cent hooked on the name Oscar for my first baby but then swerved to Freddie when I met him. I always feel this is my 'one that got away', so snap up the award for best name with Oscar.

Otto - 'Wealth'. Rich with history throughout Germany and Scandinavia, Otto is playful and fun and really stands out for its upbeat, cute sound.

Reed - 'Red hair'. What a sweet name meaning. I love the nature connotations too with minimalist reeds of grass, and for music lovers there's also reeds in many woodwind instruments. Unique, unusual and minimalistic at its core.

Soren - 'Stern'. A Danish boy name, Soren is a quiet crush of mine and is rising quietly in popularity. Søren Kierkegaard is a Danish philosopher who was famous for writing about existence.

NEUTRAL

Drew - 'Strong'. A Hollywood star of a name, this one-syllable moniker is a lovely modernization of Andrew.

Folke - 'Chief'. Pronounced Foll-Kar, it's a traditionally Danish male name which also means 'protector of the folk', and I love that it is so unique in meaning and sound.

Lane - 'Passage'. Lane has a bit of glamour while retaining a simplicity. It reminds me of going off the beaten path in a beautiful city to find a local restaurant where the food is pared back and delicious. Lane has personality and is perfect as a gender-neutral name.

FOUR-SYLLABLE NAMES

A long name is a great pairing to a short or common surname and gives your child multiple nickname options.

GIRLS

Alexandra - 'Protector'. A classic, sophisticated name, Alexandra has been worn by royals since ancient times and is reminiscent of Alexandra the Great in Greek history.

Amariah - 'Said of God'. Pronounced a-mar-iyah, this Hebrew name is a rare alternative to Amelia or Olivia.

Amarillys - 'To sparkle'. To sparkle or shine, a floral name that is so lyrical and evocative it really works with the meaning and will always Stand out & Shine.

Ariadne - 'Most Holy'. Ariadne was the princess of Crete who saved Theseus from the Minotaur in the Greek myth - what a cool, strong female namesake. Pronounced Arry-Ad-Nee.

Aurelia - 'Golden'. Aurelia was a Roman surname that's become a popular first name for girls. It has such a stunning, flowing beauty written on the page and once heard, it's never forgotten.

Evangeline - 'Bringer of good news'. From the Greek for getting great tidings, what name could be more perfect for your newborn baby girl arriving into the world.

Evelina - 'Light or life'. My daughter's name, pronounced Ever-Lee-Nah. It's whimsical and pretty and as soon as I heard it, I banked it for if I ever had a baby girl. Our children are the light of our lives and I always get complimented on her name.

Dorothea - 'Gift of God'. This delightful name stems from Theodore, the name of a couple of saints and my lovely niece's middle spot. Such a gorgeous and unforgettable name, Dorothea was the patron saint of gardeners and you'll often see her depicted with a garland of flowers.

Eliana - 'God has answered'. Pronounced Elly-Ah-Nah. A distinctive and whimsical name, long but not overly fussy, Eliana makes a great spin on the more traditional Emily and Anna, for Trendy with a Twist parents who want an elevated classic.

Felicity - 'Happiness'. The goddess of good luck and happiness, *felicitas* was the Latin word for joy and good fortune, a wonderful sentiment to pass on to your baby through this stunning name.

Isabella - 'Devoted to God'. A variation of Elizabeth, the name Isabella will always feature heavily in the charts for its light, pretty sound and the beautiful Bella ending.

Mariposa - 'Butterfly'. Of Spanish origin, this sweet name gives a huge sense of freedom with its 'butterfly' or 'moth' meaning. I would use Posy as a nickname.

Olivia - 'Peace'. Olivia has become a modern classic staying in the charts for decades and topping them for many years with its understated charm. The peaceful meaning comes from the Olive tree and the Olive branch being a symbol of peace.

Ophelia - 'Help'. Gaining popularity in recent years this Shakespearean classic from *Hamlet* is stunning to look at and to speak out loud.

Raphaella - 'God has healed'. I'd use the nickname Raffy, but you could go with Ella. The meaning alone makes me want to list this trendy name for its gentle healing energy.

Seraphina - 'Fiery one'. The name of the highest order of Angels, it is just as grand and luminous as its meaning.

Tatiana - 'Fairy queen'. Created by Shakespeare, it's thought he was inspired by her strength as a daughter of the Titans and he came up with the name for the Queen of the Fairies for his play *A Midsummer Night's Dream*.

Tigerlily - 'Flower'. A daring floral name, Tigerlily is colourful, effervescent and memorable.

Victoria - 'Victory'. An elegant investment piece of a name that never goes out of style. Less popular than it was in the nineties your little girl could be the only Victoria in her class.

Valentina - 'Strong'. With a huge link to vitality and strength, I adore the vibe that Valentina brings. Linked to Saint Valentine, it's a name that celebrates love and is easy to fall for.

BOYS

Alabaster - 'Crossbow'. An occupational name for someone who made crossbows, it makes a bold name choice but feels like a mix of Alastair and Sebastian which makes it really wearable.

Alexander - 'Defender or warrior'. A fourth-century king, Alexander has stood the test of time as a punchy and powerful classic. The name came from a verb meaning 'to defend', an evocative meaning for a baby you'll always be fiercely protective over.

Bartholomew - 'Ploughman'. A stand-out name, Bartholomew has countryside vibes in its meaning wrapped up in an impressive yet flowing name.

Emilio - 'Rival'. The surname of an influential Roman family, the name is popular in Europe and has a cool mix of sounding soft with the vowel beginning and popular 'o' ending, but also sounding a bit fierce with 'lio' meaning 'lion'.

Emmanuel - 'God with us'. Gentle sounding Emmanuel has been enduringly popular. For a long name it doesn't sound complex - just the opposite, as it flows so beautifully.

Fitzwilliam - 'Son of William'. Fitzwilliam is such a mouthful of a name, in a good way. Fitz is old Norman denoting a son. It's striking but playful and would make an especially good choice if you're honouring a beloved William.

Horatio - 'Timekeeper'. The Italian version of Latin Horatius, Horatio has retained its popularity as Horace increasingly fell out of favour.

Montgomery - 'Mountain'. Timelessly Tasteful namers will enjoy Montgomery. It balances a shorter name as a combo and gives modern Monty as a nickname.

Nathanial - 'God has given'. The nickname Nate makes this high on my list of long names for little boys.

Sebastian - 'Revered'. A classic boy name, I love the short form Seb or Bastian is also super trendy.

Zachariah - 'God remembers'. There was a time when every popular boy in a nineties TV show was called Zack. The cool mum's alternative to Jack perhaps, Zachariah in its full form has that maximalist cool.

Zebadiah - 'God has bestowed'. I love the ending of Zebadiah, with its unusual 'iah' sound it's truly special and memorable.

NEUTRAL

Alessio - 'Defender'. Alessio has that popular 'o' ending that updates this Greek name to something that sounds really on-trend and works for any gender.

Azariah - 'Helped by God'. This biblical name feels right up-to-date with the strong 'z'. Traditionally masculine it makes a Stand Out & Shine name that works perfectly as a unisex option.

Domenico - 'Lord'. Often given to babies born on a Sunday in the Roman Catholic faith, Domenico is one of my favourite maximalist sounds with the strong letters giving it star quality. Short form Dom packs the same punch.

ONE-SYLLABLE NAMES

Perfect as middle spots as well as stunning first names, one-syllable names stand strong and really complement a long, complex surname.

GIRLS

Blair - 'Plain or meadow'. This is a nature name that sounds like it belongs in a chic capital city. Originally a Scottish surname, Blair has travelled far and wide and made it onto a lot of contemporary girl name lists.

Dot - 'God's Gift'. Your cute little dot will soon be in your arms and it's a lovely term of endearment name that makes a super-vintage first name.

Fleur - 'Flower'. The French word for flower, it was often given as a name by French nobility, as it was associated with elegance and grace, traits it still holds today. Simple but stylish Fleur ticks all the boxes.

Maeve - 'Intoxicating'. This Irish girl name is one of the newly recycled vintage names making a comeback in the name charts. The soft-sounding 'v' at the end is enduringly beautiful, and the intoxicating meaning draws you in.

Nell - 'Shining light'. Short for Helen or Eleanor, Nell is so charming and down to earth. Such a happy name that shines strongly in line with its meaning.

Neve - 'Snow'. From the Latin word for snow, Neve is often loved for winter babies. Traditionally Irish and often spelt Niamh, it's pronounced Nee-ve. It has a crisp, stunning sound and quite magical meaning.

Tess - 'To harvest'. From Teresa, Tess has an old-world feel and earthy roots with its meaning 'to harvest'. It's a sunny name also meaning 'summer', so its upbeat charm would suit anyone looking for an underused vintage classic.

BOYS

Ash - 'Fortunate or happy'. The Ash tree was a tree of protection and good luck, and the name is a popular short form for Ashley or Ashton. My children love it for the Pokémon character Ash, so it's well-loved by kids and grown ups alike.

Beau - 'Beautiful'. This French name is so simple but stunning. I enjoy how modern it feels, yet with a whimsical vibe from its meaning.

Finn - 'Fair'. A very sweet boy name I chose for my second son. It's got a lot of spirit and substance for such a short name. Although simple, it never sounds dull, and it embodies a bit of cheeky personality from its meaning of 'fair' or 'good'. I added Finn to my Literary Names list, so check it out for similar inspiration (page 154).

Gus - 'Exalted'. Mostly known as being short for Scottish Angus, Gus as a standalone is packed with charm and really works as a name from babyhood through to adulthood.

James - 'Supplanter'. Classic James still remains one of the enduringly popular boy names. It's gentle sound will never go out of style.

Jax - 'Son of Jack'. The name Jax has been trending onto the name charts in recent years as a modern take on Jack. It works well as a trendy middle for a traditional boy name and I love combos like Casper Jax or Hugo Jax.

Josh - 'The lord is salvation'. From Joshua, Josh has leapt out as a cool one-syllable 'nickname as first name' in its own right.

Kai - 'Sea'. The name Kai, to rhyme with 'sky', is gaining a lot of popularity and it has a few meanings - the most popular being the Hawaiian meaning of 'sea' or 'ocean'.

Mac - 'Son of'. Often used at the beginning of surnames because of its meaning 'son of', Mac is super-sweet and has a similar vibe to Jack and Zack.

Miles - 'Soldier'. A mile was originally 1,000 Roman soldiers' strides, and the name makes it into the top name charts for those looking for something a little offbeat, but simple and easy to say. I'd list it alongside a Finn or Arlo - it has a spring in its step for sure.

Rafe - 'Wolf'. Pronounced Ray-F this is so trendy, and the whimsical meaning will be one he'll grow up loving. Who wouldn't want to include the wolf pack as part of his tribe?

Rex - 'King'. The ultimate little boy's name for dinosaur fans, Rex has that perfect blend of strength in its sound but ultimately feels quite playful and adorable.

Rhys - 'Enthusiastic'. Welsh Rhys really stands out for its meaning. It reminds me of a happy, bubbly person, but the name still feels quite romantic and regal.

Seth - 'Appointed'. Seth dates back to the bible but peaked in popularity in the mid noughties. If you're looking for Trendy with a Twist, Seth sounds established, but it's not as well-used as many names of its type.

Tadhg - 'Philosopher or poet'. Pronounced Tyg like the beginning of Tiger, this classic Irish name is ultra-trendy. The meaning adds such depth, but it feels playful and sweet.

Zach - 'God remembers'. Zach, Zack or Zac are all spellings that work. An eye-catching and commanding name, Zach should appeal to Timelessly Tasteful parents who want a laid-back and stylish name.

NEUTRAL

Drew - 'Strong'. I love this gender-neutral name. It's Welsh in heritage or short for Andrew and also translates as 'wise' and 'courageous'. It always sounds modern and fashionable.

Joss - 'Member of the Gauts'. Jocelyn was a gender-neutral name which became more widely used for girls. It has a fascinating gothic history coming from a northern Germanic tribe called the Gauts, the original 'Goths'. The given name for the tribe was Gautzelin, which then morphed into Jocelyn. I'd associate Joss with incense, which comes from another variation of the word for 'God', as joss sticks were burnt during religious ceremonies. All that for a very simple word, but perhaps all this history might make Joss sing out for you.

Sloane - 'Warrior'. I've always loved the name Sloane. Reminiscent of Sloane Avenue, it sounds fashionable and glamorous while staying classic.

Wilde - 'Uncultivated'. A new word name that's so spirited. Wilde is perfect if you're after a fashion-forward option with huge personality. One for the Stand Out & Shine namers out there.

WORD NAMES

The idea of using words for a baby name has become more and more popular as generational norms shift and we like the sound and associations they bring. I've curated some ideas I think tick all the boxes. You'll be sure to find your passions here and explore your fun naming side.

GIRLS

Echo - 'Reflected sound'. Echo may not sound like a name, but it's the name of a Greek nymph who was cursed by Hera to only be able to repeat back the last words that were spoken to her. It's daring but one to keep an eye on, see similar names in my Fantastical Beasts & Mythical Creatures list (page 107).

Fable - 'A moral story'. A Fable was passed on through generations as a tale with a moral lesson. It works so well as a name, as it's not far removed from Faye and Mabel, both vintage girl names.

Honey - 'Nectar'. Also a term of endearment as it's synonymous with being sweet, it's on so many name lists when I ask people to send me those names they love but aren't daring enough to use.

Lively - 'Full of energy'. In a name chart full of 'L' and 'V' names for our girls, Lively has a place as a braver name option, full of character and expression.

Reverie - 'Daydream'. To walk in reverie is to walk in a daydream and I absolutely think this is a dream name. I love whimsical word names and with Everly being so in fashion, perhaps you'd prefer Reverie. I for one would be listing it and telling no one until I announced it, the ultimate name envy!

Sonnet - 'Little song'. A sonnet was a 14-line poem that could be sung. It's daring but perfect if you're looking for a literary name that's totally unique.

Winsome - 'Appealing or charming'. A word that's fallen out of fashion right onto my baby name list is Winsome. It was used to describe someone who is open and charming, and I love it for a little girl. Winnie makes a delightful nickname.

BOYS

Axis - 'Imaginary line around which the world rotates'. A quirky word alternative to Alex, it's just as wearable as Atlas which has become so popular. What appeals to me is that deep meaning of your world spinning around your newborn.

Blaze - 'Flame'. This is such a great word name for a little boy, blazing his own path in life. It can also be spelt Blaise, the French way, for extra cool points.

Buster - 'To break'. This term of endearment for little boys started as a nickname after a cheeky comic strip character bore the name. Rugged but cute.

Horizon - 'Where the earth meets the sky'. The more you look at this word as a name, the more it works. I adore the meaning; your longed-for baby will be here in your arms. The name feels perfect for a daring nature-inspired word.

Spike - 'A long nail'. Spike has been used as a playful nickname name since mid-century. It's so hipster and different, perfect for a cheeky little boy.

NEUTRAL

Cove - 'Coastal inlet'. It feels like protection and wild nature to me, the perfect combo reminiscent of the sea.

Cricket - 'Insect'. I think this is so playful, both the sport and the insect have strong associations. It's already in use with a few baby Cricket's registered in the UK. The insect noise is one we love and think of on summer nights. A Stand Out & Shine name.

Hero - 'Brave defender'. Cited as a name for those with the characteristics of a hero, it's rare but not wacky. Its heritage lies with Shakespeare, and Hero would be a wonderful name if you're honouring someone or a journey you've been on.

Jetty - 'Break water'. A cool choice, Jet has been around as a brave name for a while and Jetty, a pier made of wood across water, feels like a sweet name with Betty vibes. It could be a jaunty choice for a water baby.

Lux - 'Light'. The Latin word for 'light', also associated with 'luxury', it makes a lively and stylish one-syllable name.

Psalm - 'A sacred song'. An intricate word name with religious roots, Psalm would make a meaningful name for many church goers.

Story - 'A large tale'. For the love story of your life, your baby, the name is so whimsical and romantic.

HOW TO MAKE SURE A NAME WORKS WITH MY **SURNAME**

When it comes to big baby name mistakes, it can surprisingly be the one that we've been born with that comes to trip us up - your surname. It could be tricky for so many reasons; word surnames, name surnames, long complicated surnames and just the comical ones that are nearly always rude. It's not clever but it is funny, so you need to sidestep any pitfalls and I'm here to help.

There are some tricks when choosing a first name for a difficult surname that I've developed into a kind of rule book over the years of name consulting. Here's my guide to getting over the troublesome surname roadblock.

- If your surname is a common word, make sure the first name and surname don't mean anything together. For example, I know a May Reed who wasn't thrilled when people made a connection, and if your surname is Turner you want to avoid Paige. I know this could sound obvious, but I did get a panicked call from parents who were about to go with Ophelia Cox and an actress once confessed to changing her child's name from Gene Atell, a body part she didn't think would serve them well as a name, so bad names happen to good namers.
- If the surname is a colour, I wouldn't pick another colour such as Indigo Brown or Scarlett Black. It sounds a little too much like a character in a kid's book, but equally that could be what appeals to you and, if so, go for it. Keep in mind that it does exaggerate the colour theme.
- If it's a name surname like George or Scott, consider if their first name sounds different enough so they don't get

muddled. Using a surname/firstname like Hudson Scott or Emerson George could lead to a lifetime of corrections.

- It's a good idea to check the initials the whole name makes, including middle names, and see if they spell anything. It could be you want their names to spell a word like LOVE, which is quite sweet and something I would 100 per cent have tried to sneak past my husband had I needed to. One mum was upset when her baby's name spelt TURD, which would take quite a bit of polishing to get over.
- If you want to deflect from a quirky surname, use a name that doesn't repeat any sounds. I've heard surnames like Roast, Parrot and Onion (pronounced O'Nion) and of course British gem, Longbottom. Olivier Onion or Nancy Onion repeat the prominent sounds, adding more attention to the surname. Whereas James Onion or Audrey Onion deflects. I'd also pick a longer name with a strong sound to outshine the shorter surname, for example Emmeline Parrot or Alexander Parrot. Each have their own strong letters that become more prominent, drowning out the surname you might want to hide. I also tend to avoid recommending a word name as a first name if your surname is a word. Summer Roast or River Parrot just points to the fact they're both 'things'.
- It's good to consider quite early if you like alliteration, so having the same letter for both surname and first name. It can sound beautiful like Bronwyn Brown or Stanley Smith. Or it could be a big 'no' for you and, if so, that's good to have decided early on so you can discount those names.

It's an art not a science, do what works for you; as long as you're checking and are happy with the initials, flow and balance of sounds – you've got it right.

AESTHETIC TRENDS

My absolute favourite type of name list is one that evokes an aesthetic trend. Think of a mood board – if you wrote the word HIPPY in the middle, you might stick up photos of festivals, open roads and people being authentically themselves and having fun.

When I'm writing aesthetic name lists, I do just this, but I jot names down instead of using pictures. The link may be due to the meaning, but it is also the sound and style of the name that brings them together. It's a fresh way to find names that connect to the subcultures and lifestyle cues that you love to immerse yourself in.

Aesthetic trends are becoming more visible, moving upwards in favour and getting a lot of those 'likes'. It's a way of showing our personality and connecting to a community of likeminded people. It's so much fun and an amazing source of inspiration for me – whether that's the Romantasy books dominating the stores or 'Quiet Luxury' whose old-money fashion tropes are taking social media by storm. I've included my favourites for you to gather some top picks for your own baby name list.

HIPPY AESTHETIC NAMES

The Hippy aesthetic is all about names that are uninhibited and full of passion. They celebrate free-living and a yearning for a more natural lifestyle. This list is the peace sign of names, the festival field with a touch of spirituality. I know you'll find some names you'll love within it.

GIRLS

Calloway - 'Place of pebbles'. A dreamy name for someone who loves to go their own way. Calloway is upbeat and memorable and perfect for raising an independent spirit.

Joplin - 'Son of Job'. Janis Joplin gives this the seventies, festival vibe for your little girl.

Marnie - 'From the sea'. Marnie conjures up the image of running freely along the beach or diving into waves.

Nixie - 'Water sprite'. As if Pixie wasn't a spirited enough name, along comes Nixie, the female version of a pixie in mythology. I like the strong yet soft 'x' sound. Being similar in some ways to traditional Nicky helps Nixie to be more wearable.

Pandora - 'All gifts'. In Greek mythology Pandora was created by the gods who all put their own characteristics into her. Famed for opening a box which let evil into the world, Pandora still carries the essence of being a plucky and high-spirited character.

Sybil - 'Oracle, prophetess'. This was an occupational name for people who interpreted visions. I find Sybil so stylish with its vintage feel mixed with its magical meaning. It really suits a free-spirited little girl.

Thalia - 'Festivity'. Thalia is such an amazing name, with celebration and joy at its heart. Thalia was also one of the Greek muses of comedy and idyllic poetry. So many reasons to love this beautiful name.

Tiggy - 'Tiger'. This nickname name has the long form Antigone. Very playful and free spirited.

BOYS

Billy - 'Helmet'. Billy is a cheerful and friendly name, the multiple meanings remind me of a rambunctious little boy - 'helmet', 'protection', 'will' and 'desire' - all the things I need for a day out with my two sons.

Harvey - 'Battle-worthy'. Harvey is a Breton name that is upbeat and outdoorsy.

Jaxon - 'Son of Jack'. Jaxon is a modern twist on Jack, the contemporary 'x' makes it super-playful, perfect for a free-spirited feel.

Leonardo - 'Brave as a lion'. I love the lyrical quality of Leonardo, it has a lovely sound and isn't afraid to stand out loud and proud.

Rory - 'Red king'. Rory from Irish and Scottish descent honours the last High King of Ireland. Full of personality, Rory is perfect for the outgoing and independent boy in your life.

Teddy - 'God's gift'. Teddy is a vintage nickname full of joy. It brings to life a bouncy and vibrant little boy with a carefree spirit.

Toby - 'God is good'. Toby has a definite spring in its step and feels like a laid-back classic, perfect for Timelessly Tasteful namers with a touch of the hippy vibe.

NEUTRAL

Arden - 'Valley of the eagle'. Also heard in Shakespeare's *As You Like It* as the name of the mythical forest. This and the meaning are amazing reasons to use Arden as a free-spirited, gender-neutral name.

Larkin - 'Fierce'. A spirited name that brings to mind bird names and the British poet Philip Larkin, who was also a jazz journalist and librarian.

Stevie - 'Crown'. This stand-out name is on a lot of lists, inspired by Stevie Nicks. Why not use it as a quirky alternative to Evie?

QUIET LUXURY AESTHETIC NAMES

Your baby's name is the ultimate investment piece. The Quiet Luxury aesthetic evokes wealth, but with an ethos of pared-back simplicity. The look has gained popularity as an antidote to fast fashion and the showy world of influencers and celebrities that has been growing in the previous years. Quiet Luxury has an understated glamour and effortless style. I've chosen statement-piece names that aren't overcomplicated but have an innate beauty.

GIRLS

Agnes - 'Pure'. Patron saint of young girls, Agnes is confident and simple with a touch of French luxe adding that effortless style.

Audrey - 'Noble strength'. A medieval name, Audrey has a unique sound that is so elegant and glamorous. It has the pared back style of Audrey Hepburn which ticks the tropes of this aesthetic perfectly.

Ava - 'Birdlike'. Ava is as timelessly stylish as the perfect white shirt, a classic that always gets compliments.

Bianca - 'White'. Stylish and simple, the name Bianca takes me to an island with white sandy beaches or a stylish home with lots of neutrals. Bianca is a touch of glamour and a hint of retro cool.

Estrid - 'Fair and beautiful goddess'. Scandinavian's are renowned for having a minimalist, fashion-forward style which feels quintessential for this trend and Estrid is a super-chic girl name from Sweden.

Evelyn - 'Life'. Evelyn is one of the classic beautiful names and it has many name translations depending on which line you follow. It comes from both French 'hazelnut' and Eve meaning 'life'. Evelyn's popularity is unlikely to wane and the fact it has travelled so well is a testament to that.

Ines - 'Pure'. The Spanish variation of Agnes, Ines has a graceful sound that always feels on trend.

Ingrid - 'Beauty'. If Margot is too popular for you, Ingrid should be hitting your list. Glamorous and luxe with Scandinavian roots to the goddess of fertility, it's a true Stand Out & Shine name.

Margot - 'Pearl'. From Margaret, the name Margot has taken over and it really is a beautiful and distinctive name. With a silent 't', the traditional French variation was spelt Margaux. Both are perfect if you're after an effortless classic.

Marta - 'Pearl'. Classic and sophisticated, Marta is the Swedish form of Margaret. I've always loved the distinctive sound of Marta and it's a name that will get a lot of compliments.

Meredith - 'Great ruler'. Originally a male name, Meredith is now a strong and stylish girl name. Of Welsh origin, Meredith feels sophisticated and has bags of power behind its meaning. See my Water Names list for other options like Meredith (page 88).

Ottilie - 'Wealth'. French name Ottilie is so graceful, it hits the Old Money feel of this aesthetic. Attention-grabbing but friendly with the pretty 'l' sound, Ottilie is a perfect Trendy with a Twist name.

Pearl - 'Precious'. When it comes to understated glamour, Pearl is the perfect name. It combines a vintage edge with a classic gemstone, the quintessential Quiet Luxury name.

Romilly - 'From Rome'. Pronounced Rom-illy, it has class and elegance and sounds really feminine, but the stronger beginning stops it being too frilly as a name. It gives a quiet luxury vibe.

Sophia - 'Wisdom'. This beautiful name is perfect for parents with mixed heritage, as it's actually the number one girl name across the world, meaning it's travelled far and wide and has a real elegance to it.

BOYS

Barnaby - 'Young warrior'. A vintage boy name, Barnaby is full of personality with lots of charm - upbeat and bouncy while retaining a classic style.

Darwin - 'Dear friend'. With 'surname as first name' cool, Darwin has an Upper East Side swagger but it's a historical name which stops it from being fast fashion.

Elias - 'The Lord is my God'. Elias was a miracle worker in the bible. It's got a soulful feel with a calm and assured style.

Evan - 'God is gracious'. A variant of John, Evan is the elevated version. Subtly cool without being overstated.

Ezra - 'To help'. Ezra is on point as a Quiet Luxury name; it is modern and smart with loads of biblical history behind it.

Gabe - 'Hero of God'. From angel Gabriel. I adore this one-syllable version for a Quiet Luxury aesthetic name. Gabe is a true statement piece that doesn't try too hard.

Henrik - 'Ruler of the home'. The Swedish version of Henry, the 'k' ending adds that extra Scandi vibe and makes for a great twist on a classic. My husband is called Henrik and I've always loved his name so much.

Ibrahim - 'Father of many'. One of the most important prophets in the Quran, Ibrahim remains an elegant classic name.

Jacoby - 'Supplanter'. A variant of James, Jacoby has a bit of a luxury twist. It sounds fashionable, stylish and fun.

Luca - 'Bringer of light'. Luca is the epitome of pared-back cool, it always sounds slick while still being a simple and interesting name. It's flown up the charts in popularity and deserves its spot as a favourite.

Mateo - 'Gift of God'. The Spanish form of Matthew, Mateo has a more luxe and elevated style.

Macsen - 'Greatest'. From Welsh mythology, Macsen is a charming and quite distinguished name worn by a Welsh Roman Emperor. Pared back cool and hugely memorable.

Noah - 'To rest'. Enduringly popular, Noah's laidback style is popular for a reason - it oozes cool.

Otis - 'Wealthy'. Otis feels trendy for a name with so much heritage. Used for centuries, its meaning of 'fortunate' or 'abundant' are lovely virtues.

Otto - 'Wealth'. Stylish Otto has a regal feel with its namesake being Roman Emperor, Otto the Great. It slots right into this aesthetic with its simplicity but unforgettable sound.

Rayan - 'Luxuriant'. Rayan *has* to appear on this list with its meaning of 'luxuriant'. The Arabic boy name has so much elegance, also meaning 'flower from heaven'.

Reuben - 'Behold, a son'. Reuben is such a cool name that has an even more amazing meaning. It's a traditional name that remains chic and contemporary in sound, perfect for Timelessly Tasteful namers.

Theodore - 'God's gift'. Theo and Ted make great nicknames for this enduringly popular boy name that sounds so well-established and sophisticated.

William - 'Resolute protector'. William The Conqueror introduced this name into Britain and it's been passed on via royals ever since, becoming a popular name throughout the country. With Will, Bill and Billy, the name is versatile and feels both grand and elegant while remaining unfussy and gentle with its pretty double 'll'. A classic for a reason, you'll always love his name.

NEUTRAL

Blair - 'Plain or meadow'. Scottish Blair was originally a male name. It has an Upper East Side New York sound coupled with a simple and untarnished nature meaning.

Curtis - 'Polite'. An Anglo-Norman surname meaning 'polite' or 'well-bred', Curtis is a big crush of mine as a gender-neutral name. It's got that luxury feel being an Old Money surname, but is fresh as a first name.

Drew - 'Strong'. A Welsh variant of Andrew, Drew is stylish and simple and doesn't try too hard for attention. However, it's a Stand Out & Shine name with a high-class, elegant feel and intellectual meaning.

COSY 'HYGGE' AESTHETIC NAMES

Hygge is the Danish word for 'contentment in comfort'. I love this aesthetic for a baby name, as there's so much said about the chaos of newborn life; and of course there's the endless feeds, an occasional overflowing nappy bin (don't judge me) and days hoping they sleep long enough so you can just read that book on how to get them to sleep. However, I'm all for calling out how much calm a newborn brings to your home as well. It's truly the time to shut the door, let the world spin outside and get cosy in your nest with your baby. Whether they come straight home or it's a while to wait. Whether those first weeks bring an undesirable side order of mastitis or tongue tie and a lot of 'how do I do this?' moments. There will also be the times when it's just the two of you at 2am, or the fleeting feeling of pride when you realize that you actually *did* this. Or the peaceful photo someone takes of you half dozing in the obligatory ghastly dressing gown with your baby on your chest that really make up the moments that matter. That's where the hygge happens. It's contentment not perfection we're aiming for as parents, and these names bring that feeling to life.

GIRLS

Caraway - 'Spice merchant'. This warming spice is a dreamy hygge name and a long-time crush of mine. It sounds so whimsical, and I've always loved vintage name Carrie. The root word is occupational, probably from someone who travelled selling spices. I so wish I'd heard this name before picking my daughter's name as it would have been a real contender, Caraway just has so many lovely associations to me.

Chappell - 'Sanctuary'. A name for someone living by a Chapel, Chappell is a Middle English word and has all the style of a modern Virtue name with the enticing sanctuary meaning.

Enya - 'Fire'. The Irish name Enya brings that cosy warmth and vibrant red of its 'fire' meaning, which is so hygge. It's a gentle name that celebrates twilight moments.

Levora - 'Homebody'. The season of comfort and slowing down, Levora celebrates staying home and getting cosy. For those of us with JOMO (Joy Of Missing Out), Levora is a compelling name.

Sunday - 'Sun goddess'. I have to rank autumnal Sundays as my favourites, coming home for a roast after a walk or just spending time resetting and resting. Sunday is the ultimate family day, and the name will always make you beam.

BOYS

Emory - 'Home strength'. Emory is cosy and friendly sounding and I love the meaning, taking me straight to cosy nights at home with your little babe.

Hamlin - 'Lover of home'. I adore this name. It's so unique but not complex and the meaning is really comforting and full of heart.

Hugo - 'Heart or spirit'. Hugo appears in my Ready for Revival Names list (page 202) as well but I had to include it here, as the meaning really elevates this classic name. I had this picked out had my third baby been a boy, with nickname Huggy of course (which I may have let them drop when they turned 15). The spirit of family, heart and home feel bound up in sweet Hugo.

Jabir - 'Comforter'. A beautiful meaning, Jabir is an Arabic name that means 'to comfort' or 'to settle'. A perfect pick for that soothing, warming feel.

Rocco - 'To rest or repose'. Rocco is that perfect blend of sounding edgy with a soft centre. The name meaning came from catholic Saint San Rocco who cared for people who were unwell and gave them respite. I love the meaning and the name has always been such a playful and happy one.

Stellan - 'Calm'. Stellan hits so many big style ticks, being both unique and straightforward. With its gorgeous meaning, it's a Scandinavian name with so much heart.

NEUTRAL

Billy - 'Helmet'. Billie is all the reasons I love vintage nicknames. We use the spelling Billy more for boys and reserve an 'ie' for girls, but neither are fixed as they sound identical. I love the cosy feeling of protection and how down to earth Bill/Billy/Billie is as a name.

Carmello - 'Orchard'. Carmello is an eye-catching name, taken from Carmel. In its longer form it means 'orchard'. I'm really drawn to the soft 'ello' ending - it takes me to peaceful, cosy nights in with 'calm' right at its heart.

Noa - 'To rest'. One of our most timeless names, it's now become more gender-neutral, particularly if you drop the 'h'. Its meaning 'to rest' is the perfect nod to a hygge, cosy lifestyle.

Shiloh - 'Tranquil'. Pronounced shy-low, I could say this name all day long and never get bored. It feels tranquil, just like it's meaning with those soft sounds and has a kind of minimalism that makes it very pared back and cool.

COTTAGECORE AESTHETIC NAMES

Cottagecore has been a huge trend over the last few years, with slow living becoming aspirational as an antidote to the busy lives we lead. This idealized look and feel of rural life began to take off, inspiring fashions, hobbies like baking and sewing and interiors which are quaint and wholesome. I've interpreted the aesthetic into a name list which gives the exact same vibe.

GIRLS

Carrie - 'Free man'. A symbol of freedom and life well lived, Carrie has such an earthy, cottagecore spirit. It's amicable and full of joy.

Cosette - 'Little thing'. A French nickname steeped in cosiness, Cosette is world famous as the character from *Les Mis* named after French word *chosette* meaning 'little thing'. It's full of warmth and love.

Dervla - 'Poet's daughter'. Irish name Dervla has such a beautiful, unique sound. The meaning is so wholesome and with poetry really having its revival, this whimsical name feels fashion forward.

Ellerby - 'Village or farmstead'. Ellerby originates from an Old English settlement in Yorkshire and became a surname that literally takes you to the heart of village life.

Evadne - 'Good'. A beautiful figure in Greek mythology, Evadne fell in love with Apollo and bore his baby out in the woods. She left him there nestled in a bed of violets where he was raised by honeybees until she could prove Apollo was the father. Then she returned to get him. The name sounds like Evelyn and Daphne had a baby, and produced Evadne. Pronounced Ee-Vad-Nee.

Katinka - 'Pure'. From Katherine, Katinka is so joyous and Tinks is of course the iconic Fairy in *Peter Pan*. Tinkerbell may not be the most wearable name, but Katinka has its same magic.

Leni - 'Light'. Leni is a minimalist, bright and vibrant name from Helena. It is so stylish in its simplicity, whimsical and unforgettable.

Mindy - 'Sweet honey'. Mindy is so simple and wholesome; extremely pretty with a pared back charm Mindy would make an adorable name.

Rosenwyn - 'White rose'. I adore the name Bronwyn and Rosenwyn just makes me fall right into the pages of a fairy tale garden.

Rue - 'Road'. Rue has sprung into fashion as a perfect, simple girl name. Meaning 'road' in French, Rue is also the name of a herb, taking you a walk a country lane. If we 'rue the day', we regret misspending our time, which perfectly harks to the values of the Cottagecore Aesthetic, of taking our time back for the simple pleasures in life.

Sierra - 'Saw'. Sierra has such a rich tapestry of meanings for Cottagecore lovers; coming from the Spanish word for 'saw' and 'jagged', it also translates as 'mountain range'. I like the connection to creativity and craftmanship with sawing wood, plus the incredible feeling of being up in the mountain wilderness for this style of name.

BOYS

Abbot - 'Priest'. An occupational name for a priest, Abbot became a common surname in medieval Britain and as a first name it feels like a great twist on Robert or Albert. Reminiscent of a country parish and rural villages, Abbot is a wonderful cottagecore name.

Augustus - 'Majestic'. The name August is well-used, but Augustus with the 'us' is a fresh way of using it. It has the same name roots as Sebastian which would make a great sibset. Auggie and Gus are adorable nicknames, but Cottagecore is all about going back to classics, so vintage Augustus feels right on-trend. He was the Roman Emperor who took over from Caesar and did a lot of social good.

Axel - 'Father of peace'. The peaceful meaning of Axel gives it a quiet, classic energy that befits the aesthetic of cottagecore. Axel is a twist on traditional Alex, and is gaining a lot of popularity.

Clifton - 'A town by a cliff'. This name takes me straight to a gorgeous cottage garden with a view.

Fletcher - 'Arrow maker'. An occupational name, Fletcher has a lot of charm with its evocative meaning.

Hart - 'Stag'. The name of a deer under the age of five, it's so strong and of course loveable sounding - like 'heart'. It's captured mine as a rare but full-of meaning baby boy name.

Ivo - 'Yew tree'. Such a great name - if you like Ivy for a girl, Ivo could also be on your baby list for a boy. Its yew tree meaning really connects it to outdoor living, as the yew is known as the archer tree. It was traditionally what they used to make arrows. How Cottagecore is that?

Jacopo - 'Supplants'. Another variation of James that hasn't made it to the heights of Jacob, I covet this spritely name. It has a playful spring to it that somehow makes it perfect for a cottagecore vibe.

Jasper - 'Treasurer'. Jasper is perfect for your little treasure, plus the name is also a gemstone. Jasper is a dark red stone and is the symbol for protection and strength, used for grounding.

Jesse - 'God exists' A vintage name that sounds so modern, super-outdoorsy and spirited. Jesse is right at home in the countryside.

Pippin - 'Awe-inspiring'. A pet name for Philip, Pippin is happiest in the countryside. Really upbeat and lyrical, little Pip would always make you smile.

Rufus - 'Red or red haired'. Latin name Rufus has all the qualities of the Cottagecore aesthetic, feeling earthy and full of life.

Virgil - 'To flourish'. There was an Irish Saint Virgil and a Roman poet sporting the name. Virgil has a homely and warm feel and its 'flourish' meaning makes me think of plants blooming.

Walter - 'Power of the army'. A retro 1920s gem having its popularity resurrection, Walt is a great nickname and ideal for a Disney fan. It's very down to earth, and originally this name was pronounced water, such a beautiful element to link it to that conjures up rivers and streams.

Wilbur - 'Wild boar'. A brilliant throw-back vintage icon, Wilbur is still a little unexpected and super charming.

NEUTRAL

Anderson - 'Son of Andrew'. Synonymous with Hans Christian Andersen, it's a name straight from the pages of fairy tales. I love the nickname Andi for girls and for boys you get Scandi Anders or Sonny.

Forest - 'Woods'. Sheltering and magical, forests appear throughout books and movies as whimsical and magical places. Such a cosy meaning for your little Forest.

Lowri - 'Laurel'. Gender-neutral Lowri means 'Laurel', which is the symbol of peace and victory. Its soft, boho sound feels right at home in the cosy, cottagecore trend.

ROMANTASY NAMES

Romantasy is the genre of romantic fiction set in another realm, bringing in the sci-fi and fantasy aesthetic. So many of us have become huge fans of this genre; loving the aesthetic of other worlds similar but different to our own. These names are exotic, strong and have an ethereal edge.

GIRLS

Alva - 'Elf'. So many faerie and elfin fans will adore this name as its meaning sounds so whimsical. Alva Belmont was a famed suffragette in America who helped fund the movement and makes a great namesake with the aesthetic of strong, game-changing females.

Antiquity - 'Ancient times'. If you love classics and antiques this name will spring out at you, it sounds so exciting and interesting as a girl name. Antiquity takes us to a place of ancient rituals and laws, perfect for the Romantasy aesthetic.

Delilah - 'Delicate'. Delilah is such a pretty name with a dark tale. In the biblical story of Samson and Delilah, she tempted him to cut off his hair and he lost his strength. The sound of Delilah is always intoxicating and it captures hearts.

Evaluna - 'Life and moon'. This invented name has newly appeared as shortened Luna, which parents seem to love, but full name Evaluna has a midnight romance to it.

Ferryn - 'Adventurer'. A strong Stand Out & Shine name, Ferryn instils a love of adventure for a little girl and is truly magical. It's an old English name that can also be used to mean 'protected on your travels', so has a comforting feel of safety as well as its more spirited adventure side.

Guinevere - 'White shadow'. From Arthurian legend, Guinevere is such a romantic name. It doesn't sound overly daunting or too complex for new parents as it's such a well-known name.

Neith - 'Mother goddess'. The longest worshiped goddess in Egyptian history, Neith was the goddess of everything and is depicted in hieroglyphics which steeps this all-powerful name in history and romance.

Ophelia - 'To help'. The romantic love interest of Hamlet, Ophelia was a tragic heroine in the Shakespeare play and the pretty name has inspired songs and paintings.

Theodosia - 'Divine gift'. Made popular by the musical *Hamilton*, pronounced Theo-do-sha, it's meaning makes it a true gem of an ancient name that's due a revival.

Trinity - 'Triad'. Triads occur across the classics and religion as a strong symbol. I love the sound of this three-syllable name and there are so many reasons you might embrace the symbol of three for your baby.

BOYS

Cormoran - 'Giant'. Cornish name Cormoran - pronounced Coor-Moor-An - has all the glamour this aesthetic requires with a big dose of fantasy in its meaning. Cormoran was the name of the Giant in the original tale *Jack the Giant Killer* and is a Romantasy powerhouse of a name.

Eric - 'Eternal ruler'. A solid and handsome boy name and long associated with royalty in Scandinavia, Eric has been overlooked but it's such an everlasting name around the world for its pared back cool.

Gruffydd - 'Strong lord'. Welsh Gruffydd brings in mythical creature Gruff, which refers to a Griffin and a history of legends and warriors.

Keiran - 'Dark-haired one'. The name of an Irish apostle, Keiran has romantic hero swagger and sounds traditional without being too well-used.

Malakai - 'My angel'. A biblical name, Malakai brings the winged strength of angels to your names list, and angels are linked to messengers, which feels perfect for story lovers.

Owen - 'Young warrior'. Owen is a classic with a strong backbone. Familiar but not overused, it has an understated but powerful sound.

Troy - 'Foot soldier'. The love story of Helen (of Troy) and Paris was said to have sparked the Trojan War and the name has all the elements of a Romantasy classic. An ancient place, love strong enough to start battles and a poetic telling in Homer's *Odyssey* are all packed into this stunning name.

Vincent - 'To conquer'. Vincent is such an evocative name, with Van Gogh cutting off his ear being one of the most iconic legends in art. It feels like this brooding name is due a revival with its dark romance.

NEUTRAL

Azriel - 'God is my help'. Traditionally a male name but I prefer it as a gender-neutral name spelt Azrael, with its slightly different meaning - the benevolent angel of death who carries the souls of the deceased to the afterlife. A daring choice that stands out.

Glennon - 'Cloak'. Irish Glennon has a dreamy Romantasy feel with a strong sound. A glen is a narrow valley that has that vast, sweeping nature vibe which suits a genre obsessed with journeys into the unknown. Plus, the magical meaning of 'cloak' adds so much mystery.

Nyx - 'Night'. Originally the female personification of the night in mythology. It's a short, sweet name with a hint of darkness that would work brilliantly for Stand Out & Shine namers.

Tarmo - 'Energy'. Estonian name Tarmo has all the feel of a Romantasy character name plus the spellbinding meaning of 'energy' which brings a mystical, storytelling essence to this cute name.

MAIN CHARACTER ENERGY AESTHETIC NAMES

The Main Character Energy aesthetic captures that joy of being truly ourselves. A child who is self-assured and confident are values we aspire to instil. Names with Main Character Energy are strong and vibrant, encouraging the wearer to live loudly and

boldly as the hero of their own story. I've created this list with names that have those values at their core. They're unapologetically ***stand out.***

GIRLS

Athena - 'Wise'. The goddess of wisdom, warfare and art, your little girl seems destined for greatness with this powerful name.

Billie - 'Helmet'. Traditionally a nickname for William, the name Billie is now firmly on the girl lists for those looking for a name that is playful with its 'ie' ending, but doesn't blend into the background.

Clover - 'Meadow flower'. A Stand Out & Shine girl's name with love right at its centre, Clover is a contemporary and beautiful name.

Dusty - 'Sand-coloured'. I adore the singer Dusty Springfield and have met a couple of cute girls with the name. It stands out from the crowd and captures attention. The meaning comes from Norse name Torsten, which morphed into Dustin and Dusty as the nickname.

Juniper - 'Evergreen tree'. I was obsessed with the name Juniper for years - I love its hippy vibes. In the flower garden of girl names, the Juniper berry just pips the post for a braver pick.

Novalee - 'New meadow'. A modern name, Novalee combines to take you straight from the starry sky to nature. Made for Stand Out & Shine parents.

Sunday - 'Sun goddess'. I love the boldness of a word name and Sunday is one of the day names that really works. Our favourite family day brings weekend vibes to your name list.

BOYS

Atticus - 'Rugged coast'. From Athens, Atticus is a stunning boy's name that feels uber trendy with historic and literary roots. I love the sound of Atticus, it has that main character energy while bringing that natural coastal meaning for lovers of the outdoors.

Boaz - 'Strength'. This biblical boy name sounds right up-to-date, truly unique in sound but with all the cool of Noah and Ezra. Such a brilliant name.

Devin - 'Poet'. Poetry is the language of love and it's having its resurgence online. Devin is an Irish name with literary vibes that gives pure Main Character Energy aesthetic to your little boy.

Evander - 'Good man'. I love how distinct Evander is in sound while not being complicated. It pops out of the page and should be front and centre of your name list if you want a soft and characterful name.

Osian - 'Little deer'. Osian is a Celtic name pronounced Osh-An. It's a true stand-out name, Osian was an Irish demigod giving such main character energy.

Romeo - 'Pilgrim to Rome'. We all know the name from Shakespeare, Romeo being a name we often use to describe someone who is romantic and handsome. A brave but characterful name.

Theo - 'God's gift'. Theo is a strong, classic name with the coolest meaning and loads of spirit.

Xavier - 'New house'. The name Xavier pronounced Zay-Ve-Ah is big and bold and the meaning is gorgeous, as your heart is their home.

Yahya - 'God is merciful'. An Arabic name that also means 'one who lives', Yahya is enduringly cool for a baby boy.

Zayn - 'Beauty and grace'. The meaning brings so much to this striking name. Zayn is a showstopper of Arabic origin, also spelt Zain.

Ziggy - 'Victory, protection'. Taken from Sigmund (which I'm also loving), Ziggy has stardust sprinkled all over it.

NEUTRAL

Arrow - 'Fired from a bow'. Used for hunting, but also to give us direction, Arrow is such a meaningful name, especially if this baby has turned your life around. Your baby will be your strongest purpose and biggest guide and Arrow hits the target as a cool, boho baby name.

Harlow - 'Army hill'. Once a popular boy's name, now a shining star that's used mainly for girls. It has leading lady glam written all over it.

Lowen - 'Joy'. Lowen is a Cornish name. The meaning makes it an immediate winner and the unique soft sound will always stand out.

Quinlan - 'Strong'. The unique letters and sounds are phonetic, so Quinlan isn't hard to spell or say, but it really stands up to the simplicity of its strong meaning.

GOTH GLAM AESTHETIC NAMES

We used to call it a phase, but goth glam is a full lifestyle. Gothic is well known as an architectural style from France, but originally the Goths were a nomadic people from Germany who brought down the Roman Empire. Whether you love dark academia or Halloween is your happy time, this list is the 'black velvet bow and dusty library' of baby names. Recently Goth Glam has had a huge resurgence into popular culture, and I've created a name list inspired by the themes.

GIRLS

Brontë - 'Thunder'. The Brontë sisters give this name full dark academia accolades.

Ebony - 'Dark black-wooded tree'. Ebony is the name given to dark ornamental wood and it's so reminiscent of many tales from novels and art that delve into the unknown woods.

Elsinore - 'Narrow'. The name of Hamlet's castle makes such a striking one. Reminiscent of traditional Eleanor with the literary history of Shakespeare's Prince of Denmark, Elsinore packs quite a punch.

Enola - 'Alone'. Enola spells 'alone' backwards and is the protagonist's name in a series of young adult novels where Enola is the younger sister of the infamous detective Sherlock Holmes.

Inka - 'Ancestor'. The closest I can find to a meaning for this pretty name is in Finnish, where it's linked to the word for 'ancestor'. I adore the sound of Inka and was inspired by tattoo art, which is such a strong aesthetic of the Goth Glam trend.

Isolabella - 'Beautiful lonely one'. A gorgeous name perfect for Goth Glam, it's also the name of a tiny island in Italy and I love its haunting meaning.

Roxbury - 'From the raven's fortress'. This style of goth name adds some glam and Roxbury's fortress meaning is so gothic and whimsical, with a sense of security and protection.

Solstice - 'When the Sun stands still'. The winter solstice is the darkest day of the year, which gives this name its mysterious and magical vibe.

BOYS

Casimir - 'Destroyer of peace'. Casimir has a lovely flow to it. It looks soft but has that dark academia mix of romance and edge. He may destroy your peace, but I like to think of him as someone who doesn't always follow the status quo.

Cassius 'Vain'. Of Irish and Latin heritage, Cassius has a grand sound but translates as 'vain' or 'empty'. I'd still use it - the name is just too special to let the meaning undermine it, and fans of a dark hero will love the vibe.

Dante - 'Everlasting'. From epic poem *The Divine Comedy*, Dante pronounced Dan-Tay, has all the elements for a poetic and literary name. It's a gorgeous name with Italian heritage that ticks all the right vibe boxes.

Diggory - 'Lost one'. Dark and brooding, I adore the quirky name Diggory. From Old English 'digrian' the name appears as far back as Chaucer's *The Canterbury Tales*. It has the essence of one who leads their own path and goes their own way.

Halloran - 'Descendant of a pirate'. Irish surname Halloran originated from a word for 'foreigner' or a blend of words meaning 'beyond' and 'at sea'. It's got the heart of someone who sails by their own wind and also sounds poetic as a name.

Hemlock - 'Poisonous plant'. Lockie makes a cool nickname and with Ivy being a popular girl name, Hemlock deserves a listing on our Goth Glam Aesthetic baby name pages with its rich meaning.

Jace - 'Healer'. With its caring and soothing name meaning, Jace has such a spiritual and soulful side that will appeal to Trendy with a Twist namers looking for a one-syllable wonder.

Jinx - 'Spell'. If you jinx something people used to believe you put bad luck on it. However, Jinx sounds so cool and is similar in style to familiar Jax. It could be a magical name for your baby boy.

Nemo - 'Nobody'. Once a name for those who were anonymous or nameless from ancient Rome, Nemo is now most famous as a Disney name. Its meaning gives it a real gothic twist.

Sascha - 'Defending warrior'. A shortened form of Alexander, Sascha feels right at home on this list with its protective, brave meaning.

Temple - 'Sanctuary'. Goth started with architecture, and I adore the name Temple from The Knights Templar who appear in many gothic writings.

Victor - 'Victorious'. The name Victor is so strong and powerful. The character of Victor Frankenstein wanted to discover the elixir of life in one of the most gothic novels written, Mary Shelley's *Frankenstein*.

Viggo - 'Battle'. With the popular 'o' ending, Viggo stands out for all the right reasons. Meaning 'battle' in Old Norse, it's edgy and stylish.

NEUTRAL

Rune - 'Secret'. Rune stones have an old Germanic letter adorned on them and they gained spiritual use as a way of getting guidance. Rune is such a mysterious name that feels like the more traditional Ruth and June.

Salem - 'Peaceful or complete'. A very soft-sounding name with a calming meaning that is associated with the Salem witch trials of the late seventeenth century.

Soul - 'Soul or spirit'. This simple name is being used more for boys than girls. We often call our children our heart and soul, and I love the gothic vibe of this Virtue name.

Wallace - 'Stranger'. A fascinating history, the name Wallace dates to being someone who spoke Cumbric, perhaps a Welsh person arriving somewhere new. It's steeped in the mysterious newcomer vibe of this aesthetic.

SURNAME AS FIRST NAMES

I love a surname as first name and have been so interested to see this aesthetic rise to the forefront of a lot of people's name lists. I think there's a familiarity with calling someone by their surname, although not mine - Ljungstrom confuses others and I can see fear in their eyes as they try to pronounce it, which is why some years ago I just went for Strum online. Surnames have incredible meanings. If you're from a family with a strong occupation, you'll find some amazing ideas - a character trait or a symbol, it's literally our

ancestry. Surname names feel bold and modern and aesthetically suit that urban street style so many of us love. While I've separated some names into the Girls and Boys list, the entries below are mainly gender neutral, giving you so many options.

GIRLS

Addison - 'Son of Adam'. It's interesting that this name is so traditionally male, but we adore it for girls, maybe as it's reminiscent of vintage Alison. Addison is such a modern name that it's perfect if you're looking for feminine but not frilly.

Angelou - 'Angel'. Synonymous with writer and activist Maya Angelou, the name is soft and feminine with the iconic power of her namesake bringing so much spirit and impact.

Delaney - 'Dark challenger'. I love this Irish surname for a girl - with nickname Laney, it's super romantic.

Everdene - 'Wild one'. I adore names starting with the word 'Ever', it's just so sentimental. Add in the meaning of 'wild one' and I'm sold on Everdene.

Loveday - 'Love day'. My sister chose surname Loveday for her daughter Lottie's middle name, as it was ancestral in Painswick, the village where she worked. Packed with heart and history, Loveday makes a Stand Out & Shine name.

Winslet - 'Joyful dwelling'. Yes, please! What a gorgeous name and meaning, your little girl will literally become your happy place which is what this name embodies. Even better, it has Winnie as a standout nickname.

BOYS

Callahan - 'Bright-headed'. A Gaelic surname, Callahan has been passed down by the tenth-century king of Munster and was used as a regal first name after that. Lively and fun it would suit Stand Out & Shine namers.

Carter - 'Transporter'. Trendy and simple, this occupational name for someone who used a cart to transport goods has made the leap into first name status. It's now a fashionable and strong boy name.

Clark - 'Scribe'. Clark is a solid and suave name, from someone who had the occupation of a scribe or professional secretary, the name was associated with being scholarly and intelligent. Perfect for Superman's alter ego Clark Kent.

Copeland - 'Bought land'. Copeland was a surname meaning 'land owner', but would make such a great first name.

Davis - 'Beloved'. A common surname, but I love this twist on David. I chose David as a middle name spot after my cousin David who I adore. I wanted to honour his name in my son's name, but now I wish I'd thought of going with Davis or Davey as they sound so modern.

Donovan - 'Dark hair'. An Irish surname, Donovan makes a trendy first name. It's super-wearable with Don and Van being classic vintage names, but Donovan brings that extra cool.

Harrison - 'Son of Harry'. Harrison is making moves on its classic namesake. A little bit more spirited, Harrison is a wonderful name choice if you're looking for a Trendy with a Twist option.

Hendrix - 'Estate ruler'. Surname of legendary rockstar Jimi, it's a popular first name. Stemming from Dutch name Hendrik, the 'x' adds a real rock and roll vibe.

Hudson - 'Son of Hugh'. Hudson came from the ancient name Hudde and is used mainly as a form of Hugh and Richard. Hudson could be a great choice if you're honouring someone with one of those names. It's strong, romantic and packed with main character energy (see the Main Character Energy list on p. 291 for more inspiration.).

Huxley - 'Hugh's meadow'. Huxley has followed some more traditional 'x' names to become a really popular first name. Hugh also means 'mind' or 'soul', which brings spiritual depth to this edgy boy name.

Jackson - 'Son of Jack'. One of the UK's most common surnames, Jackson originated in the borders of Scotland and England as a surname. Jackson branched from Johnson, which came from John and it remains a classic. Booming as a first name for boys, Jackson is a brilliant traditional but trendy first name. If Jack feels too safe, try out Jackson.

Jenson - 'Son of Jens'. Scandinavian Jens brings us trendy Jenson - a surname that feels just right as a first name.

Lawson - 'Son of Lawrence'. A 'son' ending always gives you Sonny as a nickname, which is such a sunny moniker. Lawson derived from Lawrence meaning 'bright' or 'shining one' and it's a name that also sounds quite regal and scholarly.

Lennon - 'Lover, sweetheart'. What a gorgeous name meaning, you'll always love telling little Lennon what their name means. I'd have heart emblems for every birthday. An iconic surname from John Lennon, this name ticks so many boxes and Lennie makes the cutest nickname.

Sawyer - 'Woodcutter'. A trade surname for people working with wood, Sawyer is an outdoorsy and personable boy name.

Smith - 'One who works with metal'. Another common surname that's jumped into the first name spot on occasion, and I think it sounds so trendy. An occupational name for someone who worked with metal it came from the action smite, which means 'to hit' - it was a very popular job, and the name became widespread.

Sullivan - 'Dark eyes'. An Irish surname that's often been used as a first name, Sullivan is so stylish and has sweet Sully as a nickname.

Tyler - 'Tile maker'. Tyler was a name derived from building houses, and a Tyler was a type of medieval landlord who guarded an inn. It's a strong name with a great background meaning.

NEUTRAL

Bellamy - 'Good friend'. This quintessentially French name comes from *belle,* meaning 'good' or 'fair', and *Ami* meaning 'friend' and 'companion'. The name has picked up popularity as an alternative to names ending in Belle.

Brooks - 'Small stream'. The 's' ending is really making surnames boom as first names - Collins, Rivers, Wells - they are all rising in style and Brooks is a common surname that would have been given where this clan were located.

Cassidy - 'Curly-haired'. This Irish surname is so cowboy-cool for boys and spirited for girls - curly-haired isn't a requisite of using the name; I'd list it and be prepared for lots of compliments.

Emerson - 'Son of Emery'. Names ending in 'son' are always lush, as Sonny makes a wonderful nickname. I had Emerson-Rose on my name list before I had kids, as German surname Emerson sounds so good when combined with a one-syllable name.

Harlow - 'Army hill'. Harlow's heritage dates to Anglo-Saxon Britain and its history makes it feel like a classic while also being so fresh. It has a soft, boho sound wrapped up in a confident and stunning name.

Madigan - 'Little dog'. What a sweet name for a dog lover. From Irish surname Madadh, Madigan is very upbeat and playful, just like its meaning.

Taylor - 'To cut'. An occupational name for someone who tailored clothes, it feels like a well-established classic already. A gender-neutral gem of a name.

BOHEMIAN AESTHETIC NAMES

I'll admit, I'm probably one of the reasons boho baby names is so highly searched as a term. It was why I started my channel,

as I really wanted my core style to be a part of my names. 'Bohemian' was coined as a phrase in the Latin Quarter of Paris, very similar to the new-build suburbs of Swindon where I grew up. A Bohemian was a term then used to describe someone who challenged conventions. It spurred a creative movement. Sometimes it's described in history as someone living in chosen poverty, which meant they lived for their art. Bohemians wore flowing clothes that allowed them to move more freely and express themselves through dance or art. As I suspected . . . leggings were a nineties Swindon staple and I've never met a comfier garment for expressing my dance style at many prestigious kitchen discos. I do adore this style, the names to me are so pretty, and the lifestyle of living for oneself and not being afraid of other people's opinions is a gorgeous place to search for a name for your little one.

GIRLS

Adelpha - 'Beloved sister'. I absolutely adore Adelpha, with its special meaning it would mean a lot to many of us - whether for our own sister, a sibling, a rainbow baby or a sisterhood. Adelpha has such a pretty sound and it's unique without being complex.

Alora - 'At that hour'. Alora has a rich history, and when you investigate its Spanish roots it means 'at that hour' which is so poetic. It also appears as a Bantu language name from Botswana meaning 'my dream'. Each meaning demands that you add beautiful Alora to your list immediately.

Arienne - 'Most holy'. Arienne is so delightfully individual, it reminds me of a really spiritual girl who loves deep chats over a herbal tea.

Avalon - 'Island of Apples'. A medieval Welsh name, Avalon is said to be the mythological resting place of King Arthur. So whimsical and the meaning just makes it ultra boho. With its graceful sound, it's so wearable and Ava is such a popular name. Whenever

I feature Avalon in any lists it gets so much love, so snap it up for the apple of your eye.

Boheme - 'From Bohemia'. Pronounced Bow-Em with a silent 'h'. Bohemia was a place in Czech where Romani people would pass through on route to Paris. These painters, artists and musicians were called Bohemians. The French word *Boheme* came to signify the movement of creative expression and this vibrant group of people. A beautiful name, Boheme has a sprinkle of Emma and a touch of Beau - it would Stand Out & Shine.

Delilah - 'Delicate'. With the pretty 'D' beginning bringing some edge to Lily, Delilah has all the elements of a modern, fresh name with deep history. Biblical Delilah gave the name its 'delicate' meaning, in that she weakened strong Samson by cutting his hair. Your little Delilah would equally bring a softness out of you in a more positive way! The name is stylish, intriguing and exotic.

Elowen - 'Elm tree'. A Cornish girl name, Elowen has one of the prettiest flowing sounds. In Celtic, Elm trees were associated with elves and a passage to the underworld, giving Elowen a magical, boho feel.

Esca - 'One who feels strongly for nature'. An incredibly unusual name that I have a big crush on, like the end of Francesca. The name suits a really boho girl who loves being outdoors.

Evanthe - 'Good flower'. Pronounced Ee-Van-Thee she was the Greek goddess of Charities which makes it so special. If you love Ava, Ivy, Emily vibes then why not list Evanthe for something super special.

Fable - 'A moral story'. Fairy tales feel like woodland magic, and Fable is so wearable, with both Faye and Mable being lovely boho names in their own right. She'll always be your love story.

Fei - 'To dance in the air'. Festival lovers will unite behind this gorgeous one-syllable name with its spirited, lyrical meaning.

Godiva - 'God's gift'. A historical boho babe, Lady Godiva is famous for riding naked through Coventry to oppose the heavy tax burden people were enduring. It's almost too iconic but if you want that free-spirited, feminine vibe - this is the name.

Lavender - 'Purple flower'. A botanical name that is so bohemian and fashion-forward amongst the pretty flower names topping the charts. Lavender symbolizes love and healing, perfect for this aesthetic.

Marisol - 'Sea and sun'. So boho, it takes me straight to an inlet in Ibiza, wearing a lace kaftan. Pronounced Marry-Sol, she will undoubtedly brighten up your life, just like the name.

Meadow - 'Field of grass'. Meadow was unranked in the nineties, feeling a bit too hippy, but with the boom of word names, it's growing in popularity again. It's a pretty name that almost sounds traditional against some of the other new word names that are more well-used, like Atlas.

Millaray - 'Golden flower'. Pronounced Me-La-Ray. A gorgeous whimsical name that sounds lyrical and confident. From the Mapuche, a group of indigenous inhabitants of south-central Chile and southwestern Argentina, Millaray is still most popularly used in Chile.

Poema - 'Poem or song' I love Poet as a name, but Poema makes it feel even more like a name if word names are for you. With vintage Emma at the end, it's so pretty.

Sequoia - 'To follow'. A tree name, pronounced Se-Coy-Yah, this giant redwood tree is a symbol of strength and makes a cool boho pick for a girl name.

Tinsley - 'Woodland clearing'. With its whimsical allusions to woodland, it sounds so pretty and would really stand out alongside more classic Tilly.

Willow - 'New life'. The Willow tree is the symbol of new life, which is perfect for your baby girl and this soft-sounding name is so bohemian in nature.

Whimsy - 'Whimsical'. We often hear people described as being whimsy, which I love because it means being expressively playful, having an offbeat sense of humour and not taking life too seriously. What a pretty name it makes too, brave for sure, but so are you.

BOYS

Albion - 'White cliffs'. Albion is of Irish origin and with Albie flying high in the charts, I love the addition of the 'n' at the end that gives it much more strength.

Calle - 'Free'. A Scandinavian version of Carl, pronounced Cal-A. Calle is spot on for a twist on a classic with its vast and pleasing meaning.

Charlton - 'settlement of free men'. A good variation of Charlie or Charles that's modern and has some extra charm.

Dante - 'Everlasting'. An amazing Italian name that also means 'enduring' or 'steadfast'. Slightly goth associations with Dante's *Inferno* but it's a name worth listing if you want a literary but edgy name. Watch out with pronunciations as some people say Don-Tay and some say Dan-tay. There doesn't seem to be a 'right' way so pick what you love.

Devereaux - 'The bank of the river'. A surname, pronounced Dev-air-Oh, it makes a dramatic and outdoorsy choice for Stand Out & Shine namers.

Donovan - 'Dark-haired warrior'. An Irish Name, I am drawn to the rugged romance of this name, plus it gives you the nickname Van.

Ellsworth - 'A great man's house'. Taking us to a noble estate, Ellsworth is a walk in the Cotswolds and a trip to a grand Manor House, giving a poetic vibe to a sophisticated name.

Emrys - 'Immortal'. The Welsh version of Ambrose, it's a magical name with its otherworldly meaning and is linked to Merlin as his traditional or 'druid' name. It's such a cool option, looks great on paper and is a real head turner that is simple to say - Em-Riss.

Falcon - 'Bird of prey'. Wild birds are popular namesakes and while we have softer Wren and Robin, Falcon and Peregrine make for more daring names at the other end of the scale. A falcon symbolizes freedom or salvation and the ability to navigate challenges.

Farris - 'Horseman'. Farris is great for horse lovers, also meaning 'knight' or 'cavalier'. It's got that spirit of riding free through the countryside.

Foxley - 'A clearing in a wood where foxes dwell'. Adding the 'ley' can make Fox more wearable as a name and certainly more original. It's super outdoorsy with an evocative nature meaning that it will appeal to Trendy with a Twist parents everywhere.

Francis - 'Liberated'. The name Francis is a variant of Frank, which became popular as a saint's name. For a boy it's a whimsical and elegant choice, complementing the Bohemian Aesthetic style so well.

Heath - 'Uncultivated land'. I adore this outdoorsy name meaning a wide-open space full of heather and grass. It's got that wild romantic spirit and makes a sweet and uncomplicated name.

Hemsley - 'Woodland clearing'. Originally from Yorkshire, this habitual surname feels like pitching up your tent amongst the trees and getting back to basics.

Keats - 'Herdsman'. We immediately think of the poet when we hear Keats, but it's an Anglo-Saxon occupational name and would be given to someone who worked with cattle or sheep. One-syllable names ending in 's' are always so stylish.

Kelby - 'Farm by a stream'. From Old Norse, Kelby takes us straight to a period drama set in farmland. It's an old surname so has classic roots and a rugged outdoorsy meaning.

Oleander - 'Evergreen tree'. One of the most romantic yet strong boy names, this one always gets a lot of love on my name lists. It's a great alternative to popular Oliver and with four syllables it has a whimsical side. Pronounced Olly-Ander.

Pax - 'Peace'. The 'x' ending adds edge to a name that means peace. Pax has that quiet strength and brings to life the harmony and tranquillity of the countryside with a punchy one-syllable sound.

Robinson - 'Bright son'. Surname as first names are so popular, and this has the ultimate outdoorsy boy namesake with Robinson Crusoe. Derived from Robert meaning 'bright', it's a vibrant and spirited name.

Rollo - 'Famous wolf'. A trendy Viking name, softer than Rocco and more modern than Olly. A short form of Roland now used by itself, I love this vintage nickname as first name. It wouldn't scare off Timelessly Tasteful namers too much either.

Thoreau - Without a defined meaning, this surname brings to mind Henry Thoreau, who wrote about breaking the rules and being free-spirited. A cool alternative to Theodore.

Valentine - 'Strong'. Irrevocably romantic, Valentine is a Stand Out & Shine name radiating health and strength - such a beautiful choice for your little love.

Willard - 'Resolutely brave'. I love this vintage name as an alternative to William. It has such a regal, elegant sound that feels very romantic.

NEUTRAL

Elliot - 'Strength'. Both a Scottish clan name and an Anglo-Saxon surname, Elliot has been in use for centuries and always sounds special. The meaning complements the sound of the name with the strong 't' ending, but it's also a romantic name with the soft 'll'. Perfect if you're after a traditional name that doesn't blend in.

Larkin - 'Fierce'. A poetic name with a songbird and poet at its heart. This Irish surname, derived from Lorcan, sounds stunning.

Rhapsody - 'To sew songs together'. This is a very edgy word name that sounds whimsical, and I love its meaning, bringing new high notes to life with the birth of your baby. It also refers to music expressing great emotion which connects beautifully to birth (see also the Music Names list on page 166).

River - 'Flowing water'. Such an evocative gender-neutral name with its vast and wide nature theme. See the Water Names list (page 88) for more gorgeous water-inspired names.

Vesper - 'Evening star'. Vespera was the goddess of the evening in Roman times and the name Vesper came to mean 'evening star' in her honour. It's a fashionable name with a starry night feel that works perfectly as a gender-neutral name.

TIPS FOR BLENDING SIBLING NAMES

Have you found it harder and harder to pick a baby name as you've had more children? I definitely got braver as I went along, but also know so many more children, which knocked a lot of names out of being contenders for me and I strangely no longer liked some of the names I'd listed. Freddie was going to be Tilda if he'd been a girl; but we had friends with a Tilde and knew lots of Matildas by then and I just had so many associations with the name by the time I had my second baby.

I really think it gets more difficult and it's also quite challenging to blend names together in a way that sounds right as a sibling set. However, there are some great ways to pick a perfect sibling name and it's down to personal preference, so grab your notepad and make some notes on ways to blend sibling names.

MEANING

Looking at the meaning of your other children's names is a lovely place to get an idea of where to start your research. The list on Story-Telling names is full of ideas (page 139).

ERAS

Consider what era your other children's names are from and try mixing them up.

- If you have a vintage name, try jotting down both a vintage classic and a modern name. Do you love the juxtaposition or swoon at the older name pairings? Mix and Match is my ultimate favourite. Modern Juniper with vintage sister Margot, classic Hugo and fresh Atlas bring both names a little sparkle of the other. I also don't discount the pairing of two classic together – think Bertie and Mabel or Connie and

Nell who are straight out of a story book. Challenge yourself to play around and see which suits your style.

EUPHONY

A Euphony means a harmonious succession of words that has the effect of the sounds being really pleasing. Yes please. It's a little bit of where the art comes in and why some name combinations don't sound complete or don't seem to go together. It's not a rule breaker, but really helps if you're facing this dilemma.

The decision guide for Euphonious Siblings

- Syllables: If you have a short and sweet one-syllable name, it blends well with most other sounds. You can even try to 'clap it out' like you did when you were little, or grab the old woodblock - I was always the woodblock in our junior school nativity play, which says a lot about my singing skills. The name will have a rhythm, how does it sound to you?
- Sounds: Repeating initials and sounds can either really work or sound too repetitive. Arlo and Milo cause a repeat of the strongest sounds in the name, which makes them more matchy. If you want to avoid this then take the strong sounds and use them in different places for example, Arlo and Roman takes the strong 'r' and 'o' sounds which gives them a flow which doesn't repeat. Olivia and Dahlia pair style-wise but the 'ia' repeat ending isn't as pleasing. You could, though, look at Olivia and Delilah to use the strong 'l' and 'a' sounds. Try this if you're hooked on a name pairing but aren't fully sure the flow is working. What other names use the strongest sounds in new ways?
- Many modern names end in 'ie' as we fully embrace the 'nickname as first name' trend. I've met lots of lovely siblings

who share this ending. With more than two children, I'd always recommend not repeating the 'ie' ending more than once. Hallie and Sylvie blend; Hallie and Sylvie and Annie becomes less rhythmic and more rhyming. My top tip is to take that 'ie' sound you love and move it to the beginning to create a prettier flow. Hallie and Sylvie plus Eden or Eliza, for example. By taking the most prominent sound from the sibling name and repeating it, the names will all sound harmonious.

RAINBOW BABY NAMES – BABY AFTER BABY LOSS

A 'rainbow baby' is a modern phrase to honour a very distinct birth order – a healthy baby born after baby loss, infant loss, stillbirth, or neonatal death. I have a rainbow baby after miscarriage and have experienced that devastating moment of being told in a scan that the heartbeat had stopped. I'm very proud to be a part of a generation of parents who have opened up about baby loss in all its forms, including the most tragic ones. We don't turn away from it, we lean in and support each other, raise awareness and create charities whilst supporting research and scientific progress. For me, the main change is how we speak to each other with so much more care and compassion. I've put that compassion into this guide. Whether tethering your lost

child into their sibling's life or recognizing how dear it is to hold a healthy baby after a previous loss, each of these names is heartfelt.

GIRLS

Abella - 'Life breath'. A wonderful, poignant name meaning with a gorgeous and familiar 'bella' ending.

Aisling - 'Dream or vision'. This charming Irish girl name embodies the dream coming true, pronounced Ash-Lin.

Aruna - 'Dawn light'. The Hindu god Aruna was the charioteer who drove the sun god across the sky bringing the morning light, such an evocative meaning full of hope.

Avabelle - 'Beautiful life'. This combination of two well-known names creates a strikingly unusual name telling of the beautiful life you will create with your little one.

Eliana - 'My God has answered'. Eliana is a gorgeous, celebratory name pronounced with a long middle vowel, so Elly-Ah-Nuh vs Elly-Anna.

Eloise - 'Healthy'. A captivating vintage name, Eloise has the dual meaning of 'healthy' and 'warrior'. An unforgettable name for a strong little girl that would suit Timelessly Tasteful namers.

Heather - 'Protection and wishes come true'. This botanical name of an evergreen flowering plant has the perfect meaning for your rainbow baby and I love its classic feel.

Iridiana - 'Rainbow'. A whimsical long form name derived from Iris the goddess of the Rainbow which would truly honour your rainbow baby's story.

Iris - 'The goddess of the rainbow'. The term rainbow baby for baby loss and miscarriage represents beauty after a dark time.

The goddess Iris was a messenger between the gods and humans, which I personally love when thinking of our babies who are no longer here on earth with us, but very much loved. Irisa is a pretty alternative.

Leilani - 'Heavenly flower'. A Hawaiian name that connects heaven and earth and a Hawaiian lei is a floral garland given to honour love and friendship. Leilani pays recognition to the special status of a rainbow baby.

Nadia - 'Hope'. A name that inspires optimism and positivity. In Arabic it also means 'call', as in a call to those powers above to align the paths so our dreams come true. A distinct and strong sounding name, Nadia is not one to be overlooked.

Neoma - 'New moon'. When the Earth, Sun and Moon are perfectly aligned we get a new moon. Your world begins to spin again, and the stars have come together to bring her here.

Samantha - 'God has heard' or 'flower'. Samantha is a blend of Hebrew name Sam meaning 'God has heard' and Greek *anthos*, meaning 'flower'. It's unsurprising given the meaning that it's become such a well-loved name, and it fits perfectly into this list as that new life you've so anticipated blossoming. With gender-neutral Sam as a nickname, it ticks a lot of modern name boxes.

BOYS

Alfie - 'Ready'. Alfie has such a meaningful translation of readiness and I adore the sentiment that he's ready to arrive at the ideal time.

Amariah - 'Promised by God'. The flow of Amariah is so lyrical with its meaning of promise, pronounced Ama-Ryah.

Aster - 'Patience'. We sometimes wait so long for our miracle baby that patience can be hard to come by. I also love the symbol of this tree for your baby boy.

Calian - 'Warrior of life, honour and eternal hope'. A wonderful name that honours the journey of your baby's life from conception to their happy arrival.

Finley - 'Courageous one'. Courage is a great way to describe this path, and Irish Finley encapsulates the meaning, also translating as 'fair hero'. A soft and beautiful boy name.

Jason - 'Healer'. The name Jason was such a popular one that is becoming less common, but the meaning of 'healer' will hit home for so many of us. Jason is such an underused gem that is due a revival.

Jebediah - 'Beloved friend'. Pronounced Je-bu-Dee-Ah. A companion to heal and a beloved friend for their lost sibling who I'm sure will be a force in their life.

Kamau - 'Quiet warrior'. Kamau is from the Kikuyu language native to Kenya and gives off peaceful and protected vibes which feels like the perfect sentiment for your rainbow baby.

Keao - 'The light of the day'. Pronounced Kay-Ow. A fresh light on a new day, this Hawaiian boy name brings that joy to life.

Lorcan - 'Little fierce one'. Irish Lorcan was given to the bravest in battle and makes a great name for your much-loved baby boy.

Lorien - 'Dream flower'. Traditionally masculine, this is a Tolkien name used for an elvish realm from his book *The Lord of the Rings* which I think sounds so soft and whimsical.

Neo - 'New beginning'. Neo makes a fantastic name to really celebrate your beloved baby finally being here with you. It's meaning is both 'new' but also 'gift', from the word *neos* which marked new beginnings.

Raphael - 'God has healed'. One of the archangels associated with healing, Raphael is such a beautiful sounding name.

Samuel - 'God heard'. In the Bible, Hannah prays for a baby and Samuel is born, making the name such a moving choice, full of sentiment.

Saul - 'Longed for, prayed for'. A lovely Hebrew name with a spot-on meaning for a rainbow baby when they finally reach your arms.

NEUTRAL

Bali - 'Strength'. This name pairs a place name with the meaning 'strength' and lends an air of spirituality and peace to your baby.

Esper - 'I waited'. What a stunning Spanish name with a meaning that goes so deep. I waited is one of the most gorgeous name meanings, and Esper feels ideal for that naming moment.

Phoenix - 'Mythical bird'. This is a popular name in my community for rainbow babies - it symbolizes the mythological bird rising from the ashes and is such a strong name for your child.

BABY NAME CONFLICTS & DILEMMAS

Once you have a baby name chosen it hopefully brings everyone else as much joy as it does you. However, as with so many emotional choices, it can spark fallouts that are often totally unexpected. Working as a name consultant, I've come to realize these altercations are so common. All the dilemmas are totally solvable, and you shouldn't feel alone if you've navigating the choppy waters of name stealing, negative comments about your chosen name or even feeling that you yourself are having second thoughts. I'm here to chat them all through.

BABY NAME REGRET

This almost feels like a taboo topic, but it's way more common than you may imagine for parents to experience baby name regret. Not just a small feeling of finding it hard to let another name on your long list go, but a very upsetting and difficult time for many people where the name they chose just feels totally wrong.

I hear from parents who can't bring themselves to use the name, or who feel embarrassed to tell people the name of their baby and it's causing at best a niggling doubt, but mostly it's really distressing. If you're feeling like this, whether your baby is a newborn or even a toddler, I totally understand that it feels a bit insurmountable to deal with. And I also want to reassure you that there's still time to change the name.

How does that work? Legally it's a simple deed poll certificate in the UK that costs under £100 at the time of writing. It needs both parents' signatures, and you can do it online.

But that isn't what stops people; it's more a fear of other people's reactions. Being seen as a diva is something I've heard women worry about and other people thinking you're a bit weird. However, I want to reassure you that they absolutely will not. How would you respond if you heard a friend or family member had changed the name? You would likely give it no more than a few minutes conversation are those few minutes of chat enough to stop you going with your heart on a name you really haven't connected with?

Also think about how many times you go to visit a friend and have to ask each other - what's their baby's name again? If you're like my husband I need to remind him frequently, not because he doesn't love our friends' children, just that their names haven't featured that heavily in his mind. So don't worry about their reactions, your baby's name is only top of *your* mind and it's only for you to decide if it's the right one or not.

If you decide to go for it, here are my tips:

- If you're particularly self-conscious, you could say the new name was always the baby's middle name. We're very used to people going by their middle names and I wonder how many people we know are going by their middle name or an invented name and we have no idea. That's my new conspiracy theory.
- A simple text is enough, you do not need to apologise or be bashful. 'Hi, hope you're well? We decided that baby Rose was more of a Sienna, so we're leading with that name now - hope you can come visit soon!' Easy, breezy. You don't need to add any more explanation other than it being your decision based on getting to know your baby.
- Getting your partner on board is often a sticking point; when one parent can't connect with the name but the other parent still likes it, it can cause a lot of tension and dread at bringing up the topic all together. Did you know one in ten parents in a recent survey admitted to regretting their baby's name? If you already have an alternative name that you feel much happier with, make your case calmly for why you love it and ask to introduce it at home for a week or two to see if it

sticks. If you feel a weight has lifted off your shoulders, then it's worth tackling the hard conversation.

- You can rename your child at any age, but if you're on the fence I do recommend that deciding before they start school and have that wider community of their own is ideal. Any later and the change could impact them negatively, unless the decision is coming from them.

So, tackle the conversation, open up about how normal and surprisingly common this is and don't overthink other people's reactions. Happy renaming.

WHAT TO DO IF . . . YOUR FAMILY DON'T LIKE THE NAME

Getting a negative reaction to your baby name idea or actual chosen name is really hurtful. When a name is suggested as an idea, for some reason everyone seems to whip out the virtual white board and wrongly assume we're in some kind of brainstorm situation. There's no other situation I can compare it to and the baby name pile-on is real. Often it will come from someone outside your generation like a grandparent or your own parents; remember that styles have changed so dramatically I would venture a guess that while you love them deeply, you may not have the exact same taste. Consider the conundrum, your grandma or father-in-law takes you shopping and they pick an outfit in their style, for you - would that go well? Even your very best friend could match you in so many ways, but you have different things you love. You do not have to please anyone else with your child's name - if it's very 'you' then it's ideal for your beloved baby. If you're concerned about reactions here's some tips:

- Agree with your partner whether you're going to share your name list or not. There is literally nothing worse than hearing from someone that they've ditched their favourite baby name because Andy and Brian at their husband's place of work said they didn't like it and now they've got cold feet. A simple, 'we're still thinking of names', is enough.

- Choose your name inner circle. I had my sister and two pregnant friends in my inner-name sanctum. It was a circle of trust where mucus plugs, night sweats and the name Marigold were held with a reverent secrecy, even the illuminati would be proud of. This is your place to throw around ideas and get feedback. Make sure they are as invested as you and love 'name chat'.
- Don't put up with negative comments. It's very hard in the hormonal stages of being a new parent not to let opinions bother you, and we also get told to brush them off or let them go in one ear and out the other. Which I think is okay if it's a one-off comment - but if you have someone in your family continuing to tease or negatively talk about the name, you have *every* right to let them know that's unacceptable. Remind them either face to face or on a call that you're a new parent and need support, love and care right now and that their comments are upsetting and need to stop. Some people can be insensitive or unaware of how personal and precious your baby's name is and they need to hear that they're in the wrong. If you don't feel like having the conversation yourself, ask a mutual friend or family member to step in, but do not spare their feelings or worry you will make them feel bad - if you're upset, they need to know and hopefully make amends.

BABY NAME STEALING – WHAT TO DO WHEN YOUR FAVOURITE NAME GETS PINCHED

Sharing out family names, sibling battles over who gets the good 'Family Tree name' or who gets to honour a special loved one are a pretty common dilemma I hear in the Baby Name Envy online community. One family even had a sit down and divvied out the names before they'd all had children as it was such a hot topic. I've had three sisters as clients who all wanted to bagsy Daisy after their great granny and none were backing down. If you've picked your mum's name in the middle for a daughter, are you then duty bound to use your dad's next time? Honestly, it is a bit of a family political nightmare and feuds do happen. Most families can navigate this themselves, but I think a first-come-first-served policy seems fair - it's literally the way name heritage works. So if your little cousin warns you off Connie or your brother wants Bruno after dad, have that chat and explain why you're going for it and why it's important to you and let them stew on not getting there first.

MY FRIEND LOVES THE SAME NAME AS ME – SHOULD I SAVE IT FOR HER?

I have to confess at this point that I am . . . a Baby Name Stealer. To be fair, before you slam this book shut for ethical reasons, it was an accident. We were all set on Oscar for our baby. A uni friend of ours, who already had a daughter, had let us know that had her little girl been a boy she would have called him Freddie. I'd totally forgotten this chat - pinky promise - and when we swerved to Freddie from Oscar last minute it wasn't even mentioned, until . . . two years later. We were both pregnant with our second baby, each having boys and she shot me down with stealing her favourite name first time round. Did I feel bad? Yes, a little bit embarrassed, but had I known it was her top name I'd have still gone with it - sorry, not sorry. It wouldn't have then bothered me had they used it. We had Finn and they shortly after had a son with the middle name Finley, which was quite funny as maybe I'd accidentally done it again! She had of course kept her name cards close to her chest that time.

MY FRIEND STOLE MY BABY NAME

You've chosen your name carefully and WHAM, a birth announcement from a friend comes out and it's the same name . . . what?!

I get a lot of distraught messages about actual, legitimate examples of name stealing. Especially when it's been a unique name that has deep personal meaning which then someone in your circle repeats, it's nothing short of shocking. I understand your feelings here if it's happened to you – it's a piece of your baby's individuality and it feels like a betrayal, particularly if they haven't given you the heads-up before (which stealers don't often do). Just like in every other situation, no one likes a copycat and when they don't even acknowledge the original creator, it makes things even worse. We never 'own' a name, but in the case of your baby's name, especially when it's a creative one, parents do have a sense of 'intellectual property'. If you're in the situation of picking a name a friend has already used, you certainly don't need their permission, but a heads-up is always worth giving.

Once the initial shock of the copycat name announcement dies down, you can ultimately take pride in the fact that they liked your idea so much and comfort in all your mutual friends knowing you got there first. Your child's name has originality and authenticity and perhaps you'll start a new name trend, which is pretty cool.

YOU'VE BEEN BEATEN TO IT

Sometimes this is total coincidence. My own experience of this was proudly 30 weeks pregnant with my girl's name banked for my firstborn. My husband and I had agreed on Matilda Rose and in 2010 it was unique, vintage, a little literary and worked in both Swedish and English. I received an email at work from my best friend letting me know her other bestie, who I'm less close to, had just had . . . Matilda Rose. It shouldn't matter, I shouldn't worry as we're not that close, the girls wouldn't go to the same school or anything; but it mattered to me. I felt a bit gutted and that I'd be the second Matilda Rose of the extended friendship group. Maybe I stomped off to find comfort in a bag of chocolates and ate the suggested serving size for a family of four all by myself; but was I right to be upset? SO many people would say no, if there's enough distance it really doesn't matter. Fast forward to two colleagues announcing sons Finley and Finbar just weeks before my own Finn was born; I was less precious.

However, many people find themselves in this predicament, and I know girls who have announced their name and lost friends forever because of it, when they themselves were happy to share names. It's worth giving that heads-up to someone if you know you like and are going to use the same name as them if you're pregnant at the same time. It's easier to come to terms with and it and gives them time to change it if they're truly not happy.

Everyone has their own threshold when it comes to what they feel is an overstep. It's always worth the conversation upfront so you don't ruffle any feathers.

A FINAL THOUGHT

It's always been my hope as a Baby Name Consultant to make picking your baby name a treasured and joyful part of your journey to parenthood. I'm sure through reading these pages you've been dreaming about who your baby will be, how they will feel in your arms, what they will look like and how life will be once they're here. I'm honoured you picked up this book during those moments and am so lucky to have been beside you, hopefully helping to make this a fun, creative and meaningful experience.

A name is so precious and I know by taking all the care you have, spending time reading this book and making your list, your final pick will be bursting with love and meaning. Have a quick look at the name list you've created - right now they're words on paper, but soon one of those names is about to become your very favourite sound.

Your baby's name.

Before you pop this book up onto the shelf, make sure to dedicate this part of their story to them by writing their name here:

THIS BOOK IS DEDICATED TO

The Beginning

AND IF YOU'RE STILL STUCK . . .

Hello again; I'm so thrilled for you. You did it! I hope you're in your newborn bubble of tea and toast and maybe a big hit of all the emotions that I know can make that final naming decision feel like the last hurdle to leap.

I've created this Infographic to help you make a quick pick between the lead front runners. This was co-created with all the Baby Name Envy community on Instagram, thousands of parents. I asked them, 'What are those last few questions that helped you decide?'

STUCK WITH MULTIPLE NAMES?

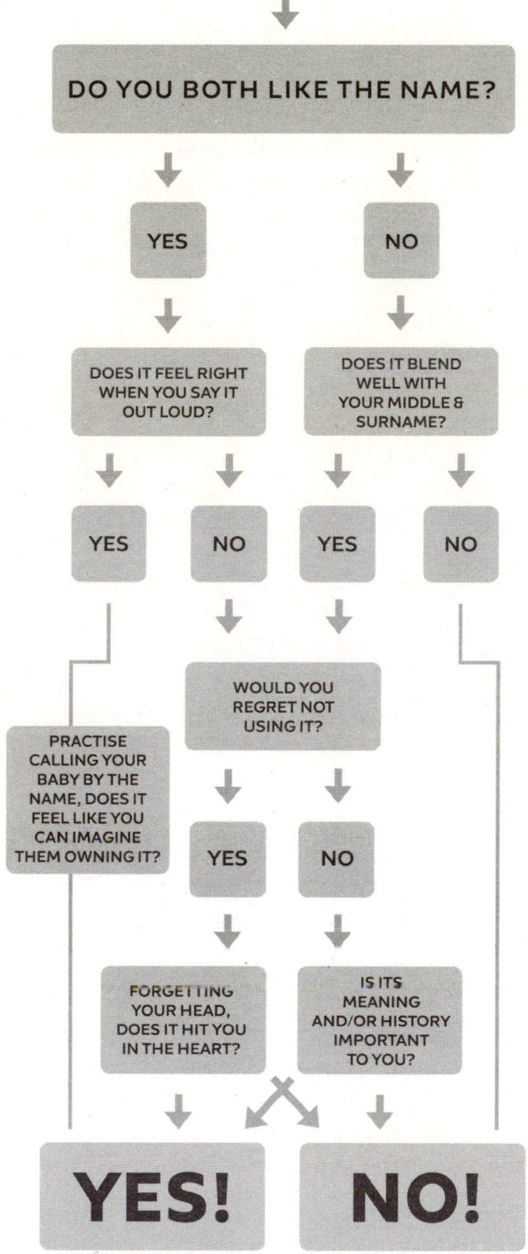